A Tide of Discontent:
The 1980 Elections and Their Meaning

Politics and Public Policy Series

Advisory Editor

Robert L. Peabody

Johns Hopkins University

Congressional Procedures and the Policy Process
  Walter J. Oleszek

Interest Groups, Lobbying and Policymaking
  Norman J. Ornstein and Shirley Elder

Mass Media and American Politics
  Doris A. Graber

Financing Politics: Money, Elections and Political Reform, 2d ed.
  Herbert E. Alexander

Invitation to Struggle: Congress, the President and Foreign Policy
  Cecil V. Crabb, Jr. and Pat M. Holt

Implementing Public Policy
  George C. Edwards III

The Supreme Court
  Lawrence Baum

Congress Reconsidered, 2d ed.
  Lawrence C. Dodd and Bruce I. Oppenheimer

Energy, Politics and Public Policy
  Walter A. Rosenbaum

The Politics of Federal Grants
  George E. Hale and Marian Lief Palley

Congressional Elections
  Barbara Hinckley

A Tide of Discontent:
The 1980 Elections and Their Meaning

Edited by

Ellis Sandoz
Louisiana State University

and

Cecil V. Crabb, Jr.
Louisiana State University

Congressional Quarterly Press
a division of
CONGRESSIONAL QUARTERLY INC.
1414 22nd Street N.W., Washington, D.C. 20037

JK
1968
1980
T53

7.50

5/62

Jean L. Woy   Acquisitions Editor
Lynda McNeil   Project Editor
Maceo Mayo   Production Supervisor

Richard Pottern   Cover Design

Printed in the United States of America

Library of Congress Catalog in Publication Data

Main entry under title:
A Tide of discontent.

   Bibliography: p.
   Includes index.
   1. United States. Congress—Elections, 1980—Addresses, essays, lectures. 2. Presidents—United States—Election—1980—Addresses, essays, lectures. I. Sandoz, Ellis, 1931- . II. Crabb, Cecil Van Meter, 1924- .

JK1968   1980.T53   324.9730926   81-4586
ISBN 0-87187-205-6   AACR2

For
Alverne and Harriet

The people are king.

—Gouverneur Morris
The Federal Convention
July 20, 1787

Here each individual is interested not only in his own affairs but in the affairs of the state as well: even those who are mostly occupied with their own business are extremely well-informed on general politics — this is a peculiarity of ours: we do not say that a man who takes no interest in politics is a man who minds his own business; we say that he has no business here at all.

—Pericles' "Funeral Oration" to the Athenians
Thucydides, *Peloponnesian War* II.6.40
431 B. C.

Foreword

Every presidential election in the United States has important consequences for the nation's politics—the selection of a presidential administration, the make-up of a new Congress, the advancement or the failure of hundreds of political careers, and the furtherance, delay, or denouement of countless programs and policies. Yet some presidential elections are more important than others, and the election of 1980 gives many indicators of being one of these.

V. O. Key, Jr. of Harvard University, who was perhaps the most able and productive political scientist of the post-World War II generation, termed such events "critical elections." He singled out the presidential elections of 1896 and 1932 as examples not only of changes in party control but also wholesale shifts in the allegiances of broad segments of the voting population. Subsequently, other scholars, most notably those of the University of Michigan Survey Research Center, have come along to modify and expand on Key's notions. A theory of "critical" or "realigning" elections has developed. Historians have extended the analyses back to include other elections such as 1800, 1824, and 1860.

With the strong Republican surge in the 1980 elections, the question has naturally been raised: Is it an election akin to these earlier watershed elections? Will President Ronald Reagan and the Republicans in the Senate and the House of Representatives continue to solidify these positions with the American electorate? Will their economic and foreign policies lead to significant advances in the elections of 1982 and 1984? Only time will tell.

In this collection of essays by distinguished experts, ably compiled and edited by Professors Ellis Sandoz and Cecil V. Crabb, Jr. of Louisiana State University, some preliminary answers to such questions are revealed. For example, James L. Sundquist and Richard M.

Scammon, two long-time observers and practitioners of contemporary politics, suggest a note of caution. They recall other great Republican victories—1952 and 1968, as well as 1946, 1956, and 1972—none of which was strong enough to overcome the period of Democratic supremacy that began in 1932. The deathknell of the Democratic party has not been sounded. Both of our major parties have remained remarkably viable institutions over the years, even in an era where the importance of parties appears to be on the decline. The authors of the other essays, too, caution us that the election may not be as clear a mandate for Ronald Reagan and the Republicans as some assume. The Republican Senate will have to work with a House of Representatives still controlled by the Democrats. In the economic and foreign policy spheres, both Stephen McDonald and Cecil V. Crabb point to the very knotty problems facing the new administration.

Meanwhile, however, Republicans have made impressive gains. In the election of 1980 they appeared to be far better organized and funded than their Democratic counterparts. The advantage of incumbency seemed to be weaker than usual, especially at the senatorial and presidential levels. In addition to capturing the White House for the fifth time in the past three decades, Republicans regained control of the Senate for the first time since 1954. In the House of Representatives, Republicans made a net gain of 33 seats, bringing them within striking distance of winning control of that body, perhaps as early as 1982. Again, only time will tell.

Each of the essays focuses on a different facet of the election and its consequences, and each is rich in historical as well as contemporary political detail. The contributors—seven political scientists, one economist, and one congressional correspondent—bring a wide range of knowledge and practical experience to this text. *A Tide of Discontent: The 1980 Elections and Their Meaning* is an important addition to our knowledge about this possibly "realigning" election as well as our knowledge of American electoral politics in general.

Robert L. Peabody

Preface

The 1980 national elections hold a paradoxical fascination that prompts us to explore them here in depth. A profoundly uninterested public, voting in a toss-up election, produced a landslide Republican victory. The public's mood was reflected in the predicted and actual low turnout of voters. The outcome stunned the nation with a rush to office of new conservative Republicans at all levels of government. What really happened? What does it all mean to our political future? How can it be understood by students of political science?

Throughout much of the long campaign, right up to election day itself, there was general boredom with the whole affair. No candidate for the presidential nominations seemed able to arouse the enthusiasm of the electorate. Republican Ronald Reagan methodically and incredibly beat out his six main competitors, one by one, as the caucuses and primaries rolled by. The wonder of it all was that a man of 69 could even survive the process. Survive he did, however, right into the Detroit convention, which he owned by July 16, 1980.

The great question of the Republican convention was not who would be the presidential nominee but what vice-presidential nominee would be chosen. There were some astonishing hours when former President Gerald Ford bargained to transform the presidency into a partnership as the price of his availability for the second spot on the Republican ticket. But reason prevailed, and the endeavor collapsed. George Bush was designated and duly nominated amid the disgruntled mutterings of Reagan's more conservative supporters. The unlikely, if not impossible, clearly had occurred. Ronald Reagan not only was nominated on the first ballot but immediately appeased the liberal wing of the Republican party in his choice of a running mate.

To make the Democrats squirm even more uncomfortably, actor Reagan then delivered an acceptance speech of power and eloquence, promising the country "A New Beginning." Reagan was persuasive, and he came across to his national audience as an altogether decent fellow with deeply-held convictions. But this is pretty thin soup for a presidential campaign.

Meanwhile, President Jimmy Carter's campaign was a Rose Garden and Oval Office affair. He busied himself in running the government and in seeking some way of gaining the release of the 52 hostages taken in Tehran by the Iranian revolutionary students in November 1979. He acted presidential and remained aloof from the rough-and-tumble partisan politics of the primaries. He devoted himself to the priority business of the country: to the intricacies of diplomacy, to the threat to peace and national interest posed by the brutal Soviet invasion of Afghanistan, to courting disaffected allies, to grappling with America's economic plight—recession, inflation, high interest rates, and unemployment—and other similarly compelling tasks.

Senator Edward Kennedy of Massachusetts livened things up a bit by his bid for the party's nomination, but *any* incumbent president, because of his control of the national organization, is virtually unbeatable for the nomination. Kennedy knew this, of course, but challenged Carter strongly. Still, even as he made the effort, a discernible note of irony and half-heartedness crept into the senator's speeches. He continually assured himself and others that he was in the campaign to stay, but it all looked and sounded a bit like the Pro Bowl of the National Football League—the last gasp of a spent season. So the Democratic party convention was as locked-up for Jimmy Carter when it convened in New York City as the Republican one had been for Ronald Reagan the month before, despite the final effort of Kennedy and his forces to have delegates released from voting for the winner of their states' caucuses and primaries. Jimmy Carter and Walter Mondale were renominated on the first ballot.

The race was on, but the country yawned. One entrepreneur manufactured bumper stickers celebrating the presidential election as a choice between "the evil of two lessers." Cartoonists made their usual contributions to the nation's political dialogue. Would the jelly bean replace the peanut as our national fruit? Representative John Anderson of Illinois, defeated by Reagan in the Republican primaries for the nomination, sought with little success to run for the presidency as an independent candidate. His only attention came when he participated in a two-man debate with Reagan in Baltimore on September 21; Carter had refused to participate. Carter and Reagan finally did meet in debate on October 28, with indecisive results. But the Republican's good humor undercut the Democratic scare rhetoric, a principal tactic that had painted Reagan as a dangerous extremist prone to violence and fits of irrationality.

"Too close to call" was the assessment of political pundits as late as one week before the election. That public view prevailed right up to election day. The electorate was uninterested. A low turnout was forecast, and a low turnout occurred. But what was not forecast was a Republican electoral vote landslide. What had been a colossal bore for the majority of the people who expressed themselves in any public forum about their feelings on the election campaign was abruptly translated on November 4 into an electrifying victory for conservative Republicans. Jimmy Carter learned that it was all over from his press secretary, Jody Powell, on the night before; and he was seen fighting back tears when he and his wife Rosalynn voted in Plains, Georgia.

Here was high drama at last. Reagan had won on November 4. And to that incredible fact was added another, on November 5, when it became certain that the Republicans now held a majority of seats in the Senate and had narrowed the gap in the House of Representatives. What did it all mean? How could it happen? Was this another watershed election, such as the one in 1932 that turned American politics in a new direction, a course generally held to ever since then?

Whom have we elected? What does the new administration want to do? Will it be able to accomplish those goals? If so, how? If not, why not? What is this conservative philosophy that now appears to have triumphed? Is this the triumph of an idea, a new national constituency? Or is it merely a protest vote, a fluke?

These perplexing and suspenseful matters are addressed in this volume. Experts in various aspects of American politics raise, and explore with care, the cardinal questions of the 1980 elections in a sequence of essays beginning with a general introduction in Chapter 1. Chapter 2 contains an election profile and historical overview, placing recent events in the long perspective of American political history.

Chapters 3 through 5 discuss the president and presidency, the struggle for the House of Representatives, and the capture of the Senate by the "New Right" Republicans. The changed roles of the parties, the media, and the pressure groups are subsequently discussed in Chapter 6, and some challenging conclusions are drawn about the uncertain future of traditional American politics.

Stephen McDonald, an economist, explains in Chapter 7 what all of the contributors to this book agree about—that more than any other factor, economic issues decided the 1980 elections. Here in brief compass is the how and why of it, and what the Reagan administration may (or may not) be able to do to correct intractable domestic problems. But diplomatic and foreign affairs, too, played a key role in the campaign, and they are discussed in Chapter 8. The Iranian hostage issue unquestionably crippled Carter's presidency. The United States's place in the world arena, the directions national policy can take under new leadership, and the chances of success of alternatives are assessed to round out the presentation. Chapter 9 sums up the viewpoints of all of the contributors and compares and contrasts the highlights of their main arguments.

We find, after all our experts have spoken, that there are some conclusions to be drawn, but that so much more is inconclusive. The larger question remains. Is a new political era beginning? What will this new era be like? Clearly there is *something* different about the tenor of politics in 1981, with implications for the American future.

Ellis Sandoz
Cecil V. Crabb, Jr.

Contents

1 Introduction: Revolution or Flash in the Pan?
   Ellis Sandoz   1

2 The 1980 Election: Profile and Historical Perspective
   James L. Sundquist and Richard M. Scammon   19

3 Presidents, Ideas, and the Search for a
   Stable Majority
   Erwin C. Hargrove and Michael Nelson   45

4 The New Conservative House of Representatives
   Neil MacNeil   65

5 The New, New Senate
   Charles O. Jones   89

6 The De-Institutionalization of Electoral Politics
   Clifton McCleskey   113

7 Economic Issues in the Campaign
   Stephen L. McDonald   139

8 The Reagan Victory:
   Diplomatic and Strategic Policy Implications
   Cecil V. Crabb, Jr.   157

9 Conclusion: Electoral and Policy Realignment
   or Aberration?
   Ellis Sandoz and Cecil V. Crabb, Jr.   191

Presidential Messages   211

Data on the 1980 Election   235

The Contributors   239

Suggested Readings   243

Index   247

1

Introduction:
Revolution or Flash In the Pan?

Ellis Sandoz

This book is devoted to the election of 1980. While nearly all the rest of the country slept in the early morning hours of November 4, the people of some of the hamlets of New Hampshire went to the polling places at midnight, as they always do, vying to be first to vote. Most prominent among the contested offices were the presidency and the vice-presidency of the United States, all of the House of Representatives, one-third of the Senate, and governorships of 13 states.

Just as the day began early on this election so it ended early, too, in the contest between Ronald Reagan and Jimmy Carter. Soon after midnight the word flashed from Dixville Notch, New Hampshire: 17 for Reagan, 3 for Carter. That was a straw in the wind, setting a trend that never changed as day spread westward across the country. President Carter abruptly conceded the election that the pollsters said was too close to call at 9:50 p.m. EST, in a nationally televised statement made long before polls closed in the western states. This was so surprising to Mr. Reagan in his Los Angeles hotel suite that he came to the telephone from the shower, dripping wet and wrapped in a bath towel, to take the president's call (at 5:35 p.m. PST, over an hour before the public statement) and to acknowledge the concession and congratulations.

Ronald Wilson Reagan would be the 40th president of the United States, come Inauguration Day, January 20, 1981, and the final phase of the peaceful passing of power to govern the world's greatest democracy.

WHAT HAPPENED?

Much of the rest of the country was as surprised as Mr. Reagan by what had happened. The full details of the election, its whys, hows, and possible meaning for each of us and for the country, will be explored with care in chapters that follow. But it must be said at the outset that the 1980 election was extraordinary in a number of ways. A tide of discontent swept the country, and the election turned into a referendum of unhappiness. The end result was an electoral sweep for the Republican party's nominee. President Carter carried only six states and the District of Columbia, a stunning defeat and rejection of his leadership. Reagan won 44 states and 51 percent of the popular vote for an electoral vote of 489 to Carter's 41 percent of the popular vote for an electoral vote of 49. Mr. Carter's concession came more quickly than in any presidential election since 1904 when Alton Parker conceded defeat to Theodore Roosevelt. Carter was the first incumbent elected president (Gerald Ford had succeeded Richard Nixon from the vice-presidency, before being defeated by Carter in 1976) to lose since 1932, the first Democratic president in 92 years, and only the seventh in American history of any party, to be denied reelection. The oldest person ever elected to the office, Reagan turned 70 on February 6, 1981, thereby also becoming the oldest person ever to serve as president.

A glance at the results of some of the other major elections shows that they were almost equally surprising. In the U.S. Senate, Republicans gained a majority (of seven votes, 53 to 46, plus Harry F. Byrd, Jr., of Virginia, a conservative independent) for the first time since 1954. They made a net gain of 33 seats in the House of Representatives, to narrow the split to 192 Republicans to 243 Democrats, 26 votes short of a Republican majority. The election wave of discontent surged into a tide of institutionalized political conservatism in the newly constituted presidency and a dramatically altered Congress. Michigan Representatives Guy A. Vander Jagt, chairman of the GOP's strategymaking National Republican Congressional Committee, described the election as "the most crushing rejection of a President and his party in Congress since Herbert Hoover. Democratic leaders who managed to survive had the bejesus scared out of them." [1]

Even so, the Democratic majority of 51 members in the House (although down from 117 in the previous session) was quite sufficient to permit it to establish control of that chamber's organization and committee structure and to stack the key Appropriations, Rules, and

Ways and Means committees. Despite being a minority in the Senate, Democrats (those who survived reelection, that is—nine were defeated) did not seem terribly scared of the Republican victors. Democratic Senator Russell B. Long of Louisiana, a power for decades as chairman of the Finance Committee, was so unaccustomed to his minority role that he occasionally forgot his new status and answered for Republican Robert Dole of Kansas when "chairman" was called in committee voting. Of the new Republican majority, Long chortled:

> Bless their sweet hearts. They are in such a state of euphoria, they are just pipedreaming right now. They're in control in the Senate for the third time in the 33 years I've been here. Now they're back in, in my opinion on a fluke, for another two years. And they'd like to think there's some overwhelming cry for them out in the hinterlands. To make as many mistakes as we've made, you shouldn't expect [the Democrats] to win.[2]

Overwhelming cry or not, Reagan's coattails figured mightily in the gubernatorial elections, where Republicans won 7 out of 13 races and no Republican governor lost to a Democratic challenger. This put the national tally at 23 governors for the Republicans and 27 for the Democrats, placing the GOP in a strong position to curb adverse gerrymandering of election district lines by Democratic state legislatures when reapportionment of legislative and congressional districts is made on the basis of 1980 census data. Moreover, the momentum generated by Reagan's conservative surge may carry over to the 1982 elections when 21 out of 36 governors' races will involve Democratic incumbents. Control by Republicans of a majority of statehouses across the country at that time is a distinct possibility, one that seemed pure fantasy as late as 1976 when GOP officials held power in a mere 12 states.[3]

POLITICAL PARTIES AND ELECTIONS

If we have now sketched in briefest outline what happened in the elections, let us next glance at their political and constitutional setting before commenting on the tenor of the campaign and the possible significance of the elections for the future.

Politically the periodic electoral struggles for offices of national authority are conducted in the names of opposing parties that serve to give identity (beyond personal reputation) to candidates. The party system, typically dividing political energies in the country between two rival candidates for each office in a general election, is extraconstitutional—that is, the Constitution makes no mention of them at all. Yet they have served, almost from the beginning of our independent political history, as the central mediating institutions by which the people award the power to govern to selected peers for set periods of time or terms of office.

"The reports of my death are greatly exaggerated," Mark Twain once cabled the Associated Press from Europe in mock urgency. A similar message may be in order on behalf of the American party system, however despondent Democrats feel in the wake of the 1980 elections. For whatever the changing roles of political parties in contemporary politics, and however serious some of the problems forcing fragmentation in party organization and consensus, the two party system is at least as likely to survive them as is the country itself. And this is "the petrified truth," Twain might have added.

The Republican party today appears to us more unified and capable of attracting the great body of the citizenry occupying the decisive middle of the American political spectrum than it has been since the Great Depression of the 1930s.

Party unity was a constant theme of Ronald Reagan's candidacy, in studied contrast to President Nixon's 1972 campaign or President Carter's 1980 reelection effort. The congressional and statehouse elections suggest some evidence to support the theory that a modicum of cohesion exists, however much that element may be discounted by the protest vote explanation. Even the connoisseurs of contemporary political discourse who write for *Time* proclaim that "the GOP is now by far the more interesting of the two parties. And much of the anticipation of the Reagan presidency has to do with the fact that people recognize that an idea is taking shape." [4] The Democratic party can take heart by reflecting that their party survived the long dry spell from Abraham Lincoln in 1860 to Franklin Roosevelt in 1932 (apart from respites of Grover Cleveland's elections in 1884 and 1892, and Woodrow Wilson's in 1912 and 1916) as the minority party in national politics. Disarray, factionalism, and operating at cross purposes with one another are no novelties of the present age for Democrats. Indeed, these are trademarks of the party during much of its long career, well summarized by Will Rogers' famed quip: "I belong to no organized political party—I am a Democrat."

The chief objective of partisan politics is to gain and retain public office for the purpose of effecting public policy on a pattern that serves constituents' and the nation's interests. This statement suggests that there is some kind of underlying consensus unifying each of the parties and their spokesmen, that each is composed of different constituencies with valid interests deserving attention, and that the visions of both parties are at least debatably good for the whole country. Periodic national elections are held so that the public can decide whose case is more persuasive and whose stewardship is more likely to serve their purposes as individuals and citizens.

The germ of the principle of bipartisan politics grounded in rival coalitions of interests was expressed in the spring of 1787, even before the Constitutional Convention met, by a writer in Rhode Island who took the pseudonym "Plato":

> the people of the United States are now divided, and have naturally thrown themselves into two great classes, or parties, . . . which are often distinguished by the names of the Mercantile and Landed Interests.[5]

The basic principle of a party is that it rests on a sufficiently broad consensus about public policies to be able to offer a persuasive vision to its membership and the nation. Political parties are "aggregators of national interest"[6] that must bridge the differences among individuals and groups. Any major party is inevitably an elaborate coalition resting on compromise and expediency for pragmatic purposes. If a party is to contend seriously for power at the national level, it must be a large and effective coalition commanding a degree of loyalty to the cause and its leaders in terms of time, treasure, and delivery of the vote on election day. Whatever its lesser functions, the primary purpose of a political party "is to select the personnel of government."[7]

For our purpose, we can say that four such "grand coalitions" have appeared to date in American politics as the foundations of dominant political parties.[8] The Federalists under George Washington and Alexander Hamilton were based on a coalition of mainly monied interests—largely landowners, mercantilists, bankers and businessmen. The Republicans of Thomas Jefferson and James Madison, who became the Democratic Republicans in 1828 under Jackson, were based on a coalition (perhaps 80 percent of the population) of farmers, frontiersmen, the "common man" generally, and slave-owners, distributed over the South, the West, and the frontier. Although this coalition later split to produce the Whig party in the period before 1860, the Republicans generally remained dominant; both parties shattered on the issues of slavery and secession. Lincoln's Republicans came out of the Civil War as the party of the Union, a broad-based coalition of the northern wealthy, the new freedmen of the South, farmers, and workers. The minority Democrats managed to stay alive, largely in exile in the South, as far as presidential elections were concerned. In 1896 the Republicans' winning coalition partly realigned in the face of industrialization and immigration of foreign Catholic labor into the Northeast, its principal elements becoming northern businessmen, middle-class Protestants, and Midwest farmers. Franklin Roosevelt's Democrats emerged out of the Great Depression in 1932, based on a coalition generally dominant for the past 50 years and composed of southerners, labor, farmers, unemployed middle-class persons, blacks, and other ethnic minorities.

Whether a new fifth grand coalition is in the making is the present question. If it is, then 1980 was a political revolution and not a flash in the pan—an electoral realignment of the country. Erosion of the coalition basic to FDR's Democratic party is apparent to the degree that Richard Nixon in 1968 and 1972 drew significant support from southerners, workers, and farmers, in addition to the usual Republican coalition of businessmen, suburbanites, and midwestern and western agrarian interests. The Watergate debacle damaged that coalition sufficiently in 1976 to enable Jimmy Carter to gain election. It appears to have been reconstituted in 1980, with the not inconsiderable addition of an ideologically identifiable New Right coalition of conservatives and activist evangelical Christians composing the Moral Majority, dedicated to Americanism and to the fight against "secular humanism"—as Republican Senator Jesse Helms of North Carolina terms it.[9]

A point to be stressed even in this short tour of our party system is this: political parties that command a national following—namely, the Republicans and Democrats since 1860—are invariably highly heterogeneous in composition. Sizeable fractions of the national population both for and against practically anything one can name seek the same political home, and what they share besides the party label is sometimes difficult to say. But it is noteworthy that a commanding personality is identified with each of the grand coalitions just enumerated: George Washington, Thomas Jefferson, Andrew Jackson, Abraham Lincoln, and Franklin Roosevelt. As Hugh A. Bone remarks:

> Popular and powerful figures attract voters to the party and help forge an alliance that often outlasts the tenure of the President. Dynamic leadership helps to personalize the party and the government. The man himself provides a rallying point for the partisans and for the "antis." [10]

Granted the fact that a party is a conglomeration unified for political ends, the force of one individual's vision and personality may be the vital element that generates a grand coalition rather than a minor one.

If it is true that dominant parties rest on grand coalitions, that coalitions are built on the basis of some degree of consensus, and that consensus is achieved in part from a vitalizing vision of the public interest, it remains nonetheless also true that the American political party as a conglomerate is a loose and decentralized affair. There are good reasons for this, the principal one being that the American people want it this way. Responsible party government of the kind identified with the British system is simply too disciplined for American tastes; it involves too much concession of authority to party leaders to bind the consciences and votes of rank-and-file members, especially in legislative assemblies. We do not have a conservative party that stands toe-to-toe with a liberal party, divided along clearly defined ideological lines. Maddening as this untidy situation is, it is thoroughly rooted in our civic culture as a reflection (among other things) of the diversity of the nation, the moderation of the mass of the citizenry, and the sense of toleration of rival viewpoints that acknowledges the right of the other person to be wrong. It reflects the primordial fear Amerians have of the tyranny of the majority explored by James Madison in *Federalist 10.* The representative insists on speaking the opinions of his district and voting in favor of its compelling interests, whatever the leadership may be insisting upon; and the senator claims a similar prerogative. Neither could withstand reelection challenges if he consistently sacrificed local convictions at every turn in the name of the "interest of the whole" celebrated by the British statesman, Edmund Burke, in the eighteenth century. Minorities have their rights, too; and every citizen knows that in certain respects he is a minority of one. This means, as Lincoln said in his last public address on April 11, 1865: "Important principles may and must be flexible." While shrillness and banality are widely evidenced in our politics, zealotry is a lethal reproach when it is convincingly lodged in a presidential campaign—as it was (rightly or wrongly) by Johnson against Goldwater, and as it was attempted by Carter against Reagan.

THE CONSTITUTION

Our electoral system is determined by the system of representation established under the Constitution. Any grand coalition and consensus embodied in a party are necessarily only distinctive articulations of the larger national coalition and consensus that derive from the people's unifying allegiance to the living Constitution and its particular hedges and fences. As E. E. Schattschneider wrote:

> The parties are bound to come into close and continuous contact with the Constitution because the parties were formed to control the government established by the Constitution. . . . If the parties are the river of American politics, the stream of the living impulse to govern, the Constitution is the river bed, the firm land whose contour shapes the stream. In the long run the river can transform the landscape, but it is also the prisoner of the land.[11]

The Constitution, as the fundamental instrument of government in the United States, establishes the legislative, executive, and judicial powers. It defines their scope and relationship to one another in the intricacies of separation and checks and balances, prescribes offices and qualifications to serve, sets the terms of tenure and modes of selection, traces divisions of authority between national and state governments comprising the federal system, and lists some of "the great rights of mankind" (Madison's phrase) secured by it for persons who are American citizens or are domiciled in the country. The document itself, a mere 6,000 words long, has been extensively interpreted—most prominently by the Supreme Court, whose decisions, opinions, and orders now fill 445 volumes of *U.S. Reports.*

No mere layout of powers, ours is the oldest written constitution in existence, an object of veneration to successive generations, a monument to our civilization, and a part of the civil religion of all sensible Americans. If the public was startled to learn that Ronald Reagan had removed the portraits of Jefferson and Lincoln from the walls of the Oval Office and replaced them with likenesses of Dwight D. Eisenhower and Calvin Coolidge, at least some solace could be drawn from Coolidge's comments on human rights and the Constitution:

> The Constitution of the United States is the final refuge of every right that is enjoyed by any American citizen. So long as it is observed those rights will be secure. Whenever it falls into disrespect or disrepute, the end of orderly organized government as we have known it . . . will be at hand. The Constitution represents a government of law. There is only one other form of authority and that is a government of force. Americans must take their choice between these two. One signifies justice and liberty; the other tyranny and oppression. To live under the American Constitution is the greatest privilege that was ever accorded to the human race.[12]

Such appeals form the basis for Ronald Reagan's "New Beginning," and strike a responsive chord among the so-called silent majority.

The chord struck was faint, it is true. Leading pollsters called 1980 "a negative-cast election. . . . We [Democrats] gave them no sense of the vision . . . we really had roughly two negative candidates."[13] Election turnout for the presidential contest, after hovering around 60 percent during the 1950s and 1960s, fell into the 55 percent range during the 1970s, and in 1980 dropped to a new low of about 53.9 percent of the 160.2 million Americans in the voting age population. (The drop of about five percentage points between the 1968 and 1972 contests is attributable to ratification of the Twenty-sixth Amendment in 1971 that enfranchised citizens 18 years of age and older; the youths promptly stayed away from the polls in even larger droves than had their elders.)

But after all of this has been noticed by way of qualification, it remains true that some vision of American splendor was communicated with some success, and the candidate most effectively communicating it won, tepid election that it was. The Republicans called for more self-reliance and less government. There was a sense of revolving back again to conceived national origins, of getting back to the old-time religion of the American Beginning. This appears to be the "idea taking shape" and animating the vision of American renewal in the minds and hearts of the conservative revolutionaries who won the election. It is a revolution *cum* reformation, on a pattern familiar to students of Western and specifically American political thought.[14]

ELECTORAL PROCEDURES

To place the events of 1980 in firmer context it will be useful to describe the institutional and political hedges and fences of American elections.

The cardinal feature of our electoral landscape is bipartisan or two-party politics. Third parties in American politics have had some impact, but the fate of John Anderson's independent candidacy for the presidency on the National Unity ticket is rather typical. Anderson polled about 7 percent of the popular vote but carried no state, hence received no electoral votes. He had to spend most of his campaign funds just to get on the ballots in all 50 states, along with his vice-presidential running mate, former Democratic Wisconsin governor Patrick Lucey. By psychology, tradition, custom, and constitutional reason a two-party system operates in our politics and has done so since Federalists and Anti-Federalists faced off against one another in the fight over ratification of the Constitution in the 1780s.

The constitutional reasons why we have a two-party rather than a multiparty system lie mainly in the combination of two principles controlling elections for national offices: single member constituencies and winner-take-all elections.

The single member constituency principle applies in elections for the House of Representatives; each congressional district in each state (or the entire state, if it has only one representative) elects a single representative. The winner-take-all principle means that the candidate with the largest number of votes is elected—a majority is not necessary, a plurality suffices. The first principle tends to keep the field narrowed to two candidates in the general election, typically those of the two major parties, as a contest between the strongest contenders for office debating issues on a pro-con basis as a means of sharpening the voters' choices of persons and policies. The second principle badly damages the attractiveness of third party candidates, since also-rans get no share of representation: they simply lose. Voters faced with a three-person race in the general election are inclined to view the third party candidate as a bad risk for election, under these circumstances, and may prefer not to chance throwing their votes away. The same psychology makes fundraising extremely difficult for third party candidates.

Similar considerations tend to operate in senatorial and presidential elections. Each state is guaranteed two senators by the Constitution. But while all House members are elected every two years, only one-third of the Senate members are elected every two years and then for a six-year term. This means that a senatorial race, to represent an entire state, is run under essentially the same conditions as a race for the House: preliminary or primary races narrow the field to the two candidates of the principal parties, and the general election is a winner-take-all race for the seat. Because of the staggered terms in the Senate, a state's two senators are never obliged to run for election at the same time, unless there is a special election for an unexpired term.

The constitutional requirements for election to the presidency are more intricate, but the same two principles can be seen at work at the level of the popular vote. This is because the contest for the presidency is decided in the two stages of a general election (popular vote) followed six weeks later by the vote of the electoral college. In the general election, the candidates of the Democratic and Republican parties (plus any third party candidates who have qualified to be on the ballot in the various states) are each represented by a panel of electors in every state equivalent to the sum of representatives (apportioned to states on the basis of population) plus the two senators. Thus California, with the largest representation in the House, has 45 electors—one for each of the 43 representatives and its two senators. In casting their votes for president, the voters in each state are doing so only indirectly; they actually vote for the panel of electors pledged to vote for the candidate of their party. The significance of the federal system in presidential elections immediately becomes apparent at this point. For a presidential election is not, strictly speaking, national; rather it is a state-by-state affair, as Madison explained in the classic statement, *Federalist 39.*

The single member constituency principle applies here in that only one slate of electors (candidate) can win in each state; the winner-take-all principle means that the slate of electors polling the highest number of votes wins all of a state's electoral votes, whether that amounts to a majority or merely to a plurality of the votes cast. In other words, there is no distribution to second and third place candidates of any electoral votes on the basis of the proportion of the popular vote received in a state. In most states the names of the electors do not even appear on the ballot, and all states except Maine permit straight ticket voting for presidential electors. These electors are morally bound to vote for the presidential candidate chosen by the convention of the party they represent, although there is no legal way to enforce this.

In mid-December the winning ticket's electors assemble in each of the states' capitals to cast separate ballots for president and for vice-president; these are sent to the president pro tempore of the Senate and on January 6 opened by him and counted in the presence of the assembled membership of the House and Senate meeting in joint session. A majority of the entire number of electors is necessary to win, or 270 electoral votes: 435 electors allotted for the 435 members of the House, 100 for the membership of the Senate, plus 3 electors alloted to the District of Columbia for a total electoral vote of 538. The results are announced, and the winners at that point become the president-elect and vice-president-elect. They are sworn into office on the following January 20 to complete the cycle.[15]

The electoral vote is decisive to the election and the popular vote decisive to gaining a majority of the electoral vote, but only in state-by-state contests. In this way the constitutional requirement, which ties together the apportionment of representatives on the basis of population and the awarding of the same number of electors to each state as it has representatives and senators, has a decisive effect on presidential elections and on the campaigns leading to them.

We have stressed that a party fielding a national ticket must have support that is both wide and deep; that is, it must be a *national* party, not a regional, or class, or ideological one. On that consideration, the competition for votes in the general election will tend to be keenest in the key states—those with the largest numbers of electoral votes. In 1980 these included California (45), New York (41), Pennsylvania (27), Texas (26), Illinois (26), Ohio (25), and Michigan (21). The arithmetic is obvious: a candidate carrying these seven key or pivotal states (all with strong two-party traditions) wins 211 electoral votes in the process—only 59 short of the majority needed for presidential election. Many other factors, of course, influence a campaign strategy, but the contest for the key states is the heart of the matter in close elections. The continuing shift of population from the Frost Belt states of the North to the Sun Belt states of the South and Southwest, induced by energy costs and other economic factors, promises to reshape the map of key electoral states in this and the next decade.

THE CONTEST FOR THE PRESIDENCY

Chief Justice Warren Burger administered the oath of office prescribed by the Constitution to Ronald Reagan at noon on January 20, 1981. With his left hand on the Bible and right hand raised, the president-elect repeated these words: "I, Ronald Reagan, do solemnly swear that I will faithfully execute the office of the President of the United States, and will, to the best of my ability, preserve, protect, and defend the Constitution of the United States. So help me God." At that instant he became the 40th president of the United States. Four ruffles and flourishes, followed by a chorus of "Hail to the Chief," and a 21-gun salute sounded across the gathered throng for the first inauguration held on the west front of the Capitol. The inaugural address was delivered, and the ceremony concluded at 12:23 p.m. eastern standard time. The text of the inaugural address is set out in the Presidential Messages appendix.

Theodore H. White once reflected that "there is no way of becoming President of the United States—no avenue as clear as the classic parliamentary ladder that takes men to leadership in Western Europe, or as naked as the tyrant's strike for power in antique and modern despotisms." [16] The way that Reagan found to the White House certainly made a unique political success story, whatever else his presidency might portend. His acting career over, he had eventually entered politics at age 55 to serve eight years as governor of California and twice had been denied his party's nomination for the presidency (in 1968 and 1976). By 1980 he was plainly too old to run, and he always had been acknowledged as too conservative to succeed in being elected even if he somehow should be nominated. Yet here he was—and is—president.

For the nomination Reagan had faced six opponents, starting with the 1980 Iowa state Republican precinct caucuses that opened the campaign. George Bush edged out Reagan 32 percent to 29 percent. Reagan's first big win came in the New Hampshire primary on February 26 where he polled 50 percent of the vote. Then, in one contest after another, Reagan won until he drove the last of his challengers (Bush) from the field at the end of May; John Anderson by then had launched an independent campaign. Reagan was nominated on the first ballot at the Republican convention with 1,939 votes (1,130 needed), after winning 28 of the 34 state primaries.

He then faced incumbent President Jimmy Carter in the general election. Carter had come to the Democratic Convention after winning 24 of 35 primaries; 60 percent of the delegates were pledged to vote for him on the first ballot. He had out-distanced Senator Edward Kennedy after April 30 when he abandoned his "Rose Garden campaign" and

Reprinted by permission of the Chicago Tribune-New York News Syndicate, Inc.

took his candidacy for renomination to the people. But Carter clearly was in political trouble, as was indicated when he lost five primaries in one day (June 3) to Kennedy, even though on the same day Carter won a majority of the convention delegates and cinched the nomination. Carter's trouble was reflected by the fact that he lagged 20 percentage points behind Reagan in the polls on the eve of the Democratic convention. In fact, his popularity stood lower with the American public at that time than had any president's since opinion polling began— lower than Harry Truman's after the Korean War, lower than Richard Nixon's after Watergate.

Always an effective campaigner, however, Carter closed the gap, and a tight race developed down to the weekend before the election. He used incumbency to maximum advantage through ready access to the press, leaking announcements on invigorated military policy and weapons systems, awarding contracts in key states for federal projects, approving loans for drought afflicted states in the Midwest and Southwest, appealing to ethnic voters by bestowing the Congressional Medal of Honor on a World War II veteran of Italian-American descent, and extending a $670 million credit guarantee to beleaguered Poland. He attacked Reagan as reactionary, inexperienced in national politics, and a warmonger whose election would endanger peace in the nation and in the world. He projected himself as a president of experience, judgment, peace, honesty, and compassion.

The Reagan campaign drove home the "time for a change" theme. It made the most of the candidate's successes as governor of a state that is larger than many countries and bore down on Carter's record in domestic policy, especially his failure to curb inflation and rising unemployment. Reagan hardly had to mention the Iranian hostage crisis beyond the reiterated resolve, sounded in his acceptance speech at the convention, to "make America great again." Newspaper endorsements favored Reagan by a margin of 443 to 126, and independent Anderson received 40. But there was little enthusiasm in their endorsement of any candidate: the *Washington Post* endorsed the president despite his "unrelieved awfulness," while the editor of the *Miami Herald* came out for Anderson because he favored a "one-eyed man over two who are blind."

A river of money flowed into the campaign. Leaving aside the great costs of the primaries, each candidate of the major parties was entitled to spend $29.4 million in federal funds during the general election race, and each of the national committees might spend another $4.6 million to support its candidate. A separate source of funds came from individuals and organizations who might spend unlimited amounts to elect or defeat a candidate, provided there was no direct connection with either official campaign organization or national party. Reagan greatly benefitted from this, because of a high degree of Republican organization at the state and local levels of political action committees (PACs) and the significant activities of such new organizations as the Reverend Jerry Falwell's Moral Majority, Paul Weyrich's Committee for the Survival of a Free Congress, Senator Jesse Helms's Congressional Club, and other "new right" groups. As Democratic Senator Daniel Patrick Moynihan of New York summed up after the election: "There were two things that hit us. First was money, money, money, money. . . . Then there was . . . organization and technology. . . . We are so far behind that we . . . are in danger of becoming the permanent minority party." [17] Organized labor sustained the Democrats' campaign at the grassroots, and the only private groups to contribute more money to Carter than Reagan were the labor unions at an estimated $15 million to $1 million.[18]

The seesaw contest for the presidency came to the surprising conclusion we observed at the outset. On Sunday before the Tuesday election Carter fell five percentage points behind in the polls, and by Monday evening he was ten points down. Whatever the complex explanation for the collapse that became reality the next day, a simple one should not be ignored. As Republican Governor James Thompson of Illinois phrased it: "A lot of people, the so-called silent majority, went into the voting booths and said, 'To hell with it, I'm not going to reward four years of failure.' " [19]

REVOLUTION OR FLASH IN THE PAN?

"The November 4 election returns constitute the greatest victory for conservatism since the American Revolution." [20] "The biggest perception Reagan had going for him was that he wasn't Jimmy Carter." [21] "The 1980 election was not a voice for a change . . . [but] a call for order and stability . . . things were out of control . . . let's bring some control back into the system—whether it was in foreign policy, which Iran obviously enters into very much, our prestige in the world, or the economy." [22] "On Sunday, after the hostage thing began, we found one of the biggest one day drops . . . in the campaign. . . . At the same time, we saw the President's rating on how he managed the economy take a huge drop. The kind of volatility and jerking back and forth we saw suggested more the nature of a primary than a general election and tended to suggest more of a protest than anything else. . . . At the end . . . a large percentage of the voters decided, 'I'm mad as hell, and I'm not going to take it any more.' " [23] "In a time of trouble at home and abroad, the President has become the lightning rod for all the discontents of the citizenry." [24] "If Mr. Reagan had been running against someone who had failed less often than Jimmy Carter he likely would not have made it at all." [25]

The tenor of most of these comments is that a tide of discontent was decisive in Reagan's and the Republicans' election victories. The view was buttressed by the *New York Times*/CBS News exit poll. When Reagan voters leaving their precincts were asked why they had voted for him, 38 percent said their main reason was because "It's time for a change." Only 11 percent claimed that their reason was because "He's a real conservative." These were the sentiments expressed on election day or within a few days after it. Poll results published on March 1, 1981, however, showed a shift in the public's views that the pollsters found "striking." Three separate polling organizations (*Washington Post*/ABC News, the Gallup Poll, and Richard Wirthlin, Reagan's pollster) noted a strong increase in the number of Americans who identified themselves as Republicans and a comparable decrease in the number who identified themselves as Democrats. Did this mean that 1980 was a realignment election? Wirthlin had not thought so previously, but his three nation-wide polls in January and February of 1981 totaling 6,000 interviews convinced him "that the change has occurred." [26]

While waiting for history to be decided, we can only speculate and wonder. Are we observing the formation of a fifth grand coalition? A realignment election? What difference would that make in American politics? What would remain largely as it has been in the recent past?

Various answers to these questions can be proposed here and others will be suggested in the chapters to follow. Hints of what 1980 may mean already have been given in the broad strokes of this introduction, insofar as we have considered the intentions of the Reagan administration and the present and anticipated circumstances conditioning political action in the nation and the world. After all, the Republicans not only want to save the country; they also want to be reelected. As candidate Reagan shouted at one belligerent audience in an urban ghetto, "I can't do anything for you unless I'm elected! " This chastening sentiment assures that common sense will rule policy decisions. The Democratic party will curb extremist tendencies among the New Right supporters of the Reagan Republicans: "We're not going to let them tear asunder programs we've built," said House Speaker O'Neill after reviewing the Reagan budget. John Anderson's fear that Reagan's "blunderbuss approach" to budget-cutting at the expense of social programs "may tear apart the social fabric of this country," can only be unfounded if a new grand coalition is in the making.[27] Battle lines already had formed by the end of February 1981, when the AFL-CIO announced formation of a Budget Coalition of 157 national organizations to fight against announced spending cuts.[28] Reagan's image as a conservative in the public's eye had been modified by March 1, 1981, according to an Associated Press/NBC News poll: in April 1980, 62 percent of those who knew of Reagan thought he was a conservative, 17 percent thought he was a moderate, and 14 percent thought he was a liberal; in February 1981, however, 47 percent thought he was a conservative, 33 percent thought he was a moderate, and 12 percent thought he was a liberal. Equally to the point, 78 percent thought he was "the kind of person who gets things done." [29]

Any successful American political leader has to be a trimmer in some degree; and the Republican party under Ronald Reagan can be counted on to trim the apocalyptical excesses from its policies—domestic and foreign—in the interest of fostering a workable consensus. In the midst of the Civil War, Abraham Lincoln made the point more than once, for example:

> My paramount object in this struggle is to save the Union, and is not either to save or destroy slavery. If I could save the Union without freeing any slave, I would do it; and if I could do it by freeing all the slaves, I would do it; and if I could save it by freeing some and leaving others alone, I would also do that.

Strange words from the Great Emancipator? Not at all. He explained himself on another occasion this way:

> It was a time when a man with a policy would have been fatal to the country. I never had a policy. I have simply tried to do what seemed best each day, as each day came. [30]

One can be fairly certain that a similar pragmatism will guide the new Republican administration.

This is, of course, not to say that a consensus that can sustain the faith of the nation can be built exclusively out of trimming and compromising. There must also be vision and force of personality. Nor can there be much doubt that the consensus in the offing (if it is) will be structured by Reagan's own convictions. Adam Smith's "invisible hand" [31] doctrine lurks just beneath the surface of budget-cutting, tax-reducing, and deregulation policies already announced for the economy; it is a primary article of faith, but one tempered by 200 years of economic development. Nor can there be much doubt that the sustained secular drift of the country is a matter of deep concern to a substantial segment of the American population, many of whom see Republican conservatism as a suitable political medium for combatting it. Nor, finally, can there be much doubt that those presently in office in Washington perceive international communism and the Soviet Union to be real and even sinister threats to all that Americans cherish, and they intend to act decisively to protect national interests against these dangers. But all these convictions will have to translate into policies supported by a national consensus and moderated by the dictates of reason—if a grand coalition is to emerge. This adds up to a tall order indeed.

NOTES

1. *Time* (November 18, 1980), p. 61.
2. Joan McKinney, "Sen. Long Enjoying New Role," *Baton Rouge Sunday Advocate*, 1 February 1981.
3. The data cited herein are largely drawn from *The World Almanac & Book of Facts: 1981* (New York: Newspaper Enterprise Association, 1980) and *U.S. News & World Report* (November 17, 1980).
4. *Time* (January 5, 1981), p. 13.
5. *U.S. Chronicle* (Providence), April 19, 1787, quoted from Jackson Turner Main, *Political Parties Before the Constitution* (Chapel Hill, N.C.: University of North Carolina Press, 1973), p. 407.
6. Charles G. Mayo and Beryl L. Crowe, eds., *American Political Parties: A Systematic Perspective* (New York: Harper & Row, 1967), p. 487.
7. Hugh A. Bone, *American Politics and the Party System*, 4th ed. (New York: McGraw-Hill Book Co., 1971), p. 20.
8. James MacGregor Burns, J. W. Peltason, and Thomas E. Cronin, *Government By the People*, 9th ed. (Englewood Cliffs, N.J.: Prentice-Hall, 1975), Chapter 11; Robert H. Blank, *Political Parties: An Introduction* (Englewood Cliffs, N.J.: Prentice-Hall, 1980), Chapter 3.
9. Quoted by Helen Dewar, "Sen. Jesse Helms—Archangel of the Right," *Baton Rouge Sunday Advocate*, 22 February 1981. Copyright 1981, *The Washington Post*. For pertinent discussion see Blank, *Political Parties*, pp. 296-304. Also see Kevin P. Phillips's provocative books: *The Emerging Republican Majority* (Garden City, N.Y.: Doubleday & Co., 1970) and *Mediacracy* (Garden City, N.Y.: Doubleday & Co., 1970.

   A further word may be said about the emergence of the evangelical Christian political activists who, in myriad organizations, have taken a leaf from the handbook of religious and secular liberals who zealously have pursued such causes as racial equality, women's rights, the environment, and opposition to the war in Vietnam. Candidates Reagan, Carter, and Anderson all professed to being "born again" Christians during the 1980 campaign; 30 million evangelical Christians were recognized to be a potentially great political force. The election proved this to be the case—to the general benefit of conservative Republicans.

   Religion in American politics is nothing new, however, despite this most recent and well-organized latest manifestation of it. Alexis de Tocqueville, in his book *Democracy in America*, said: "It was religion that gave birth to . . . America. One must never forget that. In the United States religion is mingled with all the national customs and all those feelings which the word fatherland evokes. For that reason it has peculiar power."

   That religion, and specifically evangelical Christianity, promises to be a potent source of communication for the formerly silent majority in the Reagan years can scarcely be doubted, but it is merely one more voice in the massed choir of American democracy.
10. Bone, *American Politics and the Party System*, p. 32.
11. E. E. Schattschneider, *Party Government* (New York: Holt, Rinehart & Winston, 1942), p. 124.
12. President Calvin Coolidge as quoted in Ralph H. Gabriel, *The Course of American Democratic Thought*, rev. ed. (New York: Ronald Press, 1956), p. 444.

18   *Revolution or Flash in the Pan?*

13. Robert M. Teeter and Patrick H. Caddell as quoted in *New York Times,* 9 November 1980, p. E-3.
14. Ellis Sandoz, "Classical and Christian Dimensions of American Political Thought," *Modern Age* 25 (January 1981): 14-25.
15. The constitutional requirements for electing the president and vice-president, together with related matters, are set forth in the 12th Amendment (1804) as modified by the 20th Amendment (1933) and the 25th Amendment (1967). For an excellent summary see "ABC's of How a President is Chosen," *U.S. News & World Report* (February 18, 1980).
16. *The Making of the President 1960* (New York: Pocket Books, 1961), p. 31.
17. Quoted in Peter Ross Range, "Thunder from the Right," *New York Times Magazine,* 8 February 1981, p. 25.
18. Richard A. Watson, *Promise and Performance of American Democracy,* 4th ed. (New York: John Wiley & Sons, 1981), p. A12.
19. *Time* (November 17, 1980), p. 24.
20. Howard Phillips, "Election is Biggest Win for Conservatives Since the American Revolution," *Conservative Digest* 6 (November 1980): 5.
21. John P. Sears, quoted in *New York Times,* 9 November 1980, p. E-3.
22. Peter D. Hart, quoted ibid.
23. Patrick H. Caddell, quoted ibid.
24. *Time* (November 17, 1980), p. 24.
25. Paul Weyrich, "Election Proves Conservatives Don't Have to Abandon Their Principles to be Victorious," *Conservative Digest,* 6 (November 1980): 4.
26. Barry Sussman, "Surprising change in political alignment noted," *Baton Rouge Sunday Advocate,* 1 March 1981.
27. O'Neill as quoted by *Time* (March 2, 1981), p. 14; Anderson as quoted in the *Baton Rouge Morning Advocate,* 11 February 1981.
28. William J. Eaton and George Skelton, "Labor-led Coalition to Fight Budget Cuts," *Baton Rouge Morning Advocate,* 28 February 1981.
29. Reported for AP by Evans Witt, "Reagan Gets Positive Rating in Overall Work," *Baton Rouge Sunday Advocate,* 1 March 1981.
30. The first Lincoln quotation is from his letter to Horace Greeley, dated August 22, 1862; the second is from Carl Sandburg's unpublished foreword to *Abraham Lincoln: The Prairie Years* (1925) which appeared in newspapers on February 12, 1954; quoted from *The Mirror,* Part I, p. 4.
31. Adam Smith (1723-1790), the Scottish economist, published the great work on natural liberty and free enterprise (laissez faire) economics in 1776. At its center lay the principle of faith in the operation of an "invisible hand," which he explained in these words: "As every individual . . . endeavors as much as he can both to employ his capital in the support of domestic industry, and so to direct that industry that its produce may be of the greatest value; every individual necessarily labours to render the annual revenue of the society as great as he can. He generally, indeed, neither intends to promote the public interest, nor knows how much he is promoting it . . . he intends only his own security . . . he intends his own gain, and he is in this . . . *led by an invisible hand* to promote an end which was no part of his intention. Nor is it always the worse for the society that it was no part of it. By pursuing his own interest he frequently promotes that of the society more effectually than when he really intends to promote it." *Wealth of Nations,* Book IV, Chapter 2, ed. C. J. Bullock, Harvard Classics, vol. 10 (New York: P. F. Collier & Son, Co., 1909), pp. 351-52. Emphasis added.

2

The 1980 Election:
Profile and Historical Perspective

James L. Sundquist and Richard M. Scammon

The immediate reaction to the 1980 election was that the results were far from ordinary. "It is plainly the end of an era," author Theodore H. White intoned on election night television. "Republicans and Democrats Alike See New Era in '80 Returns," was a Thursday morning headline in *The Washington Post*, over a story by veteran political analyst David S. Broder that described "all the appearances of an era ending—and a new one beginning." Consumer advocate Ralph Nader saw a "power shift so significant" that the previous Republican victories of 1952 and 1968 paled by comparison.

We have, however, heard all of this before. Those of us who are old enough to remember some other great Republican victories—not only 1952 and 1968 but 1946, 1956, and 1972—recall that each of them was hailed as the end of the long period of Democratic supremacy that began with the first election of Franklin D. Roosevelt in 1932. On each of those occasions, the Roosevelt New Deal coalition had "finally broken up." In 1969, *The Emerging Republican Majority,* by Kevin Phillips, offered a book-length explanation of the inevitability of it all.[1] Yet when things settled down after each of those elections, the Democratic party had survived, and remained the larger party in the country.

Reprinted with permission of the New York Times Syndicate.

So we can say yes, categorically, a new political era has arrived—but only if an era is defined as something short, such as four years, say, or maybe eight. If the term is assumed to mean something longer than that, the White-Broder-Nader interpretation is challenged by nearly a half century of experience.

Still, one day the prophets of political revolution will be right. The country's normal Democratic majority in party identification will not last forever. So the possibility that 1980 did indeed mark the beginning of the long-awaited realignment of the American party system cannot be dismissed out of hand. Was 1980, then, another 1932, when the party that had been the minority in the country for two generations—the Democrats—was turned into the majority party for the next two? Or was it more like 1952, that flashiest of all Republican victories that turned out to be just a deviation from normal political behavior, corrected shortly afterward? Or, perhaps, was it something in between, or something quite different from either?

WHAT HAPPENED IN 1980

The central circumstance of the 1980 election was the unpopularity of Jimmy Carter. In the summer of 1979, his approval rating in the

Gallup Poll was under 30 percent; it was boosted temporarily in the rally-round-the-president reaction to the seizing of U.S. hostages in Iran and the Soviet invasion of Afghanistan, but by the following summer it had slumped again. In July 1980, it set a record for the four decades of the poll's history—21 percent, lower than Harry Truman's rating in the midst of the unpopular Korean War, lower even than Richard Nixon's just before his resignation. Carter's disapproval rating at that time was exactly three times his level of approval—63 percent.[2]

All that saved Jimmy Carter at that point was that the Republicans chose a nominee about whom the public likewise had grave reservations. In retrospect, it seems clear that if the GOP had settled on a more typical politician as their candidate—George Bush or Howard Baker— there never would have been a contest. But Ronald Reagan carried some heavy burdens. A few weeks after inauguration, he would become the oldest president in American history. He had the image of an extremist; his origin, and his zealous support, were in the far right of the Republican party. Like Carter, he had no experience in governing a nation, no background in foreign or military or economic affairs, and people could not forget he was a movie actor by profession. He had a reputation for reckless statements, including a penchant for brandishing a military solution for every international crisis.

After the conventions, more than half the people polled said that they were unhappy with the choice the two parties had given them. That gave a momentary glimmer of hope to independent candidate John Anderson, whose essential platform was that he was neither Jimmy Carter nor Ronald Reagan, but inevitably that hope faded. Meanwhile, Reagan was denouncing the Carter record, while Carter was saying, "Let's talk about Reagan instead." The Democrats did the best they could to reinforce the reservations of the voters, especially on the "warmonger" question, but in the end the antipathy to Carter outweighed the fear of Reagan.

The Carter-Reagan debate in the final week of the campaign was crucial. With more than half the television sets of the country tuned in— and presumably all the sets of the conscientious undecided—Reagan won the personality contest. He reassured the waverers that he was not a right-wing nut, that his youthful vitality had not all vanished, that he had a command of economics and world affairs, that he was a man of peace. So the voters felt free to do what they had wanted to do all along—throw Jimmy Carter out.

Presidential Vote

Yet landslides are won by small percentage shifts. By all the evidence, a large majority of the voters stayed fixed; most Carter voters of 1976 were still Carter supporters in 1980, and almost all Ford voters went naturally to Reagan. Gallup Poll figures indicate that 10 percent of voters calling themselves Republicans voted for Carter in both elections, and many of these, undoubtedly, were the same people. Among Democrats, 18 percent were for Ford in 1976, 26 percent for Reagan in 1980— that difference being the decisive switch. Independents, increasing their Republican vote by little, split 57-38 for Ford over Carter in 1976 and 55-29 for Reagan over Carter in 1980, with 14 percent going to Anderson.

So 1980 basically replicated 1976, but not closely enough to keep Carter in the White House. The swing to the Republicans was by no means of abnormal strength; Reagan's percentage of the popular vote was a full 10 points under Richard Nixon's margin in 1972. His enormous electoral college majority appears a bit misleading; of the 10 states that were very close, Reagan eventually carried all but Hawaii. Five of the close states were in the South, and another was Kentucky, which makes the new Republican South look less solid than it had appeared at first.

Moreover, the basic alignment of the party system created in the Roosevelt era was still apparent. Liberals, big city voters, union families, blacks, Hispanics, the youngest electors, the unemployed, the lowest income groups, those with the lowest school completion rates, Jews—all of these groups stayed with the Democrats. To read this list is, of course, to note the duplication of categories, such as unemployed and low income, or black and big city voters. In addition, and unfortunately for President Carter, voter turnout in a number of these groups is traditionally low, and the Democratic margin in 1980 was smaller than in 1976.

Among labor union families, for instance, a Democratic break of 63-36 in 1976 was cut back to 50-43 in 1980, with 5 percentage points going to Anderson. Thus, the Democratic margin of 27 points was reduced to but 7, and in a very substantial element of the voting population. All of the television exit polls taken on election day placed the Carter vote among Jews at less than 50 percent, far lower than in any recent national campaign, with at least one-third supporting Reagan.

Among one important group, Roman Catholic voters, the normal and often heavy Democratic majority disappeared. Both Gallup and the exit polls agreed that Reagan carried the Catholic vote by a small margin, compared to a 15-point plurality for the Democrats in 1976.

One of the most striking phenomena of 1980 was the difference in voting behavior between men and women. In the Gallup data, the women gave Reagan a 5-point margin over Carter, not much of a change from the 3-point edge they gave to Ford. But men went for Reagan by a difference of 15 points, compared to an 8-point Carter margin in 1976—a swing of 23 points.[3] Most analysts attribute this difference primarily to the greater sensitivity of women to the "warmonger" charges made against Reagan, with his opposition to the Equal Rights Amendment a secondary factor. If men had behaved like women, the 1980 election would have been a squeaker; the other way around, it would have been nearly as overwhelming as the Nixon reelection victory of 1972.

Congressional Races

In the congressional elections, the Republicans did not fare as well as in 1952, when they captured both houses of the Congress along with the presidency. But they did do better than in 1956, 1968, and 1972, when they won the White House but lost both the Senate and the House. This time they gained the Senate only, picking up a dozen seats. The usual combination of reasons can be found—some national, some local, some ideological, some personal. But two at least can be regionalized. In the West, four liberal Democratic senators were "targeted" by conservatives for defeat, and were beaten. A sort of liberal "Gang of Four," these incumbents—Birch Bayh, Frank Church, John Culver, and George McGovern—all represented states clearly more conservative than they. All four states—Indiana, Idaho, Iowa, and South Dakota, respectively—have voted for the Republican candidate in every presidential election after they went for Lyndon Johnson in 1964. Even more significant, in the long run, may well be the Republican Senate victories in four southern states—Alabama, Florida, Georgia, and North Carolina. This brings the southern Republican representation in the Senate up to 10 seats, and if one adds to this number Senator Harry Byrd, Jr., of Virginia (who was elected as an independent, endorsed Reagan in 1980, and normally votes with the Republicans except on organizational matters), the southern seats are split 11-11. As late as 1961, the score was 22-0 in favor of the Democrats. Other significant implications of the election of 1980 for the Senate are analyzed in Chapter 5.

In their national advertising campaign, the Republicans emphasized that the Carter record the voters so plainly disapproved of was not his alone; the Congress also shared the blame, and it had been controlled by the Democrats almost continuously for half a century. The message evidently got through to the voters, as far as the Senate was concerned. Senators, after all, are national figures, identified with the making of national policy.

Democratic House members fared better, maintaining their majority, presumably because they are associated more with district matters and constituency service. Bearing out this thesis is the fact that conspicuous among the losers were some of the more prominent, nationally known Democratic figures, including the majority whip, John Brademas of Indiana, and the Ways and Means Committee chairman, Al Ullman of Oregon. Chapter 4 calls attention to other significant aspects of the election for the House.

THE ANALOGY OF 1932

The favorite Republican scenario, at this point, is that 1980 will turn out to be another 1932. Ronald Reagan will be another Franklin Roosevelt, able to forge a durable coalition out of the disparate groups that supported him in his initial victory. He is a master of television, as FDR was of radio; his first talk to the nation as president was inevitably dubbed a "fireside chat." Under his leadership, that long-delayed Republican majority will finally emerge, and stay.

The Republicans can start with hope, for the election of 1980 does bear resemblance to that of 1932. But that is only a start, for in the realignment of the 1930s the 1932 election was but the beginning point. True, 1932 is often bracketed with 1860 and 1896 as the years of critical, realigning elections, but to interpret 1932 (or 1860 for that matter) in that manner is misleading. The triumph of Roosevelt over Herbert Hoover was a massive protest against the record of the party in power— similar to the Reagan victory of 1980 in character though far exceeding it in scale. The protest was expressed rather uniformly among all segments of the electorate, with little of the diverse movement of population groups that defines a realignment of the party system.

That came later. In the election of 1936, various population groups behaved quite differently. The enormous gains made by the Democratic party in 1932 in working class and lower income areas stayed put, and were even expanded, while the gains made by the Democrats in upper income voting precincts were largely lost—those voters returned to the Republicans. Between 1932 and 1936, then—perhaps to a considerable extent by 1934—the party system realigned along class lines, and that configuration has remained.[4] In 1980, the Democrats were still commanding the allegiance of a disproportionate share of blue-collar workers, minorities, and lower-income groups in general, while the Republican party remained the political home of most upper-income people, professionals, and business executives. And because, to paraphrase Abraham Lincoln, the Lord made so many more common than uncommon people, the Democratic party has been in the majority in the new alignment.

If 1980 is to be the precursor of a Reagan realignment, the history of the 1930s will have to repeat itself in two respects. First, the Republicans will have to put forward a program that is perceived by the protesting voters of 1980 as the solution to the problems that beset them. Major obstacles confronting Republican policymakers in two key spheres—economic and foreign policy issues—are identified more fully in Chapters 7 and 8, respectively.

Second, the Democrats will have to oppose the program. Then the differences between the parties will become stark, and the conflict bitter. The country will be divided, polarized. Presently unattached voters, especially the younger ones, will discover that parties have meaning after all. They will identify, intellectually and emotionally, with the party that is waging the political battle on their side. Some who have considered themselves Democrats will conclude that it is the Republicans who now share and represent their views, and will change sides, outnumbering those who cross the party line in the opposite direction. For reasons identified more fully in Chapter 6, this prospect faces a number of fundamental obstacles.

That is the process that took place after the 1932 election. Clearly by 1936, probably as early as 1934, Roosevelt had convinced millions who had voted against Hoover that the new president was truly on their side, that he was determined to feed the hungry, put the unemployed to work, and repair and reform the failed economic system. He did not have to achieve all those ends. Roosevelt's New Deal did not vanquish the Great Depression; only World War II did that. But he had to be seen as trying, and trying hard. In that, he succeeded. Those who were suffering had no doubt that the man in the White House was their champion. And so was the Democratic party that he led.

But to be seen as battlers, the president and his party have to have an enemy. And this the Republicans provided, as—still under the leadership of Hoover—they fought FDR's programs, measure by measure, throughout the realignment period. As the parties were polarized, so was the country. Political conflict was more intense and harsher, the difference between the parties wider and clearer than at any time in the recollection of most voters. Partisan opponents were more than just competitors for power; they were the enemy. Economic questions became issues of morality, cast in terms of good and evil, right and wrong. Little room was left for political independence, or neutrality. People had to decide where they stood, and with whom. And they did. Millions of new voters entering the electorate had no doubt which party they adhered to, and established voters were forced to reconsider their allegiance. Most of those who joined, or changed, parties in that period did so for life. In the emotionally-charged political atmosphere, the bond that formed between voter and party had the durability of the tie between a parishioner and his church. In 1932, to pursue the metaphor, those who voted Democratic for the first time were visiting a new political church. As the New Deal developed, millions remained and were baptized. Many were born again.

Even to recall the events, and the temper, of the 1930s is to suggest the difference from the 1980s. In Jimmy Carter's record is nothing so cataclysmic as the Great Depression. He was unpopular, but he was not hated. The mood may be grim now, but it is not desperate. Many people have suffered a loss in real income, but they are not hungry. And, unlike in the 1930s, many have not been hurt at all, or have only felt the impact very slightly; in the inflation game, there are winners as well as losers, while during the years of the Great Depression hardly anyone was insulated from the general catastrophe.

Nevertheless, if discontent is not as deep today, that would only make a resulting realignment less profound; it would not forestall it altogether. So what of the two basic conditions that produced the realignment of the 1930s: first, the perceived program of the winning party; second, the position of the losing party?

As Roosevelt did, President Reagan will have to convince his 1980 backers that he has an economic program that is well designed to work. More than for any other reason, Jimmy Carter lost popularity—and therefore the election—because he lost the battle with inflation. In his four years, he changed course too many times; the people eventually concluded that he had no sense of direction. Ronald Reagan begins his administration with a much firmer ideological base. Throughout his political career, he has confidently prescribed cutting government spending and reducing taxes as the solution for every economic ill, and he has shown every sign of being wedded to consistency. But he is contending with a very skeptical electorate. The people voted to give him a chance to test his theories, and their verdict will await the outcome of that test.

The fact is that Americans are highly ambivalent on taxes and spending. Unfortunately for the purists, solid majorities can be found for balancing the budget *and* for continuing public services. In the struggle between retrenchment and entitlement, the result tends to be a draw, with the great majority supporting *both* viewpoints simultaneously. As for tax reduction, polls have shown for years that a solid majority of the people oppose cutting revenues, if that means increasing the budget deficit and, therefore, the national debt. At last report, a popular majority was against the Kemp-Roth plan (named for Representative Jack Kemp and Senator William Roth) to cut taxes by 10 percent a year for three years—which Reagan has embraced—because the budget would be further out of balance.

For these reasons alone, it will be more difficult for Reagan to bring about a party realignment than it was for Roosevelt. Those who became the New Deal coalition agreed on the basic issue that split the country; they demanded that the federal government act swiftly to provide relief for the destitute and jobs for the unemployed. All Roosevelt had to do to cement his coalition into the Democratic party was to respond energetically to that demand. But in Reagan's case, those who supported him are not agreed upon the course. The doubters will not make a commitment to him, and to his party, until the Reagan-Republican philosophy is proven right.

If, then, Reagan's policies succeed in cutting the inflation rate, reducing interest rates, and stimulating productivity, he will assuredly make some permanent Republicans out of all those temporary ones. If that is done at the expense of increased unemployment and cuts in health and education services and environmental protection, he will make new Democrats as well, although—assuming these effects are not severe—they will probably be fewer in number. The hazards are obvious. Tax cuts take effect quickly; spending reductions slowly. If tax cuts swell the deficit, the Federal Reserve Board clamps down on credit, interest rates soar, and inflation is exacerbated while the president and Congress are still arguing about where and how to slash the budget, then those who voted for Reagan despite grave misgivings about his economic program will go right back to whatever political home—Democratic or independent—they came from.

Moreover, the suspicion of the Republicans as the party of big business, which contributed much to Democratic strength and solidarity in the 1930s, could be revived (as it was for a time during the Eisenhower era). The economic program then will be seen as having been conceived and administered by men from big business, and can be easily portrayed as delivering its benefits predominantly to the corporations and the rich.

There are similar hazards in other Reagan policies. If "getting the government off the backs of the people" means giving them fouler air, dirtier water, more industrial accidents, and more consumer fraud, then probusiness policies will be seen as antipeople. Environmental issues alone could be enough to reverse the Reagan gains in his own heartland, the West.

Nevertheless, it is possible that Reagan and his Republican party will succeed in skirting all of these obstacles. They may master inflation, put the unemployed back to work, retrench government, or at least be seen as making a good start in these directions, all without adverse, offsetting consequences. If so, they will have fulfilled one of the conditions for cementing a large proportion of the 1980 protest voters into their ranks. But tall as that order is for any president and party, even that will not be enough. The outcome depends on Democratic behavior also.

The New Deal realignment would not have occurred on anything like its ultimate scale, and perhaps not at all, if the Roosevelt measures had been enacted with cheerful bipartisan support. The bitter Republican resistance, which polarized the party system, was an essential circumstance. It forced people to reconsider their political allegiances and make new choices, with the GOP the loser. But there is little reason, as of 1981, to believe that the Democrats will make the same mistake.

True, the Democrats hold a majority in the House of Representatives, but it would be a surprise if they tried to use their power there to block the essentials of the Reagan program. In the first place, they are not well enough united. If the Republicans line up solidly behind their president, and on central issues they surely will, it takes only 26 Democratic defections to give them a majority. And the newly-invigorated conservative wing of the Democratic party has considerably more House votes than that. In the second place, the Democrats are too scared. They read the election returns, too. They saw their liberal brethren in both houses mowed down along with Carter. So they will respect the voters' mandate. And third, they will see it as bad politics. They will not want to give the Republicans the issue of "obstructionism" to flail them with in 1982. The wise course, politically, is to play the rather long odds that if given their way Reagan and the Republicans, for all the reasons set out earlier, will turn more people into new Democrats than new Republicans.

The House Democrats will, of course, find points on which to differ with the Republicans—though their ranks will not be solid—and the number of such points will increase each year, but probably the issues will be marginal rather than central until after the 1982 election. They will modify the Reagan program in the interest of their traditional constituencies, and many of their spokesmen will shout their misgivings, but they will not block it. A big Democratic gain in 1982 would inspire the House majority to a more vigorous and united opposition, but barring that eventuality the House Democrats are likely to be timid in confronting Reagan. As emphasized in Chapter 4, House Democrats are mindful of the public mood, as expressed in the results of the 1980 election.

If that turns out to be the Democratic posture, then, the distinction between the parties will be blurred; massive shifts in party allegiance are not produced by fuzzy issues. Democratic voters, in short, can feel they are giving President Reagan the support he needs while remaining Democrats, as long as their representatives in the Congress are doing that. The same is true of independents. With no reason to become Republicans in order to advance the causes for which they gave Reagan their votes in 1980, they will stay put.

THE NEW CONSERVATISM

While inflation, and the loss of real income associated with it, were the most powerful forces behind the protest vote of 1980, there were other issues as well. One was a cluster of foreign policy and national security questions—the feeling that the United States was being "pushed around" by small nations, especially Iran, that it was not standing up effectively to the Soviet Union, and that it was taking second place in military strength to the Soviets. In late September 1980, an NBC/Associated Press poll showed that 78 percent of the respondents rated President Carter's handling of foreign affairs as "only fair" or "poor" (almost as many as the 85 percent who marked him that low on his handling of the economy), and 60 percent disapproved of his handling of the Iranian situation. Beyond these were a series of social issues—abortion, busing, affirmative action, gun control, the Equal Rights Amendment, and other questions associated with crusading "single interest" groups, and broader organizations such as the Moral Majority.

In the nearly 50 years that the New Deal party system has existed, foreign policy and social issues have usually been peripheral. The confrontation between Democrats and Republicans has centered around the role of government, the economy, and the conflicting interests of different occupational and income groups. As explained more fully in Chapter 8, during much of that time, foreign and national security policies were essentially bipartisan, based on a high degree of national consensus. And social issues, including even civil rights, were hardly on the government agenda at all.

Political Conflict Redefined

But events of the past 15 years have tremendously broadened the range and scale of political conflict. The war in Vietnam shattered the national consensus on foreign policy and thrust fundamental questions about the country's posture and conduct in world affairs into the center of political debate. Other events and trends sent shocks through the nation that compelled attention to social issues—among them the Supreme Court decisions on school desegregation, busing, abortion, and school prayer; the civil rights revolution; the urban and campus riots of the mid-1960s; the feminist movement and the Equal Rights Amendment; the rise in crime and drug abuse.

In the past decade, it has been on these new issues—rather than on such traditional ones concerning the role of government—that political heat has been generated and large groups of voters have been polarized. A new body (or, as Chapter 4 explains more fully, several new groups) of conservatives has appeared, quite different in class and social origin from the traditional conservatives of the corporate boardrooms and the northeastern suburbs. The new conservatives are strongest among some of the voting groups attached since the 1930s to the liberal Democratic party—notably, white southerners and Catholics.

It is to these new conservatives that many Republicans look for recruits to make them the majority party.[6] That would produce a party realignment in the full meaning of the word. A new line of cleavage would be formed. People would choose their party on the basis of a new set of policy differences beyond the old ones of economics, role of

Table 2-1.   Classifications of Voters According to Conservative-Liberal Issue Positions.

Issues	*Groups*							
	1	2	3	4	5	6	7	8
Economy/Role of Government/ Class	C	C	C	C	L	L	L	L
Foreign Policy/National Security	C	C	L	L	C	C	L	L
Social	C	L	C	L	C	L	C	L

government, and class. The whole structure of party conflict, the rationale of the party system, the substance of the rivalry between Republicans and Democrats would be altered fundamentally. The two-party world would shift on its axis.

But the old conservatives, who are predominantly in the Republican party for the traditional reasons, are not necessarily new conservatives. And there is a new liberalism, too. In foreign policy, it is reflected in détente, the Strategic Arms Limitation Talks agreements, an emphasis on human rights, support of foreign aid and international organizations generally, and a disposition to question the wisdom of heavy military expenditures. In social policy, it tends to support the Equal Rights Amendment, gun control, integration, and affirmative action, and to oppose writing antiabortion and pro-school prayer amendments into the Constitution.

Neither the new conservatism nor the new liberalism is monolithic, of course. People can be conservative on some of these issues, liberal on others. In particular, there is little necessary correlation between what is called a conservative or liberal view on foreign policy and national security, on the one hand, and social issues on the other.

Table 2-1 illustrates the divergent conservative (C) and liberal (L) views voters can have. The electorate is seen as falling into eight distinct groups, ranging from Group 1 which is consistently conservative (CCC) on all issues to Group 8 which is consistently liberal (LLL). In between these poles are a number of variations such as those voters in Group 2 who are conservative on economic and foreign policy issues but liberal on social issues (CCL), or those in Group 7 who are the reverse—liberal on economic and foreign policy issues but conservative on social issues (LLC). The scheme is oversimplified, of course, because of the intermediate positions between conservative and liberal that produce an infinite variety of borderline cases. Yet, most voters can probably be classified within one of the eight categories.

Category 1 thus includes voters who are conservative on all three sets of issues; President Reagan himself can be chosen as the prototype. At the opposite extreme are the voters in category 8—liberal on all three —and here former Senator George McGovern of South Dakota of may be seen as typical. In between are those who are conservative on some matters and liberal on others. Senators Henry Jackson of Washington and Daniel Patrick Moynihan of New York, for instance, are traditional liberals on economic and role of government questions who parted company with the McGovernites on foreign and military policy, and at least some social issues as well, and belong in Group 5 or 6. Similarly, Vice-President George Bush is anathema to many activists in Group 1 because of a liberal position on social issues and belongs, probably, in Group 2.

At a time when foreign policy was bipartisan and the current social issues had not yet arisen, political identification was based on the first set of issues and groups 1 through 4 found their natural home in the Republican party and groups 5 through 8 in the Democratic party (although there remained regions, especially in the South, that were slow in conforming to the national party alignment established in the New Deal period). Now the new issues have cut through the traditional voting blocs, scattering them in new configurations, giving unaccustomed and disturbing meanings to the old, comfortable words Democrat and Republican.

It is in the nature of political organizations to emphasize the issues that unite them, and to straddle and evade when new, cross-cutting, divisive issues come along. The professionals who used to run the Republican and Democratic parties understood the necessity for that and behaved accordingly. So their platforms—except when reiterating traditional themes—were strong on generalities, weak on particulars, and their speeches full of ambiguity.

But with the political revolution that has culminated in the past decade—the disintegration of party organizations, the proliferation of primaries, the democratization of caucuses, the mass marketing of candidates by television, the rise of political action committees with their ample treasuries—the amateurs have taken over both parties. And they come at politics from a different direction. Unlike the professionals, their primary interest is not the preservation and strengthening of party organizations as such; it is the ends those organizations serve—the public policies to be adopted. To advance those ends, they disdain the generalities; they want the party to commit itself as specifically as possible. They assume it will be helped by doing so, for if a cause is righteous it is bound to be popular as well—ultimately, if not at once. In the meantime, what happens to the party is a secondary matter. The amateur is, of course, the single-interest group or person who sees political parties as instruments to be used or discarded as tactics at any given time may dictate.

With the decline of party organizations and the professionals who lead them, the new conservatives and the new liberals—issue-oriented, well-organized, single-minded, often fanatic—have been able to move into the established parties en masse. They have been able to dominate many of the caucuses, conventions, and platform committees. Cross-cutting issues, then, far from being avoided, have been embraced. In the Republican party, the CCCs (Group 1 in Table 2-1)—most numerous probably, and most zealous surely, of the four blocs that mainly make up the GOP—have been able to take command. On the Democratic side, the LLLs (Group 8 in Table 2-1) captured the party in 1972, wrote the platform, and nominated George McGovern. Discredited by the failure of that campaign, they gave way to the much paler liberalism of Jimmy Carter. Now that that has failed in turn, the party is confused, divided, and rudderless.

The historical significance of Ronald Reagan is that he is the first person whose origins were in the extreme wing of either party to reach the White House since the scope of the political conflict has been redefined. Reagan is the archetype of the new conservative. He entered public life just as the new issues came over the horizon, and he became their spokesman. They propelled him, and he them. The rank and file of the New Right discovered him after the defeat of their original hero, Barry Goldwater, made him their leader, and carried him on their shoulders to his eventual triumph. His ideological purity was his appeal. Every other competing leader was compromised to some degree, with a liberal record on at least some issue, some time—but not Reagan. He succeeded in making Republicans with perfect conservative voting records in the traditional mold look like moderates—even Gerald Ford, whose deviations from the true faith impelled the Californian to challenge him for renomination in 1976. Four years later, under the tutelage of political strategist John Sears, Reagan softened his rhetoric in order to broaden his appeal, but the new conservatives were able to accept that as a tactic. They even accepted his selection of George Bush as vice-president, because they knew that Reagan, in his heart, remained their own.

But how does President Reagan now hold together the disparate elements of his support? One choice is to follow the instincts of the professionals. Submerge the new, divisive issues: stay away from any that can be avoided, such as a constitutional amendment on abortion or school prayer. Compromise some of the others: mellow the harsher lines of previous foreign policy positions, for example. Concentrate, then, on the issue that unites the party—its economic program. That course would disappoint the CCCs, but it would placate the CCLs, the CLCs, and the CLLs, who otherwise might begin to drift away. In particular, Reagan's goal would be to hold the Democrats who remain liberal on foreign policy issues or social issues, or both, but who crossed the party line in 1980 to get a change in economic policy, and whose flirtation with Republicanism is highly tentative. They are the temporary CCLs, CLCs, and CLLs who can be quickly alienated by CCC extremism.

The danger in that course is clear. It will enrage the CCCs. They did not follow Ronald Reagan for years, and make him president, in order to see their goals abandoned. And they have the capacity to thwart and sabotage him. About one-third of the Republican majority of the Senate, numbering 17 or 18 members, can be classified as CCCs. If the president strays conspicuously from the party line as they define it, at least some of them can be expected to employ the power of their committee posts to haul him back.

The alternative is to follow the course the new conservatives have been advocating for two decades with great intensity. Go after the LCLs, the LLCs, and especially the LCCs. They are the Democrats who have been disgusted at their party's seeming weakness in confronting the Russians and the Cubans, who hate busing and hiring quotas and gun control and abortion, but who have stuck with the Democrats over the years because of the party's reputation as the friend of the worker in its economic policies—until 1980, when even those had failed. Now, argue the conservatives, the LCCs see that one party is no better or worse than the other on economic matters. They will vote their foreign policy and social convictions, and that will make permanent Republicans of them—provided only that the president does not forget or compromise his positions on those matters.

This argument, however, makes some assumptions about numbers. It takes for granted that there are more LCCs than CLLs—more Democrats and independents to be attracted than the Republicans and independents who would be repelled by militant conservative positions in foreign affairs and on social issues. The evidence is far from clear on this, however. The polls have consistently shown majorities in favor of the Equal Rights Amendment and gun control, for instance, and against a constitutional amendment to ban abortions. As for those aspects of the new conservatism that clearly command popular support, the main body of Democrats is sure to go along. On these issues, then, there will be no apparent party difference; Democrats and independents will find no cause to become Republicans in order to further those policy objectives.

If President Reagan and his party set out to realign the political system on the basis of the new conservatism, there is no doubt they can succeed to some degree. New lines of cleavage would be drawn—not to supersede, but to supplement, the existing one. Some voters would take their stands on opposite sides of the new lines, and attach themselves to the two parties accordingly. But there is no assurance that in the process the Republican party would be the gainer. Some Catholics, blue-collar workers, and others who have been LCCs for years would become Republicans, but there might be as many, or more, CLL Republicans and independents—women, suburbanites, younger voters—who would cut their ties with the Republican party. Many of the voters driven from the Republican party because of its ultraconservativism in 1964 did not return. If President Reagan chooses to lead his party in that direction during the next four years, the experience could be repeated.

THE ANALOGY OF 1952

Democrats have their favorite scenario as well. In their daydreams, 1980 turns out to be another 1952.

The Eisenhower landslide of that year was, if anything, an even sharper repudiation of the Democratic party than was the Reagan sweep of November 1980. Eisenhower did not get quite as many electoral votes as Reagan, but he achieved a higher percentage of the two party popular vote, and the GOP captured not only the Senate but the House as well, with 221 Republican seats—29 more than they were able to attain in 1980. The slogan was much the same in 1952 as 28 years later—"time for a change"—and on the morning after the election, change seemed indeed to have occurred. The oft-heralded "new era" was at hand. Journalists wrote solemn obituaries for the Democratic party, and looked forward to at least two decades of Republican rule corresponding to the 20-year period of Democratic dominance that had just ended.

But from that new era, the Democrats of this one can take heart. In a short two years, their party regained small majorities in both houses of the Congress. In 1956, they retained their control even while Eisenhower was being reelected overwhelmingly. Two years later, they gained nearly two-to-one majorities in both houses; in 1960 they put John F. Kennedy in the White House. In 1964 came their own great landslide, when it was the Republicans' turn to be left for dead on the political battlefield.

The two massive Eisenhower triumphs, it turned out, brought no significant number of Democratic converts to the Republican party. The proportion of the voters calling themselves Republicans, in response to the Gallup Poll's periodic question about party identification, had been running at slightly under 30 percent while Harry Truman was in office; by the end of Eisenhower's second term it was back at approximately that level and continued to drift downward. The Eisenhower years had produced only a blip of four or five points in the chart line, only an interruption in the slow Republican decline that had been apparent since World War II. Nor, in states where voters register by parties, was there a significant Republican gain or Democratic loss—in contrast to the prodigious shift in the Democratic direction in the 1930s.

The 1952 election has to be interpreted as a whopping protest vote against the party in power, like that of 1932—but with quite a different outcome. Much of the disaffection was personal; as the election approached, Truman's approval rating was dismally low, falling below 30 percent. The Democratic party as a whole was in disrepute; 20 years of continuous control of both the executive and the legislative branches had given it ample time to wear out its welcome. It was the party that created the scandals that were dubbed "the mess in Washington." It was the party of the Korean War. It bore the taint of being "soft on Communism" in spite of opposing it in Korea. At this juncture the Republicans had the good judgment to nominate a war hero in Dwight Eisenhower, and the Democrats the bad luck to choose Adlai Stevenson—a candidate who was never able to convince the public that his capacities for leadership were quite sufficient.

In 1953, the Republicans had their majorities, but the conditions for making permanent their temporary support—in other words, for a realignment—simply were not present. The country was not rent by any great issue of governmental principle. It was not polarized, or even stirred. Indeed, Eisenhower was a stabilizing, calming influence. He cleaned up the scandals—until his administration had some of its own. He ended the unpopular Korean War. He carried forward the bipartisan foreign policies of the postwar period. And, despite the Republican rhetoric over the years, including some of his own, he did not try to repeal the Democratic legislation of the previous two decades.

In their turn, the Democrats were not obstructionist. On matters of foreign and military policy, they backed the president. In domestic affairs, the initiative on legislative measures popular in that period—Medicare, aid to education, aid to depressed areas, and civil rights—lay with the Democrats, and it was Eisenhower who risked the charge of obstructionism. In his second term, especially in the last two years, he tried to sharpen the partisan conflict by attacking the Democrats as reckless spenders. However, the economic problem at that time was not inflation but recession and stagnation, and the charges did not stick.

Consequently, the political system in that period did what it always does between realignments: it continued to move in a cyclical, or pendulum, pattern. It ended the swing toward the Republicans that had been going on, in jerks and spasms, for 15 years, and began its swing back toward the Democrats.

There is a simple theoretical explanation of the normal pendular character of American politics, as well as those of other two-party democratic countries. The two parties take their stands on opposite sides of whatever cluster of issues gave rise to the party system in the first place. In the common terminology, then, one is conservative, or right-of-center, the other liberal (or progressive) and left-of-center. But the electorate as a whole is arrayed, generally, on almost a normal curve, with a large and decisive bloc of voters at or very near the center. Whichever party is in power, therefore, is inevitably either to the left or the right of the majority of the voting public. It is to some degree out of sync with the mood and temper of the people. (This discussion assumes that party competition is essentially one-dimensional, as was the case in the United States from the 1930s until the 1960s. In a multidimensional system with several lines of cleavage, the analysis applies to each of the dimensions.)

When the right-of-center or left-of-center party, as the case may be, takes power, it may try to move toward the center to bring itself closer to equilibrium with the electorate as a whole. But it cannot move far, because its active elements will not let it. They are the ones committed to the party position. They do not give their time, effort, and money in political campaigns to support centrist positions. They can threaten to bolt the party or stir up trouble in the primaries—as Senator Edward Kennedy did when Jimmy Carter took the Democratic party too far toward the center. So the activists keep the two parties anchored to either side.

When the victorious party, whether liberal or conservative, begins to make decisions and take actions, the disequilibrium between its position and that of the general electorate becomes apparent. It will be either too rightist or too leftist. It will begin to alienate the large mass of voters in the center. Its popularity will fade. The pendulum will begin to swing back. When enough dissatisfaction has accumulated, the voters will try to rectify the situation by the only means at their disposal—by putting the other party in power. Thus, as soon as a party gains power, it is on its way to losing it. It is only a matter of time.

That is what happened after 1952. Eisenhower had been swept in on a tide of dissatisfaction with the Democrats, but it was clear almost at the outset that he and his administration stood well to the right of the general electorate. It was then the Republicans' turn to make mistakes, and they did. Eisenhower's personal popularity held up remarkably well, but his party's did not. Indeed, the 1952 election—far from introducing a new era—marked the crest of the Republican wave. From that point it continued to recede for a dozen years.

Specifically, the new administration quickly revived the image of the Republican party as the party of big business, which in 1952 was still anathema to a goodly portion of the voters. It began with the "nine millionaires and a plumber" who made up the Eisenhower Cabinet, and continued with the tidelands oil "giveaway," the Dixon-Yates deal, and Hell's Canyon and other public power issues.[7] Even worse, the administration made itself vulnerable to Democratic charges that it was still the party of depression, for the economy slumped in 1953-1954, and again in 1957-1958, and remained stagnant as the 1960 election approached. Finally, it took stances far more conservative than those of the general electorate on the major domestic issues of the day, including aid to education, Medicare, and civil rights. All of these issues sped the pendulum along its leftward course, bringing Democratic gains in 1954, 1958, 1960, and finally Lyndon Johnson's smashing victory in 1964— after which it became the Democrats' turn to make mistakes. What saved the party from an earlier reaction, presumably, was that President Kennedy's margin in the Congress was so narrow that he was able to carry out but little of his program.

Hopeful Democrats searching for parallels between 1980-1981 and 1952-1953 can find them readily enough. Ronald Reagan stands far to the right of center in American politics, and always has—much farther than Eisenhower, who was the candidate of the moderate-liberal wing of the Republican party in 1952. Close to half of the people voted in 1980 for candidates to the left of Reagan, when one adds John Anderson's vote tally to that of Jimmy Carter. Even if one assumes that Reagan was at the center of his narrow majority—a dubious supposition—he was still positioned halfway between the center of the electoral spectrum and its conservative extreme. At the beginning, then, he is out of sync. As presidents before him, he will probably try to move his party and his administration toward the center, but Democrats can rest reasonably assured that he will not be able to remold the GOP as a truly centrist party within the span of two or four years.

The Reagan cabinet had the same big business coloration as that of Eisenhower. Ten millionaires were counted this time (the cabinet is larger), with no plumber in evidence. Corporate wealth and power may not suffer the same ill repute as they did three decades ago, when memories of the Great Depression were fresh, but this is far from demonstrated. Reagan's commitment to repeal of the tax on the windfall profits that oil companies would enjoy when oil price controls were ended was parallel to the tidelands oil issue, complete with the same villain. Dixon-Yates and Hell's Canyon also have their counterparts in 1981 in the far more widely ranging struggle between the environmentalists and the resource developers, and any evidence of overreaching by corporate exploiters of the public lands would drive conservationists and nature lovers out of the Republican camp. Republican tax and budget policies give Democrats the same opportunity they grasped in 1953 to place themselves squarely on the side of the "little man" against the "interests."

As Eisenhower failed to cope adequately with recession, in the public view, so Reagan will surely have his difficulties with both inflation and unemployment. If the administration program puts the squeeze on working people through unemployment, on both business and consumers through high interest rates, and on the beneficiaries of public services through budget cuts, at the same time that it does not conquer inflation and appears to distribute its tax cut benefits disproportionately to the rich, the GOP will be on the defensive in the 1980s as it was in the 1950s. At this juncture, President Reagan's problems appear far more difficult than those that Eisenhower faced, because his own position is more out of equilibrium with that of the electorate, and his approach is perhaps less flexible and conciliatory.

In this favorite scenario of the Democrats, then, the pendulum should swing back in their direction even faster in the 1980s than it did in the 1950s. The Democrats should enjoy the normal gains of the out-party in the congressional election of 1982, and hold their gains until, in 1984 or 1988, they win back the White House and complete the arc of the cycle now beginning.

THE REPUBLICAN SOUTH

The cyclical pattern of American politics is obscured, somewhat, by a secular trend: the continuing realignment of the political party system in the South.[8] The most astonishing result of the 1980 election was not the decisive victory of Reagan—that had precedents—but the Republican capture of a majority of the Senate by virtue of its victories in the South, which had no precedent at any time in history.

It would be a mistake to interpret the four Republican victories in southern senatorial races, giving the GOP nearly half the Senate representation from the once-solid Democratic South, as the consequence primarily of new forces—as the product of the new conservatism rather than the old. It marks, instead, a secular movement of southern conservatives from the Democratic to the Republican party that has been going on gradually but steadily since the days of Eisenhower. Indeed, the Senate contingent from the states of the former Confederacy is not demonstrably more conservative now that it is half Republican than it was when it was entirely Democratic. The last all-Democratic southern contingent in the Senate, in 1961, included 14 who would be characterized by most observers as arch-conservatives, and only 8 moderates or liberals. The Senate in 1981, even assuming that all of the new Republicans turn out to be solid conservatives, numbered no more than 14 conservatives and at least 8 moderates (the word liberal having disappeared from the southern political vocabulary).

The Solid South was held intact by the Democratic party from the end of Reconstruction until 1948, except for the deviation of six states in the Al Smith-Herbert Hoover race of 1928. Democratic hegemony was shattered by Strom Thurmond's States' Rights party in the first postwar election in 1948, and then by Eisenhower in 1952. But few of the Eisenhower voters considered themselves Republicans, and their willingness to give the GOP their votes moved slowly from the top of the ballot toward the bottom.

In 1961, however, John Tower of Texas became the first Republican senator from the South in modern times; in 1966 the party captured its first governorships—in Arkansas and Florida—and its strength grew gradually in state legislatures and in the U.S. House of Representatives. Two party competition is now firmly established in presidential and other state-wide elections while local politics are still Democratic-dominated. But in time that too will change. Two party competition will become normal in even the rural counties in contests for local office.

The surging Republicanism of the South represents the long-delayed falling into place of the New Deal party system. When the parties realigned in the turmoil of the Roosevelt era, the new line of cleavage between the parties, based on class interests and issues of governmental activism, supplanted the one based on geography that had been embedded since the Civil War. But it did not obliterate the old configuration everywhere at once. One party states (more accurately, one-and-one-half party states) survived in the North into the 1950s and, in a few cases, into the decade after that, before the heirs to the Republican progressive tradition flowed across the party line and vitalized the Democrats as an equal competitor in the two party system. The lag in the South was simply longer. But in every election since 1952 —except for a setback at the time of Watergate—more and more conservatives have been willing to call themselves Republicans, participate in party affairs, and support the ticket up and down the line.

Once this trend began, it was bound to accelerate. For as conservative Democrats—or their sons and daughters, as generations changes—started to move into Republican ranks, it left the Democratic party more liberal, resembling more closely the national Democratic party the conservative southerners detested. The more liberal it became, the more conservative Democrats departed, leaving their former party still more liberal, in a gathering spiral. The enfranchisement of the blacks in the rural South was, and remains, an important factor hastening this process. To some degree also, it has been furthered by the migration of Republicans from the North.

It was always to be expected that a national party system split along liberal-conservative lines would tend to be roughly in balance. If the mood of the country became more conservative or liberal—as it does during each swing of the pendulum—the whole spectrum would move, carrying both parties with it, and they would remain on opposite sides of the center. So the two parties would alternate in power, and their strength would be approximately equal—as soon as the realignment spread across the nation. In other words, it had to await the realignment of the South. In presidential voting, that happened 30 years ago, and competition between the parties has been roughly equal ever since. That the Democratic party maintained continuous control of the Congress through six Eisenhower and eight Nixon-Ford years was simply an abnormality, traceable to the reluctance of conservative southerners to accept the Republican party as their instrument of conservatism in filling offices other than the presidency.

That abnormality now may be cured, evidently, in the case of senatorial elections. When the South realigns its voting for the House of Representatives as well, both parties—and the whole political system—will benefit. The Democratic party, when it is in power, will be more homogeneous and cohesive, without a strong southern conservative minority bent on frustrating the majority. And the Republican party, when it wins at the presidential level, will have the control of both houses of Congress that is a virtual precondition of effective government.

INDEPENDENCE AND DEALIGNMENT

During the nearly five decades of the New Deal party system, three complete swings of the pendulum can be traced. The first covered 16 years or a little more, from the peak of Democratic-liberal strength in the 1934-1936 period to the Republican-conservative high point of 1952-1953—a steady movement, except for a brief setback in the surprise Truman victory of 1948. The return arc, from 1953 to 1964-1965, was uninterrupted. The third swing did have its interruption, in Watergate, but after that resumed its movement in the Republican direction. If it turns out that the Republicans reached another peak in 1980, the third cycle will have lasted about as long as the other two—15 or 16 years.

But associated with the latest cycle has been a new development, and one of critical importance. Until the mid-1960s, the proportion of voters who labeled themselves "independents" had for a quarter of a century remained consistently in the low 20s on the percentage scale—around one-fifth to one-fourth of the electorate. Democratic strength was usually in the high 40s, Republican in the low 30s. In good Democratic years, the Democratic party gained a few points at the expense of the Republicans, occasionally breaking 50, and in good

Republican years the reverse occurred. But the proportion of independents did not increase.

In the mid-1960s, however, all that changed. When, in the bad years
of riots and Vietnam, the Democrats lost support as might be expected,
most of their disaffected voters did not become Republicans. According
to Gallup, most of them became independents; according to data from
the University of Michigan's Survey Research Center (SRC), virtually
all of them became independents. The SRC showed no gains at all for
the Republicans in the 1964-1970 period, only a continuation of the slow
decline that began in the latter 1950s. When it was the Republicans'
turn to have their troubles, in the 1970s, again the opposing party was
not the gainer. In the main, the GOP defectors turned up as independents. By mid-1975, the Gallup Poll showed the independents at a
record high of 34 percent, the Democrats at 44 percent, the Republicans
at 22 percent. From one-fifth or a little more, the unattached, floating
segment of the electorate had risen to one-third. Political scientist
Everett Ladd has termed it "dealignment."

One can associate dealignment with the rise of the cross-cutting
issues discussed earlier. When social issues and questions of foreign
policy came to the center of the political debate, the New Deal party
system inevitably lost its relevance. Forged in a confrontation over the
role of government and in class conflict, the system had vitality, and the
term Republican and Democrat had meaning, as long as those issues
were the stuff of politics. On those, the parties had distinct positions and
their differences were clear. But on social and foreign policy questions,
both parties spread across the whole spectrum of opinion; there were
four combinations of Cs and Ls on those issues within each party. The
Vietnam antiwar movement produced amendments to limit or end the
war such as the Cooper-Church[10] and Hatfield-McGovern[11] amendments, ostentatiously bipartisan in their origin and identification,
opposing the establishments of both parties. Young people seeking to
express their views on the war could be pardoned if they found neither
party fully satisfactory and denounced them both.

And the same was true of people whose main concern may have
been the rise in crime or race riots in the cities. Like the young, they
could well ask: Why join a party that has neither a clear position nor a
program? Look instead for the individual candidate, of whatever party
or none at all, who comes closest to expressing the desired views.
Support simply the one who seems most honest, competent, and earnest
—or, in this age of television, especially pleasant and ingratiating.
Chapter 6 identifies additional reasons for the loss of party appeal for
the electorate.

With one-third of the voters calling themselves independents, one
could expect a corresponding rise in ticket splitting—and that has

happened. One result is 16 years of divided government, so far—1955-1960, 1969-1976, and 1981-1982. And one should expect the unattached voters to swing freely, and in massive numbers, from side to side, from election to election, like a loose cannon on shipboard lurching from port to starboard, and back again, in a storm. Independents are as likely to come off the fence overwhelmingly on one side or the other as to be evenly divided. So for each close election, such as those of 1968 and 1976, a landslide on the scale of 1972 or 1980 can be anticipated.

A Gallup Poll taken late in 1980, however, shows a startling reversal of the dealignment trend of the past 15 years. Republican strength is up, from 20 points in mid-1977 to 31 points in 1980. The Democrats are down, from 49 to 43 points. And independents are down as well, from 31 to 26 points. That is the highest score for the Republicans since the early 1960s, and the lowest for the independents.

This poll is the joyful news the Republicans have been waiting for—if it holds up. But that is less than certain, for the Gallup question has some tricky wording. It asks: "In politics, as of today, do you consider yourself a Republican, a Democrat, or Independent?" and the phrase *as of today* is critical. It appears to produce a bias toward the winning party in any presidential election year, and especially at election time. An independent who has just voted for Reagan might reasonably respond that, as of that day, he must be a Republican, however tentative his judgment. (The Survey Research Center appears to eliminate the bias through a different wording of the question.) So one must await confirmation of the spectacular Republican gains and independent losses from later polls taken further from the influence of election day.

CONCLUSION

On balance, it is easier to see the 1980 election as an analogue to 1952 than 1932. The odds seem to be against a realignment similar to that of the 1930s, for such revolutions occur rarely, and only in periods of crisis and unrest far more intense than this generation is experiencing. The protest of 1980 was, by comparison with 1932, a mild one—more similar to 1952. In any case, in any protest election, those who switch from past voting habits are giving their new president and his party a chance, not a commitment. In 1980, millions of voters visited a new political church to find out whether they might like the sermon and the music, but they did not embrace the faith and get baptized—and have not yet. Few Democrats have yet trooped to their county courthouses to change their party registration.

Eventually they may, but that depends on many things. It depends on whether the Republicans conquer inflation, revive the economy, face down the Russians without dropping bombs, and all the rest. Any reader can appraise the difficulties the GOP confronts, make a guess about the skill and wisdom of the Reagan leadership, and place his or her bets accordingly. But a massive conversion of the new Republicans depends on Democratic behavior also. And that is not wholly predictable. In the old Army phrase, "it depends on the terrain and the situation."

Perhaps the Democrats will tone down their liberal rhetoric still further, and postpone their liberal initiatives. If so, they will be seen as an acceptable alternative the first time Reagan slips. For, no matter how far the whole liberal-conservative spectrum may have moved to the right during the cycle that began in 1965, President Reagan and his administration, as well as the Republican Senate, will remain well to the right of center. The disequilibrium should become increasingly apparent. When it is visible, so too will be the beginning of the fourth arc of the pendulum since the present party system came into being.

But the Democratic left is activist and strong. It may well dominate the party dialogue of these next few years, as the left has dominated the Labour party in Britain since it went into opposition following its loss to Mrs. Thatcher in May 1979, and as the Republican activist right dominated the GOP dialogue in the Carter years. If that is the case, the voter suspicion of Democratic policies that was so evident in 1980 may linger, and the return swing of the pendulum may be delayed.

NOTES

1. Kevin Phillips, *The Emerging Republican Majority* (New Rochelle, N.Y.: Arlington House, 1969).
2. The Gallup Poll release.
3. The Gallup Poll, release, December 21, 1980.
4. For an analysis of the realignment of the 1930s, see James L. Sundquist, *Dynamics of the Party System* (Washington, D.C.: Brookings Institution, 1973), Chapter 10. The discussion there of the timing of the realignment is based upon Walter Dean Burnham, *Critical Elections and the Mainsprings of American Politics* (New York: W. W. Norton & Co., 1970), p. 56.
5. "Was the President the Issue?" *Public Opinion* 3 (December/January 1981): 27.
6. For a readable report on the self-styled New Right, see Alan Crawford, *Thunder on the Right* (New York: Pantheon Books, 1980).
7. "Tidelands oil" was an early issue, as President Eisenhower and the Republican congressional majorities set out to make good on a 1952 campaign pledge to give the coastal states ownership of oil-bearing tidelands within a specified distance from the shore. Opponents charged it was a "giveaway" to a few states of resources belonging to the entire nation and vital to national defense. They attributed the campaign to assert states' rights to pressures generated by oil interests.

Dixon-Yates was a conflict-of-interest controversy surrounding a contract between the Tennessee Valley Authority (TVA) and a private utility combine to provide power to the western part of the TVA system. The combine was formed by the Middle South Utilities Company (Edgar H. Dixon, president) and the Southern Company (Eugene A. Yates, chairman). TVA supporters viewed this proposal as a plan to block expansion of TVA generating facilities in order to let private power producers back into the business of generating electricity in the TVA area. After a severe fight in Congress and the decision by Memphis to build its own plant, the Dixon-Yates contract was cancelled.

Hell's Canyon was a major public power project on the Snake River on the Idaho-Oregon border that was opposed by private power companies. Underlying the controversy over project specifics was the ubiquitous public-*vs.*-private power dispute. Originally proposed in 1947, the federal project had the support of the Truman administration, public power organizations, and the rural electric cooperatives. The Eisenhower administration, the private power industry, and most business organizations supported the construction of three smaller privately owned dams. The fight ended in 1958 when a House subcommittee killed a Senate-passed bill to authorize the federal dam.

8. Among recent studies of southern politics are Jack Bass and Walter DeVries, *The Transformation of Southern Politics* (New York: Basic Books, 1976); William C. Havard, Jr., ed., *The Changing Politics of the South* (Baton Rouge: Louisiana State University Press, 1972); and Sundquist, *Dynamics of the Party System,* Chapter 12.

9. The Gallup Poll, release, December 21, 1980.

10. In 1971, Republican Senator John Sherman Cooper of Kentucky and Democratic Senator Frank Church of Idaho proposed an amendment to a foreign aid appropriations bill that would have prohibited the use of funds for U.S. forces in Indochina for any purpose other than protection of U.S. forces as they withdrew from Vietnam.

11. In 1970, Republican Senator Mark O. Hatfield of Oregon and Democratic Senator George McGovern of South Dakota proposed an amendment to a military authorizations bill that would have set a deadline of December 31, 1971 for withdrawing all U.S. troops from Vietnam.

3

Presidents, Ideas, and the Search for a Stable Majority

Erwin C. Hargrove and Michael Nelson

Revolution is a word whose meanings are as varied as they are important in American political history. In our day, we usually emphasize its definition as "a fundamental change in political organization, especially the overthrow or renunciation of one government or ruler and the substitution of another by the governed." The apt synonym in this case is "rebellion" or "realignment." When Thomas Jefferson, for example, is quoted to the effect that a revolution every 20 years is much to be desired, it invariably is to support the argument that there should be sudden, frequent, and dramatic alterations in government, whether by means of the ballot or the bullet.

At earlier times in our history, however, revolution usually was used to signify something quite different. Political "rotation" was thought to be similar to "the rotation of a celestial body on its axis." Far from being abnormal, revolution used in this sense is as regular and as anticipated as the movement of the earth that produces day and night. This probably is how Jefferson himself used the word and meant it to be understood in the much quoted phrase; laws and constitutions to him were 20-year contracts with each generation that ought to expire regularly.[1]

Interestingly, two popular and influential theories about the significance of the 1980 election for the American presidency correspond to these contrasting meanings of revolution. The first "revolutionary" theory regards the displacement of Jimmy Carter by Ronald Reagan as merely the latest "rotation" of the "revolving-door presidency." Evidence for this view is abundant. No president since Dwight Eisenhower, who left office in 1961, has fit the two-term presidential tradition that students learn about in civics class. John Kennedy might have, but he was assassinated in 1963, two-thirds of the way through his first term. Kennedy's successor, Lyndon Johnson, lasted only until 1969—his severe unpopularity with the voters forced him to withdraw his candidacy for reelection. Johnson's Republican successors fared no better. Richard Nixon, the 1968 winner, was returned to office in 1972 but in the process covered up the Watergate burglary that brought about his resignation 21 months later. Gerald Ford, who was appointed to the vice-presidency and subsequently succeeded Nixon, failed to win even one election. Finally, Jimmy Carter, who defeated Ford in 1976, lost his own reelection bid.

Ronald Reagan's inauguration on January 20, 1981, made him the sixth president to be sworn into office in 20 years. In contrast, the six presidents who served directly before 1961—Dwight Eisenhower, Harry Truman, Franklin Roosevelt,, Herbert Hoover, Calvin Coolidge, and Warren Harding—spanned 40 years, exactly twice as long; as did the first six presidents, beginning with the inauguration of George Washington in 1789 and ending when John Quincy Adams left office in 1829. To get a sense of the dangers associated with a political world that rotates, in effect, at double speed, it is worth noting that only two other 20-year periods in our history are comparable to the present one. The first period was 1877-1897, when the United States saw seven presidents, none of them sufficiently effective in office to mitigate the harmful side-effects of rapid industrialization; the second period was 1841-1861, when eight presidents each failed to head off the approach of the Civil War.

As we will see, those who subscribe to this first "revolutionary" theory of the 1980 election generally regard the presidency as a weak and troubled institution whose problems lie in the office and its relationship with its constituencies. There are others, though, who see the election of 1980 not as the latest in a series of political rotations, but as part of a possibly fundamental change in American politics that is revolutionary in the contemporary use of the word. To them, 1980 was the latest stage of a potential political realignment whose future success depends less on the presidency than on the president, less on the office than on the person.

Again, this is a theory not lacking in evidence. Presidentially inspired realignments are not unknown in American history. In 1800,

Jefferson's victory over Federalist John Adams and his subsequent success in office marked the beginning of a period of electoral domination by his Democratic-Republican party. The election of Andrew Jackson as president in 1828 (he defeated Adams's son John Quincy) ushered in a period of Democratic ascendancy that lasted until Abraham Lincoln's triumph in 1860. Lincoln's Republicans continued to dominate national politics until the 1930s, when the combination of severe economic depression and President Franklin Roosevelt's response to it realigned American voters in a way that gave the Democratic party a majority electoral alliance centered on blacks, southern whites, labor, and intellectuals—the fabled New Deal coalition.

In recent elections, all but the first of these components of Roosevelt's coalition have shown signs of disenchantment with the Democratic party. Even before November 4, 1980, some analysts were saying that conditions were ripe for a Republican realignment. During the 1970s, it was noted, the attitude of American voters on fundamental political issues—such as defense and the economy—had changed, and "like it or not, almost all of these changes are in general concert with perceived Republican doctrine."[2] The lesson of previous realignments, the argument went, was that all that was needed for these attitudinal changes on issues to be translated into long-standing behavioral changes at the polls—and more pertinent to our concern, to a revival of effective presidential leadership—was the successful performance in office of a "remarkable political personality like FDR."

'WELL, I'VE DECIDED !... I'VE DECIDED VOTING ONLY ENCOURAGES THEM.'

Rotation or realignment—which kind of "revolution" does the 1980 election indicate? And where do we look for clues as to what it means for the future of the American presidency—to the office or to its occupant? Our answer is some of all—and all of none—of the above. But first let us look more closely at these two theories to see which elements of each can be used as building blocks of a third, more solid theory.

ROTATION

Scholarly and journalistic assessments of the power and effectiveness of the American presidency have revolved as rapidly as has the door to the White House during the past two decades. The image of the office presented in the political science textbooks of the 1950s and early 1960s was summed up by Thomas Cronin in two words: "omnipotence" and "benevolence."[3] Experience with the administration of presidents Kennedy and Johnson, respectively, cast severe doubts on first one, then the other, of these characterizations. But even as late as the final days of Watergate, it was academically respectable to argue, as newspaper correspondent Peter Lisagor did, that "the only problem with the presidency is that it has been occupied by two clunkers in a row," meaning Johnson and Nixon. The subsequent failures of Gerald Ford and Jimmy Carter, however, have riveted the attention of many on the office itself. The reasoning is summed up by British journalist Godfrey Hodgson in a recent and influential book, *All Things to All Men: The False Promise of the American Presidency:*

> When five consecutive men—all of them, with the possible exception of Gerald Ford, men of very great political ability—all fail to operate an office, when their task seems to get progressively more and more difficult with the passing of time, then the fault can hardly be the individuals. It must be in the institution.[4]

The presidency's institutional fault, Hodgson argues (and we cite Hodgson merely as representative of a school of thought), is best thought of as a paradox, graphically expressed by President Johnson: "The only power I've got is nuclear, and I can't use that." What Johnson meant was that although presidents have vast, even ultimate power, if power is defined as the ability to alter people's lives, it is

> power to do things that no one in their right mind would have them to do: to declare martial law, to throw the world's currency into chaos, to invade Cuba, blow up the Middle east oilfields, incinerate the Northern Hemisphere. The power that eludes them is the power to do the very things people expect them to do: to end inflation, ensure law and order, to negotiate disarmament without endangering the United States, to end the energy crisis.[5]

The root of the paradox that Hodgson presents is the purported imbalance between what presidents can do and what they are expected to do. What is worse, in his view, is that the imbalance is growing. The weight of the first part of his equation—the effective power of the office—is declining. Yet demands for action from its constituencies, which seem more aware of the ultimate nature of presidential power than of its paradoxical limits, continue to grow.

Rotation theorists trace the decline in the president's capacity to deliver to two sources: its constitutional dependence on other political institutions for support, and the recent decline in the ability or willingness of those institutions to provide it. Presidents need the support of their political party, but in recent years parties have crumbled at the organizational level and have lost much of their former hold on the loyalties of both voters and other office-holders. Presidents need a Congress that is cohesive enough to lead or at least to bargain with. But since 1970, the legislative branch has so decentralized power within itself that it presently is little more than a congeries of literally hundreds of relatively autonomous committees and subcommittees. Presidents need a bureaucracy that is responsive to their policy initiatives, for executive agencies, even those headed by presidential appointees, increasingly guard not presidential interests but their own and those of their client groups. And although the media spotlight still shines as brightly as ever on the White House, the post-Watergate press seems more intent on using it to magnify presidential failures than to show off successes.

What makes all this worse, Hodgson argues, is that even as the presidency's ability to meet demands of constituents for action has declined, the volume, intensity, and complexity of those demands—the other half of the presidential equation—has been rising. The American people expect too much of their president: "He must simultaneously conduct the diplomacy of a superpower, put together separate coalitions to enact every piece of legislation required by a vast and complex society, manage the economy, command the armed forces, serve as a spiritual example and inspiration, respond to every emergency."[6]

These demands are said to be not only excessive, but often contradictory as well. When it comes to leadership, argues Cronin, Americans want presidents who are "gentle and decent but forceful and decisive ... programmatic but pragmatic ... open and sharing but courageous and independent." They want a "common man who gives an uncommon performance" and a leader who is "inspirational but doesn't promise more than he can deliver."[7] In the realm of policy, they want cheap but plentiful gasoline, lower taxes and higher benefits, national security and disarmament. They want America to be a respected world power, but don't want their children sent abroad to fight.

In his farewell address to the nation, President Carter pointed to still another source of excessive and contradictory demands: "single-issue groups and special interest organizations [whose purpose is] to ensure that whatever else happens our own personal views and our own private interests are protected." In truth, as both Chapter 4 and Chapter 6 emphasize, Americans seem politically balkanized as seldom before, not only along historically familiar geographical and economic lines, but along a variety of biological lines as well: sex, race, sexual preference, and age, among them.

The list could be added to, but only for the purpose of reinforcing the point of the rotation school: as long as the presidency is asked to do more with less, we can expect to see future presidents continue to "fail."

The prescriptions for enhancing the ability of the presidency to deal more effectively with national problems that follow from this diagnosis are those of institutional reform, reform of the office. Some, such as Lloyd Cutler, counsel to President Carter, urge sweeping changes: require candidates for president and Congress to be voted on as a single ticket; draw half of the Cabinet from Congress; and provide a single six-year term for the president, but with provisions to allow either the executive branch or the Congress to call a special election before that term expires.[8] Others advocate the rolling back of changes already made, such as a return to structured nominating conventions dominated by party leaders and elected officials.

REALIGNMENT

Though rotation theorists seem to have the evidence of recent history behind them (six presidents in 20 years, with no apparent likelihood of change in the conditions that have produced this turnover), those who assert that a lasting realignment is in the making can draw on almost two centuries of political experience to obtain grist for their mill. This second "revolutionary" theory does not deny the reality of present-day presidential institutional weakness; it merely asserts that this condition is not new in American history. In fact, it is a chronic and recurring condition, whose antidote is always effective, even if temporary. It is to be found in popular presidents who forge new electoral coalitions, as Franklin Roosevelt did between 1933 and 1936. Realigning elections are the cornerstone of this theory because it is through such elections that strong presidential candidates are said to create coalitions. This permits effective government for a time, until the coalition falls into disarray. A period of governmental weakness ensues until a new coalition can be created, but this is to be expected and certainly is no cause for wholesale institutional reform.[9]

Realignments not only happen, argue Richard Scammon and Ben Wattenberg, they happen precisely in those settings that describe the electorate of 1980: changing opinions on fundamental political issues and changing patterns of election results.

"There are few analysts these days who would deny what the general run of [poll] numbers tends to point up," Scammon and Wattenberg conclude. "Inflation has become the nation's number one concern, the bloom is off the rose for the idea of futher governmental activism, the public is substantially more hawkish than it was a few years ago. . . . Agree or disagree on substance, these have been Republican themes."[10] Further, they are themes that have produced Republican election victories at all levels of government. In terms of voter demography, these can be traced largely to a swing to that party's candidates of a group traditionally associated with the Democrats: blue-collar whites who have been distressed by their former party's preoccupation with minority rights and its failure to contain inflation. And, realignment theorists add, consider this: population shifts reflected in the 1980 census mean that the increasingly Republican Sun Belt states of the South and West, which cast 41 fewer electoral votes than the states of the Frost Belt in the 1960 election, will have a majority margin of 26 in 1984 and 1988.

The still unanswered question, of course, is whether these changes will produce the third change that theory says is necessary for realignment: a transformation in how voters perceive the parties. What is most interesting about Scammon and Wattenberg's answer is the method— simple salesmanship from the Republican incumbent—by which they see that final change coming about:

> Mr. Reagan will keep on making those pernicious and malign noises that say "*We* are the party of the people, *they* are the elite royalists."
>
> If the Republicans can make that partisan perception stick, they can remind voters of that wonderful dictum of the football fan: "fire the coach." If that happens, in that way, realignment will be on its way.[11]

Clearly, this theory gives less importance to such skills of intragovernmental leadership as coaxing Congress and managing the bureaucracy than to a leader's understanding of popular trends and the ability to articulate issues in response to these trends in ways that will cause large groups of voters to fall into line. Interestingly, Scammon and Wattenberg trace the sources of Republican revival not to new ideas, but to the party's successful capture of the New Deal Democrats' old idea: growth economics. The only important questions to realignment theorists are whether Ronald Reagan is a heroic leader and whether the 1984 election will bring about a realignment of the country and the government into a Republican majority.

IDEAS AND THE PRESIDENTIAL POLICY CYCLE:
PREPARATION, REFORM, CONSOLIDATION

Each of the explorations of the pattern that has characterized the American presidency, and thus the conduct of national government, in recent years is both plausible and partially accurate. When another thought is added, the building blocks of a third, more solid, theory are at hand. The thought is simple: in addition to heroic leaders and prior to institutional reforms, the presidency requires creative ideas about what government can and should do to solve pressing policy problems.

Nothing demonstrates the truth of this proposition better than the history of American politics and government in this century, a history that can be understood in terms of recurring presidential policy cycles. At the heart of each cycle was a "presidency of reform"—the administrations of Woodrow Wilson, Franklin Roosevelt, and Lyndon Johnson— in which a burst of creative legislation was enacted. In each case, a leader was able to introduce into politics ideas that had been developing for some time, and make the resulting voter coalition the basis for the passage of new public policies. Each such presidency of reform was followed by a "presidency of consolidation," in which reform was not rejected but rationalized, scaled down, and legitimatiized for adherents of the consolidating political party. The presidencies of Herbert Hoover, Dwight Eisenhower, and Richard Nixon were of this nature. In two of the three cycles we have witnessed thus far in this century, the reform period was preceded by a "presidency of preparation"—Theodore Roosevelt's term before Wilson and John Kennedy's before Johnson—in which new ideas were presented and articulated, but the political coalition to enact programs based on them was still nascent. The abruptness of the depression catapulted FDR into the White House without a preceding presidency of preparation.[12] Table 2-1 sets out the cycles of change.

Table 2-1. Presidential Policy Cycles.

	Preparation	*Reform*	*Consolidation*
Cycle 1	Theodore Roosevelt William H. Taft	Woodrow Wilson	Warren Harding Calvin Coolidge Herbert Hoover
Cycle 2		Franklin Roosevelt	Dwight Eisenhower
	[*stasis:* Harry Truman]		
Cycle 3	John Kennedy	Lyndon Johnson	Richard Nixon
	[*stasis:* Gerald Ford/Jimmy Carter]		

During each of the three types of presidencies there is a congruence between presidential policies and the broad alignment and preferences of voters. The New Deal represented a loose and varied coalition of workers, farmers, minorities, and intellectuals—and policy was similarly a crazy quilt of reform. In the Eisenhower years, voters were quiescent and seemingly lacking in any taste for ideological conflict, as was their president. But as political leaders began to debate alternative agendas for the post-Eisenhower years, the voters responded in kind. In doing so, they revealed a strong capacity to link voting and issues.

This is an important point. Indeed, it is the hinge of our argument that presidential elections are the action-forcing mechanisms that turn the wheel of the cycle from one type of presidency to the next. Critical elections provide a "political gateway"—a point of legislative passage for policies that have been developing and incubating elsewhere in the political system.[13] For example, most of the issues that were to be dramatized by Kennedy's New Frontier and Johnson's Great Society in the 1960s had been percolating in Congress in the 1950s under the sponsorship of progressive Democrats, just as many New Deal measures were developed and nurtured by progressives in the 1920s in reaction to Republican policies. The ideas that contributed to the 1964 tax cut, employment and training programs, Medicare, and environmental policy all had been thrown into the congressional hopper in the previous decade. These politicians, in turn, did not invent the ideas that formed the basis of their policy proposals but drew them out of the intellectual life of the times as it worked through the universities, research institutions, and advocacy groups. The stuff of politics is thus very dependent upon the common stock of intellectual capital for its vitality.[14]

A crucially important presidential skill is the capacity to discern the direction, potential, and limits on policy action that the electorate is offering at any point in the cycle. Among recent presidents, Eisenhower, Kennedy, and the early Johnson administration all get high marks for that. Each perceived what was politically possible and acted accordingly. And though this has not been as true of succeeding presidents, the explanation may be less their personal incapacities than a break in the cyclical pattern that has produced a time of political and policy disorientation.

PRESIDENCIES OF STASIS

The present period clearly has been one of drift and deadlock, of "presidencies of stasis." Stasis is used in this context to mean a period of stagnation, a stopping or a slowing down of the normal flow of events. The only twentieth-century parallels are Franklin Roosevelt's second term, when his New Deal alliance was broken apart and the "conservative coalition" of Republicans and Southern Democrats in Congress was able to frustrate his policy initiatives; and the Truman domestic presidency, which continued to suffer from the politics of deadlock that had been interrupted by World War II. In presidencies of stasis, the old governing coalition is spent, but a new one has not emerged. Policy problems are new and unprecedented. There is a great confusion about the nature of these problems and few ideas about solutions. This confusion at the governmental level is accompanied by comparable confusion among citizens.

Thus, by 1974, when President Ford assumed office, both parties were living on outdated intellectual capital. Neither bag of tricks contained ready answers to the new challenge of energy production and conservation presented by the Organization of Petroleum Exporting Countries (OPEC), to the simultaneous occurrence of high inflation and unemployment, or to the seemingly intractable problem of minority youth unemployment. There was similar disorientation in foreign policy. Cold war reflexes had been dulled by Vietnam, but the world continued to be a dangerous place for American interests. As explained more fully in Chapter 8, a balance between restraint and intervention abroad had yet to be found.

Though presidents Ford and Carter tried to address these policy problems, each was handicapped by the lack of fresh ideas from his advisers, from Congress, or from the nation's centers of thought. The depleted intellectual capital of both Ford's and Carter's economic advisers was apparent in the ad hoc and contradictory twisting and turning of economic policy that characterized both administrations. And though Carter succeeded in passing national energy legislation, official policy still contains many unresolved questions about the role of coal, nuclear power, and more innovative forms of energy; the appropriate market price of oil and gas; and the degree of emphasis that should be placed on conservation and production. Because events had outpaced ideas, neither president was able to articulate a clear sense of direction to the country. And because of this, neither was able to summon the sustained support of a political coalition, either in Congress or the country.

The Reagan presidency may attempt to create an enduring electoral majority based on policies developed in the next four years that will make 1980-1984 a realigning period similar to 1932-1936. As realignment theorists point out, the elements of such a majority already are in place—geographically in the South and West, demographically in the middle and white working class. To hold such a coalition together, Reagan—no less than Franklin Roosevelt before him—must develop and carry through policies that appear to be coping with the major issues of the day.

Yet the reason that politics and government today are in a condition of stasis is because we as a nation, not merely our two most recent presidents, lack agreed-upon ideas about how to address unprecedented policy problems. This proposition can be illustrated in each of the three crucial policy areas that shape popular and partisan politics.

First, we face a crisis of economic policy. Most notably, the economy suffers from unprecedented sustained inflation and a high rate of unemployment. According to Keynesian theory, these two phenomena are not supposed to occur at the same time, yet both seem so incorrigible as to be systemic. Evidently, mainstream liberal thought, which is grounded in the Keynesian paradigm, is deficient. Yet the intellectual armory of the right—which is to be the basis of the Reagan administration's efforts to lower inflation and unemployment, cut budgets and taxes, and raise defense spending—is hardly more imposing. It consists of a hodge-podge of monetarists, who believe that the answer is to keep growth in the money supply from exceeding growth in the economy; balanced budgeteers, who accept Keynes's idea that a budget deficit raises consumer demand and thus producer prices; and supply-siders, the authors and advocates of the Reagan-endorsed Kemp-Roth bill, which would reduce income taxes by 30 percent in three years in the belief that the freed-up capital would be used to increase industrial productivity.[15]

The supply-siders offer the most interesting case: in part, because they disagree so strenuously with the others (e.g., they want taxes cut whether the budget is balanced yet or not); in part, because they disagree so strenuously among themselves. It even is hard to tell from them what the intended effect of Kemp-Roth on the federal treasury would be: a reduction in tax revenue, or an increase?[16]

Second, the shortage of energy brought on by the vagaries of OPEC oil prices, the difficulties of reconciling the exploitation of abundant American coal with a clean environment, and uncertainties about nuclear power have presented Americans with problems for which they are ill-prepared.

In part, these problems involve conflicts of fact. Neo-classical economists assert that high energy prices will lead to the discovery of new energy resources, but we do not know this to be true. Nor do we know all the consequences of increased reliance on coal or nuclear power. We do know that higher prices induce conservation, but it still is unclear how the burdens of price are to be distributed politically.

Yet even more crucial than these scientific uncertainties is the nation's inability to think about energy in an ethical mode that involves conflicts of value. American political thought and rhetoric are not accustomed to "zero-sum" political questions, in which one group's gain means another group's loss. Rather, we think in expansionary terms, of increasing the pot for all. A zero-sum mode of thought requires rules of fairness and equity that are not congenial to a society in which individual and group claims historically have prevailed over any sense of a common community.

Third, though the social programs of the Great Society achieved much, they did not address adequately the most serious social problem of all, minority youth unemployment. Again, we do not know what to do about this problem. It is intimately related to juvenile crime, family instability, and the uncertain fate of school desegregation, but no one is quite certain how. Yet so long as it persists, blacks and other disadvantaged minorities will not be fully integrated into society, and a racial tinderbox will exist.

Thus, for each of America's three most urgent domestic problems, there is a great lack of intellectual capital from which to draw solutions. And it is not just that the experts fail to understand the phenomena scientifically, for by intellectual capital we mean more than academic expertise. Policy decisions are syntheses of value thinking and political strategies as well as expert knowledge. This is what we mean by "ideas," and this is what presidents need.

Consider the dilemmas that any president will face with regard to racial desegregation in the nation's public school system. Empirical research strongly supports the proposition that in academic terms, black students will benefit and white students will not be harmed by desegregation. Research also documents that white flight is a common response to desegregation. And finally, much of the black community is up in arms about traditional schools and home-grown school leaders that sometimes are lost in the process of integration. A president who would deal with such questions must combine incomplete insights from expert knowledge, moral sentiment, and political reality to construct a synthesis. Such syntheses form the ideas that characterize a presidency and perhaps a political era.

PROSPECTS FOR THE REAGAN ADMINISTRATION

Substance

Can Ronald Reagan identify, synthesize, and present new ideas that will address the nation's new problems in ways that will appeal enduringly to a majority of voters? The central issue on which his administration's success depends is the performance of the economy. Initially, at least, the president seems to have concluded that the new road to success is marked by familiar conservative signposts: reduced federal spending and vigorous programs of economic and social deregulation.

Reagan initiated this strategy very soon after his inauguration by asking Congress for unprecedented cuts in federal spending to bring the budget deficit under control. This, it is hoped, will improve the economy in two ways: by freeing private capital to move from federal securities, presently required to finance the deficit, to more productive investments in private economic development; and by altering public and business expectations about the inevitability of inflation, with a consequent dampening of the wage-price spiral. Whether these economic ends will be achieved or not is unclear. (Is shortage of capital the real cause of lagging industrial productivity? Will reductions in the deficit significantly reduce high wage demands and price increases?)

What is clear is that more is at stake in the new strategy than healthier economic indicators. The Reagan administration also sees budget cuts as the first wave of a direct assault on the way of doing business that has prevailed in Washington—and sustained growth in the federal government—since the early 1960s. David Stockman, President Reagan's director of the Office of Management and Budget, first attacked these norms in a 1975 article called "The Social Pork Barrel."[17] His central argument was that social programs served the political incentives of members of Congress to distribute money to their constituencies far more effectively than they served the groups they were intended to help. "The care and maintenance of the social welfare spending pipeline that extends to each of the 435 Congressional districts in the nation," he observed, "have now become a central preoccupation of members and their staffs." Included in the 435, of course, are congressional Republicans who, Stockman found, may have opposed these programs when they first were proposed, but invariably supported subsequent reauthorizations in order to keep the federal money flowing back home.

Stockman soon will learn whether his former Republican colleagues in Congress will rise to the challenge that he, with Reagan's endorsement, has presented to them. The challenge is nothing less than to reduce the size of the "barrel" and, he hopes, the volume and intensity of popular demands on the presidency. The administration appears to subscribe to a pair of political maxims in this regard. The first is that the federal government suffers from a combination of overload and incapacity: it took on too much too quickly and failed to digest it. Second, the most effective way to "dish the Democrats" is to reduce the obligations of the federal government and bring them into line with what presidents realistically can achieve. Thus, we can expect that two very important policy initiatives will follow the initial assault on the budget: economic deregulation, and the deregulation of social programs through their decategorization and devolution to the states and cities in the form of block grants.

The selection of Murray Weidenbaum as chairman of the president's Council of Economic Advisers is a sign of the importance accorded economic deregulation in the Reagan administration. A conservative expert on regulatory policy, Weidenbaum is the first microeconomist to chair the council. Again, policy and policymaker are bold, but only experience will tell whether the American people will approve the trade-offs in the proposed new balance between the federal government and private industry. Will they accept the new risks to health, safety, and the environment that come with deregulation in return for reduced costs to government and industry and increases in economic growth? For that matter, will deregulation have much effect on economic growth?

Social deregulation is an even more murky area. Economists, at least, are confident that the free market will protect the consumer in the wake of economic deregulation, but the closest analogue to markets in the deregulation of social programs is Montesquieu's two-century old theory that smaller polities are less likely to become tyrannical than larger ones.[18] Nonetheless, the Reagan administration will ask Congress to pass new legislation that will combine casually related categorical social programs into block grants to state and local governments. For example, a proposal will be made to combine Title I of the Elementary and Secondary Education Act, a program of compensatory education for disadvantaged children, with P.L. 94-142, the Education for All Handicapped Children Act. State and local agencies would be able to make their own decisions about how best to serve the clients of these programs, with minimal federal oversight. In exchange for this added discretion in the use of funds and reduction of the costs of compliance with federal regulations, it is predicted, local agencies will accept a substantial cut in funding.

As with Reagan's other policy proposals, a word of caution must be offered. The evidence of the three block grant social programs enacted by previous Republican administrations—the Comprehensive Employment and Training Act (CETA), Title XX of the Social Security Act, and the Better Communities Act—is that the social pork barrel does not disappear through devolution. It simply starts serving the political interests of state and local officials rather than those of national politicians.[19] And insofar as there are truly national social problems that require coherent federal action, the devolution strategy will be found wanting in other ways as well. It is an open question whether the Reagan administration will find the right balance between needed federal guidelines and desired local direction. It also is not clear whether Republican members of Congress will surrender the opportunity to advance their own political interests to potential political foes such as governors and mayors.

In the meantime, Democrats will be in a good position to develop alternatives of their own about how to address the nation's problems. Such activity would not have been possible if Carter had been reelected, but defeat has freed the party's mind from current responsibilities and old shibboleths. One already may discern the emerging themes of the new Democratic agenda. Republican efforts to reduce inflation through fiscal austerity and monetary tightness will be countered by new ideas about national agreements among labor, management, and government to tie wage increases to increasing productivity, thus avoiding the recessions brought by past Republican policies. The increase of productivity will not be left to deregulated markets, as the Republicans wish, but will be guided by new ideas about government initiatives to target investment. Finally, serious modes of collaboration between government and industry for the creation of jobs for minorities will be advocated.[20]

Style

To discover new and effective political ideas is a difficult enough task in itself. But for President Reagan to create a political realignment, he must do more than this. He must sell his ideas as well, in the face of opposition that we already have indicated may be formidable. Unlike Carter, Reagan certainly has the political temperament to do so. He can dramatize and explain issues. Equally important, he understands that to win the support of public and politicians alike, he must concentrate his policy appeals and strategies on the few issues on which an administration rises or falls.

Reagan will attempt to implement his policies of deregulation through a politics of public rhetoric and Washington-directed accommodation. A decade ago, Richard Nixon pursued similar policy goals by throwing down the gauntlet to Congress with a direct attack on the politics of accommodation.[21] The issue was never resolved because Watergate intervened, but the odds are that he would have failed even if it had not. The pressures of "interest-group liberalism" were still too strong in 1973.

The political climate is very different in 1981. Congressional Democrats are ideologically less confident and less protective of Great Society programs. They have experienced an intellectual failure of nerve. In addition, there is a Republican majority in the Senate, a conservative majority in the House of Representatives, and a disposition among some liberal Democrats to let President Reagan try his policies in the expectation that they will fail and be discredited.

Reagan, therefore, may be able to prevail by following his nature and working cooperatively with Congress on the few issues that truly concern him. (To do this, of course, he must control the Republican party's "moral regulators" on issues like abortion and school prayer and keep all eyes focused on his economic and social deregulation plans.)

President Reagan may be able to maintain a cohesive cabinet in which there is considerable unity about policy. Republican presidents usually find this easier to do than Democrats because Republicans stimulate fewer popular demands on government. Too many such demands create competing forces in an administration that are manifested in departmental disagreements. Unity in the cabinet also may reduce the role of the White House staff in the conduct of government, which invariably is conflict-inducing among legislators and department heads jealous of their prerogatives.

A clear style of authority has been established in the first weeks of the Reagan administration. It is guided by a coherent theory of governance which matches the new policy initiatives. The principal architect is Edwin Meese, the counselor to the president, who oversees both domestic and foreign policy. Meese has used the term "cabinet government" to describe his theory but that is not the appropriate designation. In fact, Republican-style cabinet government, under presidents Eisenhower, Nixon, Ford, and Reagan enforces collegiality among cabinet members and subordination on policy to the White House chief of staff. Eisenhower had Sherman Adams. Nixon was served by H. R. Haldeman and Alexander Haig; Ford turned to Donald Rumsfeld. Reagan has divided the job between Meese, who will oversee policy formation, and James Baker, who will handle administration.

It is already clear that cabinet members will be on a tight, central leash. Within that framework there will be free discussion through cabinet committees. But, department heads are expected to be agents of the president to their departments and the constituencies served. Meese, and others in the White House, were careful to appoint subcabinet officers who would be responsive to them, as well as to their chiefs. The bold initiatives of economic policy were taken by the White House before department heads had settled into their jobs and could raise objections in response to promptings from bureaucrats and constituents. This may appear to be cabinet government because White House staff assistants are to keep a low profile and act as analysts of policy alternatives and checks on departmental proposals rather than as policymakers or implementers. However, a high degree of collegiality among cabinet members can only be obtained by strong direction and control from the White House.

This model of government engenders unity and discipline and presents a common front on policy to Congress and the range of political interests. The capacity of the administration to implement policy is also enhanced by such cohesion. The corresponding weakness of such a system is that genuine discussion of policy is often quite limited, and the wagons are drawn in a closed circle against ideas which challenge working assumptions. This could be a serious flaw for the Reagan government if, as has been suggested, it is proceeding on the basis of weak and uncertain intellectual capital. Untested doctrine may be bolstered uncritically by pressure for intragroup conformity.

President Carter attempted to run a more open, loosely connected administration in which collegiality would emerge from debate. He tried to create a balanced tension between the White House assistants and department heads with himself as the arbiter. This is the model that all Democratic presidents inherit, not only because it derived from Franklin Roosevelt, but because Democrats represent greater social diversity than Republicans and must open themselves to both the play of ideas and interests, as represented through the many parts of government. Carter's failure was his inability to establish his personal primacy over policy in such a structure. This was due to his personal inability to set strategic goals that combined policy and political objectives and impose them on his colleagues. Reagan is determined not to make the same mistake. But presidents may make new, unforeseen mistakes in the effort to avoid committing the errors of their immediate predecessors.

Will Reagan continue to search out new ideas if the ones he tries first do not work? His record as governor of California shows him to be politically flexible. On the other hand, Reagan appealed to the past rather than the future in his election campaign. He promised to restore a time when America enjoyed abundance and national prestige. In the presidential campaign, he railed against the economics and politics of sacrifice and scarcity. He echoed the expansionist themes of the past with which American leaders are most comfortable, but which avoid discussion of zero-sum conflicts. It is an open question as to whether Reagan and his advisers know how to meet these old goals with new methods that marshal expert knowledge and link it to moral appeals and political strategies.

In sum, Ronald Reagan's chances of creating a coherent and adaptable program of governance as the basis for a partisan realignment rest on two questions. First, will his policies be enacted? Reagan's proselytizing performance puts other recent presidents to shame and illustrates the importance of the very skills that some political analysts have discounted on the grounds that the presidency is too weak for them to make a diffference. Second, will the general public and its organized groups become convinced that, if enacted, Reagan's policies are working to their benefit? Clearly, successful economic performance is of overriding importance to his other goals.

So we close the circle and return to our theme. Successful public policy has two ingredients: style (or political craftsmanship) and substance (valid ideas). We think it likely that the Reagan administration will receive high marks for craftsmanship. We feel some skepticism about the ideas. Time will tell. But if Reagan fails and a Democratic successor is elected and also fails to develop new convincing and effective ideas, then our politics will remain in disarray and our governments weak. The revolving-door presidency will continue to rotate. Instead of a Republican realignment or a Democratic renewal, the politics of stasis will be intensified amidst ever deepening popular alienation.

NONPRESCRIPTIONS

Few discussions of the modern presidency end without offering a variety of prescriptions for reform of the office. But, if our argument implies anything, it is that even the most laudable efforts at institutional tinkering may be largely beside the point. The forging of new institutional links to facilitate collective action in politics and government—the stated goals of most reform proposals—most likely will follow the development and articulation of collective purpose in the country rather than cause it. Presidents will have their way with Congress when they can present policies that the country will support, not before. Party reform, in the direction of a return to a politics of accommodation within party organizations, is likely to follow on the heels of new ideas as the basis for more cohesive electoral coalitions, not precede them.

Excessive concern with institutional design may be more than just pointless; it may be dangerous as well. The dangers are the false reformist sense that something important really is happening when lines on a chart are changed, entailing the distraction from more important tasks that inevitably follows. As David Broder points out, this is exactly what occurred after Lyndon Johnson exhausted the intellectual inventory of New Deal liberalism with his Great Society programs. "When [the Democrats] turned over the White House to Richard Nixon in 1969," he writes, "instead of restocking that idea factory, the Democrats expended their energy on 'reforming' their delegate-selection and convention rules. These were matters of consequence to some of the new constituency and leadership groups, but they were only tangentially connected to the emerging problems of the nation ... inflation or productivity or the costs of bureaucracy."[22] It would be supremely ironic if this same mistake were to be made today by those who wish to undo these reforms.

NOTES

1. Garry Wills, *Inventing America: Jefferson's Declaration of Independence* (Garden City, N.Y.: Doubleday & Co., 1978), Chapters 4 and 8. The source

of the famous quotation is Jefferson to Col. W. S. Smith, November 13, 1787: "God forbid we should ever be twenty years without . . . a rebellion." A. Koch and W. Peden, eds., *Life and Selected Writings of Thomas Jefferson* (New York: Modern Library, 1944), p. 436. Jefferson refers to Shays' Rebellion.

2. Richard M. Scammon and Ben J. Wattenberg, "Is It the End of an Era?" *Public Opinion* (October-November, 1980), p. 3.

3. Thomas Cronin, "Superman, Our Textbook President," *The Washington Monthly* (October, 1970), pp. 47-54.

4. Godfrey Hodgson, *All Things to All Men: The False Promise of the American Presidency* (New York: Simon & Schuster, 1980), p. 49.

5. Ibid., p. 14.

6. Ibid., p. 239.

7. Thomas Cronin, "The Presidency and Its Paradoxes," in *The Presidency Reappraised,* 2d ed., Thomas Cronin and Rexford Tugwell, eds. (New York: Praeger Publishers, 1977).

8. Lloyd Cutler, "To Form a Government," *Foreign Affairs* (Fall 1980), pp. 126-143.

9. Other obstacles to a party realignment in the American society are identified and evaluated in Chapter 3.

10. Scammon and Wattenberg, "Is It the End of an Era?" p. 4.

11. Ibid., p. 10.

12. Erwin C. Hargrove, *The Power of the Modern Presidency* (New York: Alfred A. Knopf, 1974), pp. 186-189.

13. Bernard R. Berelson, Paul F. Lazarsfeld, and William N. McPhee, *Voting* (Chicago: The University of Chicago Press, 1954), p. 209.

14. Hargrove, *Modern Presidency,* pp. 189-200.

15. Challenges facing Republican policymakers in solving domestic and foreign economic problems are dealt with in greater detail in Chapter 8. The text of President Reagan's 1981 budget message to Congress may be found in the Presidential Messages Appendix.

16. A minor footnote to the history of taxation: On January 25, 1978, author Nelson visited Representative Jack Kemp's office to see his aide, Bruce Bartlett, about a tax-indexing proposal that Kemp had introduced in 1977. Bartlett was helpful, but distracted; what he really wanted to talk about was a 30 percent tax cut bill he had just drafted for Kemp and Senator William Roth. "Conservatives have got to realize that they'll never be able to shrink the welfare state at the spending end," he said. "The only strategy that will work is to cut the size of the intake." Yet by the time of the bill's introduction in Congress, Kemp and Roth were arguing that their tax cut would so stimulate activity in the private sector of the economy that the tax intake actually would *grow.*

17. Stuart Eizenstat, "What the Democrats Should Do Now," *The Washington Post,* 2 January 1981.

18. David S. Broder, *Changing of the Guard: Power and Leadership in America* (New York: Simon & Schuster, 1980), pp. 477-478.

4

The Struggle for the
House of Representatives

Neil MacNeil

On November 4, 1980, there was no great doubt about the outcome of the contest for the House of Representatives. By then a consensus had been reached by the Democratic and Republican party leaders, the political managers of both parties, and the political correspondents: the Republicans were certain to make marginal gains against the Democratic majority that had controlled the House of Representatives since 1955. By this consensus, the House Democrats had no chance to enlarge their majority in the new Congress, and the Republicans had none to win enough seats to give them control of the chamber. There was a basic reason for this consensus: these observers and participants, all professionals, were examining essentially the same data.

CALCULATING THE POLITICAL ODDS

If they agreed that the House of Representatives would continue under a Democratic hegemony for yet another two years, however, the party leaders disagreed on just how many seats their respective party candidates would win. Instinctively, the Republicans assumed they would gain more than the Democrats were willing to concede. In mid-

65

October, just a fortnight before the elections, Thomas P. O'Neill, Jr. of Massachusetts, since 1977 the Speaker of the House of Representatives, offered to bet Robert Michel of Illinois, the Republican whip of the House, that the Republicans would not win more than 18 additional seats. Michel, in good humor, refused to take such an unfair advantage of O'Neill: he countered that the Republicans would win at least 25 more seats. O'Neill, a lifelong partisan Democrat, refused the better odds; he had studied the prospects for his party, and he was sure of his calculations. They shook hands on O'Neill's original proposition. The bet was for $100.

For the student of party politics, what was truly remarkable about the O'Neill-Michel wager, other than that the two opposing party leaders could have such a teasing, friendly relationship, was the very slightness of the shift each expected in the House of Representatives. After all, there were 435 seats at issue, but both leaders automatically assumed that the voters would reelect almost all of the incumbent candidates of both parties. For a host of reasons, this could not be considered a good year for the Democratic candidates; from the start O'Neill knew his problem was to minimize his party losses, and yet both leaders knew that most House incumbents, Democrats and Republicans alike, would win new terms without difficulty. This had been the pattern for more than a generation, and they had no reason now to discount the simple power of incumbency. The fact of incumbency had helped, in part, to keep the Democrats in majority control of Congress for more than a quarter century.

Of the 276 House Democrats in the 96th Congress, 249 were seeking reelection, as were 143 of the 159 Republicans. That meant that there were only 43 "open" seats, with no incumbent running, 27 of them Democratic, 16 Republican. These, obviously, were the seats most vulnerable for the party that held them, but even among these many were safe for the retiring member's party. In early October, Congressional Quarterly (CQ) published a special report assessing the prospects for the 1980 elections, campaign by campaign.[1] Of the 27 Democratic "open" House seats, CQ found 16 with the Democratic candidates clearly favored to win, only 5 running behind, and 6 too close to call. Of the 16 Republican "open" seats, CQ reported 12 still safely Republican, 2 with Republicans losing, and 2 too close to judge. Overall, for all 435 races, CQ could find only 25 Democratic seats likely to go Republican, only 12 Republican seats leaning to the Democratic candidate. There were others, in both parties, considered in some political trouble, but they were expected to survive. Overall, the CQ findings were the rationale for the narrowness of the changes expected by both O'Neill and Michel. From their own party sources they were receiving quite similar information.

"We have analyzed them all," O'Neill explained privately. "We have 25 in real tough fights and we may lose 15 to 25. Some will survive. The Republicans have 12 in tough shape, and we figure we are going to win a minimum of 6 to 8 of them. All together, we could lose 15 to 18, but I don't expect to lose that many." [2]

The reality was that many incumbent candidates from both parties had only token opposition. In fact, 37 Democrats had no Republican opponent at all, and 14 Republicans had no Democratic opponent. In sum, then, well in advance of the actual voting, by CQ's accounting and by the calculations of the party leaders as well, the Democrats seemed assured of holding at least 250 of their 276 seats in the House, a clear majority, and the Republicans at least 147 of their 159. Advance calculations like these, however skillfully drawn, can never be totally accurate; both sides knew that. There are always some surprises, some unexpected results, in every national election, but for practical, work-a-day purposes, the real struggle for the House of Representatives centered on scarcely 40 individual races, with perhaps as many again in less doubt. That did not make the struggle meaningless, by any account. The Democrats and Speaker O'Neill might well be assured, in advance, of a working party majority in the new House of Representatives, but that suggested nothing of the ideological, political bent of the new House then in the making.

In their halcyon days of the 1960s, liberal party strategists and lobbyists such as the AFL-CIO's Andrew Biemiller normally figured that they needed at least 275 Democrats in the House of Representatives to guarantee them a working *liberal* majority. They received occasional help from a score or so of moderate Republicans, but they had to outvote a strong contingent of Democratic conservatives, most of them from the South. With less than 275 Democrats, the House automatically slipped toward an ideological conservatism; the fewer the Democrats the more conservative it would be. The economic and political convulsions of the 1970s had substantially altered that once convenient measure by which to assess the House of Representatives. The 276 House Democrats in the 96th Congress did not automatically make the House ideologically liberal. Far from it. Not only had the Watergate excesses brought a new breed of Democrats to the House—a group headstrong in their independence of party leadership—but the very nature of the American economy had driven many liberal Democrats to question, and even to abandon, their party's traditional liberal responses to economic crises.

To survive politically in their 1978 election campaigns, many of them had felt forced to pledge to work for a balanced federal budget. Goaded by politically frightening grassroots pressures from their home districts, most members of the 96th House of Representatives paid more than lip-service to the demands for fiscal austerity. By the late spring of

1980, the House of Representatives had actually voted for a fiscal 1981 federal budget that was at least technically in balance. For the first time since 1969, Congress approved a national budget in which planned expenditures did not outweigh anticipated federal revenues. The House of Representatives that voted for that balanced budget was something less than a hell-bent liberal assembly. The 18-seat net Democratic loss that Speaker O'Neill conceded was possible would, of course, make the new House of Representatives still more conservative; the 25-seat net Republican gain Representative Michel foresaw would make the new House markedly conservative, even if still functioning under a Democratic party majority. In those 40-odd seats in which the stiffest competitions existed in the 1980 elections, the party leaders and their lieutenants were fighting for the ideological soul of the new House of Representatives.

PROBLEMS FOR THE DEMOCRATS

That the Democrats had severe reelection problems in 1980 was no surprise. There were warnings aplenty. Persistent high unemployment was a nagging national ailment, with pockets where unemployment was so high as to constitute actual economic depression. The energy shortage had brought more than the frustration of long lines and high prices at the gas pumps; it contributed to spiraling national inflation—the "cruelest tax," the politicians called it—that hurt almost every American citizen and voter. First in California with its Proposition 13, and then elsewhere in the country, grassroots movements protested high rates of taxation, and 30 state legislatures petitioned Congress for a constitutional convention to force the federal government to operate within its revenues and halt its huge annual deficits.

The Senate hearings on the SALT II Treaty, in the summer of 1979, disclosed a dangerous imbalance between the United States and the growing power of the Soviet Union, that in turn triggered sharp demands for an increase in American defense spending. The seizure of the American embassy in Tehran by Iranian radicals and their jailing of the American personnel as hostages proved a humiliating and agonizing demonstration of U.S. weakness. The implications of these public discontents on foreign policy issues are discussed more fully in Chapter 8. President Jimmy Carter, nominally the leader of the Democratic party, showed himself so politically unpopular and vulnerable that Senator Edward M. Kennedy of Massachusetts confidently challenged him for the Democratic presidential nomination with private and sometimes open encouragement from many congressional Democrats who were anxious about their own reelections.

THE BACK OF THE BUS

Despite popular folklore, a presidential candidate rarely helps his party's congressional candidates. A weak candidate at the head of the party's national ticket can hurt other candidates of the party, and if there are any political coattails at all, they tend to be short, indeed. For example, in the 1976 elections, when Jimmy Carter won the presidency, he ran behind 272 of the 292 Democrats who were elected that year to the House of Representatives and behind all but one of the Democrats elected to the Senate. The Democratic members of Congress could claim, as some did, that Carter rode into the White House on *their* coattails.

The disordered national economy, the disarray of American foreign and defense policies, and the intraparty quarreling among the Democrats offered the Republicans an extraordinary opportunity, one which they seized. The Republican National Committee, under the chairmanship of William Brock, joined forces with the special Republican campaign committees for the party's candidates for the House and the Senate to launch a unified assault on the perceived ineptness of the Democrats and their presumed mismanagement of the national government.

For starters, the Republicans skillfully orchestrated a $9 million national television campaign to catalogue the country's many ailments and blame them on the Democrats. Over and over, these Republican television programs emphasized that the Democrats controlled Congress, and had long controlled Congress, and that the Democrats had voted for the legislation that had brought the nation to its present difficulties. To their surprise, the Republicans had discovered, through their own pollster, that many Americans blamed Congress for the country's troubles, but did not know that the Democrats controlled Congress. For the campaign itself, the Republicans adopted a catchy slogan: "Vote Republican—for a change." That slogan not only used a clever play of words, but carried as well a subliminal message to the voters dissatisfied with the frustrations and anxieties of their own lives.

REPUBLICAN CAMPAIGN STRATEGIES

In the House of Representatives, the chairman of the National Republican Congressional Committee, Guy Vander Jagt of Michigan, brought a partisan zeal to his job unmatched in contemporary congressional politics. A political orator of admired talent, Vander Jagt was picked as the keynote speaker for the Republican National Convention at Detroit that nominated Ronald Reagan for President. Indeed, Reagan let it be known that Vander Jagt's name was on the short list from which he would choose his vice-presidential running mate. Even then, Vander Jagt was already running for another high office in his party, for in December 1979, John Rhodes of Arizona, the House Republican leader, had announced that he would not seek to continue in that position in the 97th Congress. Vander Jagt promptly declared his candidacy for Rhodes's leadership post, as did Representative Michel. Their rivalry added extra fervor to the struggle to increase the Republican membership of the House.

Long before the party convention or even the party primaries, Vander Jagt and other House Republican leaders had fully underway their initial strategies for the 1980 campaign. Indeed, the results from the 1978 congressional elections were scarcely tabulated before the partisan leaders of both House parties were already engaged in drafting plans for the elections two years hence. In the House of Representatives, reelection campaigning is an ongoing activity; the two years between elections allows scant time to prepare for the next campaign. For longer than the Democratic regulars could remember, the Republicans had had a greater ability to raise political funds and thereby provide their party's candidates with the wherewithal for their campaign. For longer than the Republicans liked to remember, the Democrats had been winning the majority of seats in both the Senate and the House of Representatives. Vander Jagt, like Republican campaign chairmen before him, intended to change that, and he devised a special strategy of his own to this purpose.

As campaign chairman, Vander Jagt had formidable resources at his command, including a campaign staff of 40 professionals and a $12 million budget. He had legal authority to allocate as much as $10,000 to each Republican candidate from his own committee's funds; from the Republican National Committee, he could commit as much as $14,720 more to each candidate. "We are giving everything the law allows," Vander Jagt said. The campaign funds, while significant, were merely the beginning of the help Vander Jagt's committee could provide. The committee regularly ran four-day schools for the candidates themselves, instructing them in the intricacies of modern campaign techniques of polling, fundraising, media communications, and precinct organization, and a similar three-day course for their campaign managers. Using its own broadcast studios, officials of the Republican committee offered to produce the radio and television spots for their candidates, to help publish their campaign literature, and to conduct their polling. "We'd do it at cost," Representative Vander Jagt said, "one-sixth of the commercial cost."

The committee staffers offered massive research on the voting records of their Democratic opponents. They could assign nationally known Republicans, such as Gerald Ford, to campaign in their districts, and they could help solicit campaign contributions for them from the political action committees of corporations and business associations.

Vander Jagt himself toured the country, as he was expected to do, to recruit likely candidates for the Republican party. When he found a prospect, he said, "I really put on the heat." He would pledge all the extraordinary help his committee could provide for every phase of the potential candidate's campaign, and he had what he called his "hard-sell pitch" to each one he sought to persuade. "I don't care about the sacrifice to you," he said. "You owe it to your country." In district after district, Representative Vander Jagt signed up candidates he believed could win.

This was a normal operation for a campaign chairman, but to this Vander Jagt added an ingredient of his own. In the past, his party predecessors offered serious party help only to those candidates running against Democratic incumbents from marginal seats, and a marginal seat was defined as one where the Democrat had won election by less than 55 percent of the vote. In the 1976 election, George Mahon of Texas, a deeply respected Democrat and chairman of the powerful House Appropriations Committee, had an unanticipated close reelection race running against an unexpected Republican opponent. For many years, the Republicans had not bothered to try to defeat Mahon. After all, he had been in Congress for four decades. "It was the classic example," Vander Jagt explained. "We learned that Democrats who had not been challenged for years could be out of touch."

CHALLENGING THE DEMOCRATIC LEADERSHIP

Shortly after the 1978 elections, Vander Jagt directed his committee staff to conduct "vulnerability studies" of the most senior Democrats, including the Democratic leadership, in the House of Representatives to learn how they were perceived by their constituencies back home. "We added a new targeting factor under my chairmanship," Vander Jagt said. "A fellow out of touch with his district was more vulnerable than the fellow who got by with only 53 percent of the vote. The vulnerability techniques showed a guy may have won by 70 percent, but he's not as solid as he looks."

From these studies, Vander Jagt resolved to conduct strenuous 1980 campaigns against all the Democratic leaders of the House, not exempting even Speaker O'Neill. "This was a deliberate strategy on our part," Vander Jagt explained. "We feel the Democratic leadership is out of touch with the country. We know they're out of touch with their constituents. All of them have been voting more liberal than their districts." Vander Jagt himself tried to recruit a candidate against O'Neill. He found a Republican named O'Neill in the Speaker's Boston district and tried to persuade him to run. One of Vander Jagt's senior staffers tried to persuade a woman to run against the Speaker. Neither would do it. "I tried," Vander Jagt said, but he had to conclude that "perhaps" O'Neill's constituents supported him more deeply than the vulnerability study had showed. "The others," Vander Jagt said, "were clearly out of step with their districts. They're all vulnerable. Any one of them could be beaten."

The House's Democratic leaders assumed that they were always subject to serious Republican opposition to their reelection, but Vander Jagt's systematic campaign against the entire Democratic leadership as a party strategy raised partisanship to a new level in the House of Representatives. His deliberate attempt to target Speaker O'Neill broke what amounted to a long-standing unwritten rule of the House that the opposition did not personally challenge the other party's leader. At the very top, the party leaders tended to be personal friends with cordial relations, despite the fact that they led opposing parties. As far back as the 1920s, Nicholas Longworth of Ohio, then Republican Speaker of the House, let the world know that his best friend in Congress was the leader of the House Democrats, John Nance Garner of Texas, later Speaker of the House himself. Every morning Longworth had his limousine pick up Garner for their trip together to the Capitol; every evening, in a back room, the two struck what Garner called "a blow for liberty" drinking Prohibition-prohibited whiskey. In the 1950s, Democratic Speaker of the House Sam Rayburn was once asked to campaign against then House Republican leader Joseph W. Martin of Massachusetts. "Speak against

Martin?" Rayburn snapped. "Hell, if I lived up there, I'd vote for him." ³

House Republican leader John Rhodes at first did not believe that Vander Jagt had entertained such plans against O'Neill. "I can't imagine that," Rhodes said. "It's not with my sanction. There's no way I'd be against Tip O'Neill. I don't agree with him on the time of day, but I love him. He's a great member of the House."

O'Neill felt the same way about Rhodes, and he was surprised at the Vander Jagt strategy. "We'd never go after them as leaders of their party," O'Neill said. "We never look at it in that manner. It's an unwritten principle of Congress that we argue and fight philosophies on the floor; at five o'clock we're friends. Another principle is we don't challenge each other." O'Neill had just returned from a campaign trip to Arizona, the home state of John Rhodes. "I didn't speak against Rhodes," O'Neill said. "I'd never do that."

"We didn't go after the leaders simply because they were leaders," Vander Jagt said, in his own defense, "but because they were vulnerable. We just feel that the Democratic leadership has to face up to the record of this Congress. They of all people shouldn't be able to say it wasn't me, it was somebody else who did it to you."

For all that, Vander Jagt had coldly appraised the impact of just such a campaign on the Democratic leaders. It would keep them campaigning hard for their own reelection, unable to travel around the country to help their less prominent Democratic colleagues, and those leaders who survived would learn by the experience to become more conservative. "Even those we don't defeat," Vander Jagt said, "we think we can make them better 'Republicans' when they get back here."

Among those on Vander Jagt's target list were: Democratic floor leader, James Wright of Texas ("We've encouraged his Republican opponent all along"); Democratic whip, John Brademas of Indiana ("We've encouraged his opponent from the start, letting him know what we can do for him"); Democratic campaign committee chairman, James Corman of California ("We've got Corman on the run"); Democratic party caucus chairman, Thomas Foley of Washington; House Ways and Means Committee chairman, Al Ullman of Oregon; House Interior Committee chairman, Morris Udall of Arizona ("We're running tremendous radio commercials against him"); and House Public Works Committee chairman, Harold Johnson of California ("I recruited his opponent.")

Foley had been targeted two years before by Vander Jagt, and when Vander Jagt campaigned for Foley's opponent, the Democratic leader unexpectedly held a public news conference to welcome Vander Jagt to the district. "I'm delighted to have him here," Foley said, and then, issue by issue, he cited how he and Vander Jagt agreed in their votes in

Congress—on positions Foley's opponent opposed. "I never got dusted off so well," Vander Jagt admitted.

Brademas dismissed Vander Jagt's campaign against him; he always had a hard campaign, and this was nothing new. "They want to kill us," Brademas said. "That's politics." Ullman felt hurt, especially in view of the bipartisan way he had always chaired his committee. Udall believed that he deserved better treatment; he had a well-earned national reputation as a talented legislator. "I expect Republicans to be with Republicans," he said, with resignation to the ordeal ahead.

When Vander Jagt campaigned in Corman's California district, a journalist confronted him with his earlier public praise for Corman as a skillful and persuasive legislator and "a very good friend of mine." "I was quoted accurately," Vander Jagt conceded, "but Jim Corman is part of the problem because he votes to put Congress under the control of the Democratic Party." Corman, like others on the target list, was forced to attempt to raise more than $500,000 to match the funds Vander Jagt and his allies were providing his opponent.

As part of Vander Jagt's campaign against Jim Wright of Texas, the Republican staffers helped prepare a pamphlet for Wright's opponent portraying the Democratic leader as "the liberals' liberal." Wright denounced it as deliberately distorted. Republican Senator John Tower of Texas sent letters to the heads of corporate and business political action committees in Washington, soliciting contributions of up to $5,000 for Wright's opponent. Wright learned about it quickly and sent them a letter of his own, coolly suggesting they read it carefully. "The one thing my opponent does not need is money," Wright wrote in his letter. "I'll be coming back to Congress, but everything you give to my opponent just makes it that much more costly to me." There was no mistaking Wright's chilling message: he would be majority leader of the House in the 97th Congress, in charge of scheduling all legislation, and they had better remember that now. When a copy of Wright's letter reached Vander Jagt's headquarters, his staff read it grimly. "There are not many Washington PACs [political action committees] that will dare go against Jim Wright," one of them said. Even so, Wright had to raise $750,000 for his own campaign and to campaign hard.

DEMOCRATIC CAMPAIGN EFFORTS

For their purposes, the House Democrats had a campaign committee of their own, but it was a feeble, ill-financed rival to Vander Jagt's organization. With only a handful of staffers and a budget of less than $1.5 million, the Democratic committee had no capacity to match the depth and variety of assistance the Republicans could offer their candidates. The Democratic committee had to limit its total help to any one candidate to $5,000 and then only in situations of dire emergency. By the end of September, the Democratic committee had provided only $334,000 to its party candidates, and it had been able to give any help at all to only 138 of its House candidates.

Plainly, every House Democratic candidate had to find his own campaign funds, and that did nothing to lessen his independence from, or increase his loyalty to, the party leaders. The Democratic National Committee, under the chairmanship of John C. White, made no attempt to help the congressional Democrats; White concentrated his efforts and party funds on trying to reelect President Carter. This was in striking contrast to Chairman Brock's extensive coordination of the Republican National Committee's work with the congressional Republicans. By the end of the campaign, White's negligence had become a matter of bitter resentment among the congressional Democrats, including House Speaker O'Neill and Senate Democratic leader Robert C. Byrd.

The Democrats had a startling further handicap in election year 1980. In February, the Federal Bureau of Investigation abruptly revealed that its agents, with the help of undercover informers, had operated a political "sting," using bogus Arab sheiks to offer substantial bribes to members of Congress in exchange for help on their alleged immigration problems. Accused, among others, were one Democratic senator, Harrison Williams of New Jersey, and seven members of the House of Representatives, six of them Democrats. The most important of these were Frank Thompson of New Jersey, a widely respected member, and John Murphy of New York, chairman of the House Merchant Marine Committee. The operation, quickly nicknamed "Abscam," raised serious questions about the propriety of the FBI's own behavior, but in election terms the accusations had to damage the Democrats' cause. All six Democratic representatives came from safe seats that Republicans normally had no chance to win. By election time, five of the Democrats had been indicted, and one of them, Michael Myers of Pennsylvania, had been convicted and expelled from the House—the first such expulsion of a member since the Civil War. The Republican, Richard Kelly of Florida, was defeated in a primary and replaced in the House by another Republican.

The Democratic 96th Congress had hardly completed its first budget resolution for fiscal 1981 than it became obvious that the technical balance it contained had already disappeared. Inflation had driven up the prime interest rate, and that in turn had devastating effects on the national economy, crippling several industries and pushing the country into a recession. The leaders of both political parties, in these circumstances, maneuvered to take election year advantage of the national distress.

The Republicans acted first and in so dramatic a way as thoroughly to embarrass the Democrats. At a meeting in mid-June, Reagan discussed with his advisers the idea of offering an immediate 10 percent, across-the-board tax cut. Quickly, the Republican advisers devised plans to act jointly in this with the congressional Republicans as a show of party unity. The very next week, from his California headquarters, Reagan made the proposal, and on the same day Republican senators and representatives endorsed it at a news conference in Washington. Senator Robert Dole of Kansas, the ranking Republican on the Senate Finance Committee, announced that he would offer the plan as an amendment to pending legislation. "We want the American people to understand we are united for a tax cut," Dole announced. "This is a Republican idea." Some Republicans, such as Barber Conable of New York, the ranking Republican on the House Ways and Means Committee, were skeptical about the inflationary and budgetary impact of such a tax cut, but they went along for the sake of party unity.

This Republican maneuver threw the congressional Democrats into turmoil. Senate Democratic leader Byrd found himself confronted with a potential political catastrophe: the Senate Republicans threatened to take over the leadership of the Senate on this sensitive issue. Byrd quickly summoned his Democratic colleagues into caucus and there devised a strategy to thwart the Republican scheme. There were 22 Democratic senators running for reelection, and he could not expect them to vote against a major tax cut just months before election day. Without consulting President Carter or the House Democratic leaders, Byrd persuaded the Democratic senators to reject the Republican plan and pledge an "anti-inflationary" Democratic tax cut of their own before the election. It was a stalling tactic, clearly, but Byrd's sudden response angered Speaker O'Neill and other House Democratic leaders. They were concentrating on trying to balance the federal budget, and they opposed any tax cut that would make their chore more difficult.

"I don't see any hue and cry for it," Speaker O'Neill said of the proposed tax cut. House Democratic leader Wright agreed: "I don't sense any stampede for a tax cut." Robert Giaimo of Connecticut, chairman of the House Budget Committee, was furious: "Let's remember that inflation is the enemy out there." Byrd explained himself. He had to offer an alternative. "You may not like the headlines you read, Mr. President," he told Carter at a leadership meeting, "but if we hadn't acted, you'd have seen headlines you liked worse."

ECONOMIC AND MORAL ISSUES

The tax cut incident disclosed anew the basic disarray of the Democrats. The Republican maneuver caused near panic in the Senate among Democrats, which prompted scorn from some of the House Democrats. "This looks like one of those elections when the Democrats are terrified," said Richard Bolling of Missouri, a Democrat and chairman of the House Rules Committee, "and the Republicans sense the kill." Under Byrd's leadership, the Senate did reject the Reagan tax package, and in his mid-year economic report, President Carter announced unhappily that the once-balanced fiscal 1981 budget already appeared in deficit by $30 billion. That made matters worse for the Democrats; before Congress adjourned, they had to approve the second budget resolution, and Budget Chairman Giaimo saw no way to persuade the House to approve it. "Who the hell is going to vote for a $30 billion or $40 billion deficit?" he asked. "Where would you get the votes?"

For the Democrats, this election year session of Congress had become a continuing embarrassment, and their intraparty dissensions only underscored the remarkable party unity of the Republicans. The Republicans emerged from their Detroit convention in such a euphoria of party harmony that momentarily they began to believe they were destined to win not only the presidency, but a majority in the Senate and even a majority in the House of Representatives. The Democrats could not free themselves from the political realities of a flagging economy and their inability to cope with its impact on the federal budget.

By September, the economic situation had turned even worse for the Democrats. Some of them, such as House leader Wright, had hoped against hope that the economic conditions would improve by late summer. Under these circumstances they knew they could not pass the second budget resolution, and so they decided they would have to postpone final action on it until after the election. They feared further political humiliation. Senate Republican leader Howard Baker, Jr. of Tennessee mocked the Democrats: "They don't want to belly up to the bar and confront a $35 billion to $60 billion deficit." House Republican leader Rhodes did the same: "They're between the rock and the hard place. They don't dare bring it up. . . . We're going to make it cost them." There was no way to pass the budget before the election; every House Republican would vote against it, and, after all the talk of a balanced budget, so would many Democrats. "You couldn't pass a budget with a deficit," said House Democratic whip Brademas, "so why shoot yourself in the foot? If we made an effort to pass a budget with a deficit, it would fail and then it would be another weapon in the arsenal against us."

Despite all these economic woes, the Democrats by mid-October still seemed in relatively favorable circumstances; they expected their election losses to be limited. Vander Jagt and the other Republican leaders likewise limited their own hopes to merely modest gains. It was at this time that Speaker O'Neill made his bet with Representative Michel. O'Neill had been out campaigning for embattled Democratic candidates in their districts, and he had been impressed by the crowds he had drawn. "Everywhere I've gone," he said, "the crowds were tremendous." He drew encouragement from that, but he knew that two groups of Democrats were in considerable trouble, a half dozen of the senior Democrats Vander Jagt had targeted and four or five of the Democrats tainted by the FBI's Abscam accusations. "Other than that," he said privately, "the groups that came here since 1972 seem secure." He was especially distressed by the reelection troubles of the party seniors, the ones who had not been challenged in years. "The people who put them in Congress in the first place are not around," O'Neill said. "Their organizations are not there."

House Republican leader John Rhodes also had been campaigning, helping Republican candidates where he could. "Things are looking fine," he said in mid-October. "I think we've got a pretty good chance, unless I'm crazy." Rhodes found little impact on the congressional races from the then strident presidential race between Carter and Reagan. "The coattail effect is not likely to be all that noticeable," he said. Rhodes had found that Republican House candidates did not regard Reagan as a "drag" on their campaign, nor much of a help. "I don't know that they're identifying with him," Rhodes said. "I don't think they're running away from him." They were concentrating on their own campaigns. So were the Democrats, and O'Neill reported that some of the party's candidates were asking President Carter to visit their districts. "None are avoiding him," O'Neill said.

The Republicans late in the campaign had an unexpected problem: Representative Robert Bauman of Maryland, one of the party's most vocal conservatives, was arrested in Washington on charges of soliciting sex from a 16-year-old boy. Bauman, previously certain of reelection, blamed his problems on acute alcoholism and was allowed by the court to plead innocent on the condition that he enter an alcoholic rehabilitation program. The publicity destroyed his campaign.

THE REPUBLICAN LANDSLIDE AND THE HOUSE

Election day arrived with both Republicans and Democrats in an apprehensive mood. "I'm hoping for a blizzard on election day in Indiana," said one Republican party manager. "I'm hoping for a blizzard in quite a few states." He was merely echoing the old truism that more Republicans vote in bad weather than do Democrats. Through the last weeks of the campaign, the national polls had shown Reagan and Carter relatively close, and many expected a close election. The two presidential candidates joined for a debate in Cleveland on October 28, a week before the election, and Reagan had done well.

On the Sunday before election day, the Iranians again reopened the frustrations over the American hostages with preposterous terms for their release. The early returns on election evening gave great comfort to the Republicans: Ronald Reagan seemed certain to sweep the election, possibly by a landslide. President Carter's pollster, Pat Caddell, had continued polling until the last moment, and the night before the election he had sent word to the president that the race was lost. The combination of his performance in the debate and the Iranians' intransigence had given Reagan an insurmountable lead.

The next morning, voting in Plains, Georgia, Carter had to fight back tears. That night the voting went the way Caddell had predicted, and by 8:15 p.m., eastern standard time, one of the television networks formally had announced that Reagan had won. Twenty minutes later, Carter, back at the White House, telephoned Reagan in California to congratulate him. Carter made immediate plans to go on national television to concede the election publicly. The president asked the White House congressional liaison chief, Frank Moore, to telephone Speaker O'Neill. "It's all over," Moore said to O'Neill, as he told him that Carter was conceding. "He can't do that!" O'Neill shouted. "They've still got two hours out there." The voting booths were still open in the West. "There's nothing you can do about it," Moore answered. "He's already announced to the networks that he's coming."

Carter's early concession bitterly angered many Democrats; his admitted defeat would discourage voters all over the western states from °voting, and there were many close races there. At his command post in the Capitol, O'Neill was receiving telephone calls from all parts of the country on the House races. Long before midnight, he knew how badly the elections had gone for the congressional Democrats, far worse than he had expected, and there were still a dozen incumbent House Democrats with their elections still undecided. "They're all going to be close," O'Neill said. By then, the Republicans had lost only 4 seats to the Democrats, but the Democrats had lost 28. O'Neill thought the net loss to the Democrats could rise as high as 30. "There were coattails," he said then. "Jimmy Carter fell apart in the last three days. The Iranian thing killed him. The American people thought it was a lack of leadership." Brademas of Indiana, one of O'Neill's closest associates, had been defeated. So had Richardson Preyer of North Carolina and Thomas Ashley of Ohio, both senior and repected members; both defeats were surprises to O'Neill. Wright had won easily, despite Vander Jagt's campaign against him; Udall and Foley had survived.

For the Democrats, before the night was over, there was more bad news from the West Coast: defeated were Oregon's Ullman, and California's Corman and Johnson, among others. Corman blamed Carter's early concession for his defeat: he lost by less than 800 votes, and he had statistics to show that normal Democratic voters had not bothered to vote after they heard Carter's concession. Brademas rejected Vander Jagt's campaign against him as the cause of his defeat. "What did me in," Brademas said, "was 15 percent unemployment in my district—twice the national average." Four of the Democrats indicted in the Abscam scandal were defeated: New Jersey's Thompson, New York's Murphy, South Carolina's John Jenrette, and Pennsylvania's Myers, although Myers was defeated by an "independent" who would become a Democrat in the new Congress.

In all, 37 House Democrats were defeated, 27 of them incumbents, and the Democrats won back only those 4 early Republican seats. Maryland's Bauman lost, and so did Ohio's Samuel Devine. The results were that the Republicans gained a net of 33 seats on the Democrats, more than any of the party leaders had guessed. The new House of Representatives would have 243 Democrats and 192 Republicans. It was still under Democratic control, but would have a strikingly conservative tilt, and Speaker O'Neill would become the highest ranked Democrat in national office. "We're going into the Democratic caucus for a lot of talk and decide what we should do," O'Neill said.

Weeks later, after his own pollster analyzed the results, O'Neill calculated that the Reagan landslide—and the Reagan coattails—had cost the Democrats 13 seats. In the debate with Carter, O'Neill said, Reagan showed "he's not an ogre; he's a decent fellow. And his question— 'Are you better off now than you were four years ago?'—that was a ten-strike." Then there was the muddled question of the American hostages in Iran. "The combination of these things made the landslide," O'Neill said. "That landslide is where my guys got lost."

O'Neill paid off his $100 bet to Michel.

THE DEMOCRATIC LEADERSHIP AND THE REAGAN PRESIDENCY

As in previous elections, the incumbents as a group fared remarkably well despite the Reagan landslide. Among Democrats, 222 of the 249 incumbents won reelection, as did 140 of the 143 Republican incumbents. That meant that well over 90 percent of all incumbents had won, although the Republicans fared far better than did the Democrats.

In the wake of the elections, the House Republicans had to choose a new party leader to replace John Rhodes who had stepped aside. Vander Jagt and Michel had been quietly lining up commitments from their Republican colleagues long before November. With 192 Republicans in the new House of Representatives, the winner needed at least 97 votes.

"I don't count them hard unless I've looked at them eyeball to eyeball and shaken their hands," Michel said. Vander Jagt followed an identical counting scheme: "I count a hard vote when he looks you in the eye and says, 'I'll vote for you.'" Vander Jagt, the partisan campaigner, ran for floor leader on the grounds that he was the party stalwart who could make the Republicans the majority party in the House in the 1982 elections. Michel ran as the skilled parliamentarian and floor tactician who could woo Democrats to the Republican bills and thereby enact the Reagan legislative program. "The bottom line is to enact the Reagan program," Michel told his colleagues. As campaign manager, Vander Jagt had a natural advantage with the 52 new Republicans in the House; he had signed their campaign checks and orchestrated their election strategies.

On the day of the party caucus, December 8, Michel believed he had 110 hard-count votes—"unless there are a lot of liars around here." Vander Jagt had what he believed were 102 hard commitments. In the secret vote, the Republicans chose Michel, 103 to 87 for Vander Jagt. Both men were energetic, Midwest conservatives, popular with their colleagues. But the party caucus, in choosing Michel, opted for traditional leadership, working cooperatively with the Democrats to achieve legislative goals, and not the confrontation politics that Vander Jagt offered. That decision, of course, would have profound impact for Reagan's legislative success in the House of Representatives.

On the Democratic side, Speaker O'Neill had been shocked by the election results, which he called a "disaster," and he knew that he had no choice but to cooperate with the new Republican president. "We're going to cooperate with the President," he said publicly. "It's America first and party second." For all that, he had grave concerns of his own. For one thing, he had to make sure of his own renomination and reelection as Speaker. A few days immediately after the election, some Republicans, including Vander Jagt, had talked openly of trying to persuade enough conservative Democrats to join the conservative Republicans to elect a conservative Speaker. Beyond that, O'Neill had to take steps to protect himself as Speaker and his command of the House schedule in the coming Congress.

From their election successes, the Republicans were properly entitled to a larger proportion of their members on the House's committees than in the 96th Congress. O'Neill gave way on most legislative committees, but with the backing of the Democratic caucus and over the anguished protests of Michel and other Republican House leaders, he insisted on maintaining top-heavy Democratic majorities on three of the House's most powerful committees: Rules, Ways and Means, and Appropriations. That would give Speaker O'Neill at least some special parliamentary advantages in this newly conservative House, especially in the coming contests over taxation and spending.

NATIONAL PARTY ORGANIZATIONS AND LEGISLATIVE ELECTIONS

O'Neill and the other House Democrats had seen what the Republican National Committee, as well as Vander Jagt's committee, had done for their party's candidates, and now O'Neill and his party lieutenants insisted that the Democratic National Committee no longer neglect the party's congressional candidates. "Today," O'Neill said in his speech to the party caucus that renominated him for Speaker, "candidates need the financial and technical support of the party. The preoccupation of the Democratic National Committee with presidential politics must cease. The congressional campaign committee must serve as a genuine political and financial resource for Democratic incumbents and challengers alike in 1982." Senator Byrd, the Senate's Democratic leader, had precisely the same view as O'Neill. In late February 1981, the Democrats were to choose a new national chairman, and well before that date, both O'Neill and Byrd summoned the candidates for the post to their respective party caucuses to let them know, whoever got the job, that the Democrats running for the Senate and the House of Representatives in the 1982 election expected extensive help from the national committee.

Despite the obvious advantage the Republicans gained from their well-financed and well-organized campaign committee, the Democratic candidates as a group did not suffer unduly for lack of campaign funds. They had to work harder to raise funds, and they had to get them from nonparty sources. In an interim report on campaign spending dated January 21, 1981, the Federal Election Commission found that all candidates for the House of Representatives had spent a total of $130,200,000 in their campaigns, and that the Democratic candidates, as a group, had spent slightly more than the Republicans. These figures were not final because the candidates had not yet reported on the last six weeks of their campaigns, traditionally the period of greatest campaign spending. The political action committees, now numbering 2,387 as compared to only 608 in 1974, had been more active than ever before, and there was evidence that the business and corporate political action committees had begun to use their "risk capital," as the politicians called it, to favor Republican and more conservative candidates.

In previous elections, political action committees tended to contribute substantially to those who held important and influential positions in Congress, thus assuring Democrats a major share of these funds. The business leaders wanted "access" to important members of Congress, and this was a way to assure it. "With a little money," said Justin Dart, chairman of Dart Industries, "they hear you better." [4] In the 1980 elections, however, the largest of the business political action committees, that of the National Association of Realtors, made important contributions to the Republican opponents of Oregon's Al Ullman and California's James Corman, both influential Democratic leaders. The political action committees of organized labor continued their strong preference for Democratic candidates in 1980 as they had always done.

According to the Federal Election Commission's report, the total contributions of all political action committees to House candidates in 1980 was $26,700,000. The very size of the expenditures on House races had long been causing alarm, and the 1980 elections did nothing to reduce that concern. In many of the hotly contested races, the two opposing candidates together spent more than $1 million; this was true of all of the campaigns of the Democratic leaders whom Vander Jagt had targeted. In at least one race, that of Republican Robert Dornan of California, his expenditures for reelection actually reached $2 million, the most expensive campaign ever for the House of Representatives.

THE "NEW RIGHT" AND THE 1980 ELECTIONS

Another disquieting element in the 1980 congressional races was the ferocity of some of the new conservative groups taking an active part in the elections. They were so-called "New Right" organizations such as the National Conservative Political Action Committee, the Conservative Caucus, and the Committee for the Survival of a Free Congress, as well as their allies among the evangelical Christian groups, including the Moral Majority, the Religious Roundtable, and the Christian Voice. Primarily they concentrated on defeating liberal Democratic senators such as George McGovern of South Dakota, Frank Church of Idaho and Birch Bayh of Indiana; their rhetoric at times became so extreme that some of the Republican candidates they were supporting repudiated their help. "We did not want their help," said Dan Quayle, the Republican who defeated Bayh. "They're a disservice to the people they claim they help."

These conservative groups did make some effort in the House races, and in one notable instance, the Moral Majority was credited with defeating the renomination of Alabama Republican John Buchanan, a Baptist minister who was not as ardent an advocate for school prayer as the evangelicals thought he should be. The Christian Voice published a "report card" grading each member of Congress on the "morality" of his voting on such questions as school busing, a balanced federal budget, creation of the Department of Education, and the Strategic Arms Limitation Treaty. Ironically, two of the Republican members of the House of Representatives rated among the highest for morality were Maryland's representative, Robert Bauman, arrested for a sex crime, and Florida's representative, Richard Kelly, indicted and later convicted for bribery. More than a few Democrats took satisfaction in pointing this out to the voters.

How effective any of these groups proved in achieving their ends was at best debatable. Neither the Republican nor Democratic candidates were willing to acknowledge that they had much impact; neither were the party campaign managers. "In many of the close races, we were helpful," said Paul Weyrich, director of the Committee for the Survival of a Free Congress. "Ronald Reagan could have been elected without our help. Many Senate and House candidates could not have been. Where we made our contribution was in training thousands of volunteers in the various states where there were races." Weyrich coordinated the campaign activities of no less than 38 conservative religious organizations, as well as acting as strategist for the New Right groups. "They created an awful lot of noise," said William Sweeney, director of the Democratic Congressional Campaign Committee. "In many of the House races, they employed rather flagrant techniques to create a distorted image of members' voting records. I'm not convinced they were a net plus for any candidates."

Nancy Sinnott, campaign director for the National Republican Congressional Committee, agreed in substance with Sweeney. She credited them with political effect in only two elections: the defeat for renomination of Republican Buchanan in Alabama and the near defeat of Democrat Mike Synar in Oklahoma. "The election was a true party election, not a Reagan landslide," she said. "As far as the House races went, the New Right wasn't all that much."

WOMEN AND THE POLITICAL PROCESS

The 1980 congressional races were noteworthy for another reason: the number of women nominated by the two major parties for seats in the House of Representatives and the Senate. In the 34 states with Senate races, 5 of the major party nominees were women, and 3 of them were regarded as serious candidates. In the House races, there were no less than 51 women running as major party candidates, of whom 15 were incumbents seeking reelection. Many of the women faced hopeless odds, but significantly 10 of the 20 nonincumbent Republican women received substantial funds from their party for their campaigns, and 6 of the 16 nonincumbent Democratic women were viewed similarly as serious candidates.

Never had the House had more than 18 women members nor the Senate more than 2. During the 1980 campaign, however, there was a distinct possibility that the new House could have as many as 30 women members and the new Senate as many as 4. Actually, only one of the women, Republican Paula Hawkins of Florida, won a seat in the Senate, and only 4 of the nonincumbent Republican women were elected, along with all 15 women incumbents. The national trend obviously hurt the chances of the Democratic women who were not incumbents.

Even though the women candidates fared poorly on election day, their numbers in 1980 did not escape notice by the professionals. "It's been a national evolution," said Nancy Sinnott of the National Republican Congressional Committee. "They've gone through the system. On both sides, Republican and Democratic, there's been a breakdown in party organization, the organizations that used to control the nominations. The problem in the past was that women couldn't get past the smoke-filled rooms. Now there are more open primaries." Jeane Kirkpatrick, the professor of political science at Georgetown University whom President Reagan appointed U.S. Ambassador to the United Nations, saw the phenomenon in the same way. "It's an important part of a long-term trend in American society and in American politics," she said. "Women are beginning to compete for all the roles in society. There's been a growing number of women running for political office. . . . It's a changed conception of femininity, first on the part of women, second on the part of men."

Speaker O'Neill, who had seen many changes in his near half-century in politics, had hardly missed this one. "There are more activists among women now," he said. "The ERA is responsible in part. It's activated a lot of women. It's the trend that's coming."

CONCLUSIONS

In sum, the 1980 elections placed the three political arms of the government—the presidency, the Senate and the House of Representatives—in the hands of ideological conservatives, even though the House remained under the moderate-liberal management of Speaker O'Neill. That would suggest that President Reagan should have little trouble enacting his conservative program, so long as House Republican leader Robert Michel could negate O'Neill's power in the chair and take command of the House's conservative majority on the floor. Michel, indeed, argued that the decisive legislative battles in the 97th Congress would be fought in the House of Representatives. O'Neill gave credence to this idea by his insistence on keeping lopsided Democratic majorities in control of the House's three most powerful committees, the sites of the great legislative contests to come.

Speaker O'Neill, however, predicted that President Reagan's real source of trouble would be the Senate, not the House. O'Neill pointed to the Senate's Republicans, a group sharply divided into three ideological camps: the regular conservatives such as Baker of Tennessee and Dole of Kansas; the weakened but still influential moderate-liberals such as Mark Hatfield of Oregon and Charles Mathias of Maryland; and the militant, activist arch-conservatives such as Jesse Helms of North Carolina and Orrin Hatch of Utah. O'Neill expected the Republican arch-conservatives to grow increasingly impatient and unruly with President Reagan when he necessarily had to take actions that did not meet their strict criteria of conservative ideology.

On their part, O'Neill and Senate Democratic leader Byrd could read the election returns. They knew that Reagan had been elected president and elected in a conservative tide. Their public pledges of cooperation were more than political politeness: they were based on precedent and part of their own basic political strategy. Speaker O'Neill privately and deliberately counseled his House Democrats in the very words that Sam Rayburn of Texas, the party leader, had used to advise him and other House Democrats back in 1953, when Dwight Eisenhower was president and the Republicans controlled Congress: "We Democrats are not obstructionists; we're builders." Similarly, Senator Byrd was telling his Democratic colleagues to copy the example of Lyndon B. Johnson, the new Senate Democratic leader in 1953.

Rayburn and Johnson had offered their full cooperation to President Eisenhower. What were the results? Eisenhower had his principal trouble from congressional Republicans, and the Democrats won full control of Congress in the 1954 elections. That was the rationale for O'Neill's and Byrd's pledges of genuine cooperation with Reagan, that and the broader sense that they had to act for the nation's well-being. In the 1982 elections, O'Neill and Byrd want to regain working Democratic majorities in Congress. The only way they know to earn that is by acting responsibly and cooperatively with President Reagan. Whether they could successfully persuade their rank-and-file members to stay with such a strategy in the difficult days ahead remained to be seen, as did the success of the strategies of Representative Michel and Senator Baker. On their side, they would be arguing the same essential approach for their members: responsibility and cooperation toward the new administration.

NOTES

1. *Congressional Quarterly Special Report, The 1980 Elections,* 38 (October 11, 1980): 2967-3090.

2. O'Neill to the author. Unless otherwise indicated, the quotations in this chapter are remarks made to the author.

3. *Time,* October 13, 1961, p. 27.

4. *Common Cause,* October 1980, p. 13.

5

The New, New Senate

Charles O. Jones

In his 1980 book, *The New Senate: Liberal Influence on a Conservative Institution,* Michael Foley explores changes in the United States Senate from 1959 to 1972. Impressed with the "massive influx of liberals in the late 1950s and early 1960s," Foley concluded that:

> ... the liberals made the Senate a less cocooned and cloistral institution, they reduced the mystique of its introverted and private operations, and they undermined the whole notion of a structured hierarchy of personal status and privilege. Distinctions between juniors and seniors became blurred as the atmosphere within the institution became one of individual assertion. The liberals' disparate ideas and high expectations enlivened the Senate, made it more heterogeneous in composition, and brought it more into the mainstream of national political pressures and trends.
> ... the institution has experienced sufficient change to warrant the title "new Senate." [1]

Unfortunately, Foley's research extends only to the 92nd Congress (1971-1972). Of the 28 senators in that Congress who had strong liberal ratings (on five of seven issue areas), only eight (29 percent) are still members of the Senate in the 97th Congress. Indeed, a total of only 30 senators from the 92nd Congress returned in 1981—a turnover of 70 in just 10 years. Perhaps most astonishing is the fact that 55 senators in the 97th Congress are "first-termers." Eighteen new senators were elected in each of the last three elections and one senator, George Mitchell of Maine, was appointed to the unexpired term of Edmund S. Muskie. Foley was no doubt correct in identifying significant changes in the ideological and organizational direction of the Senate. But we now know that these changes do not necessarily result in permanently establishing a more liberal institution. Foley's "new Senate" in 1972 is now a "new, new Senate"—which is *not* the same as saying that the old Senate has been renewed.

This chapter will analyze the 1980 Senate elections—examining the results, comparing these results with those of previous elections, and discussing the outcome as related to recent developments in Congress. Next to the presidential election, the Senate races commanded the most attention on election night. The results exceeded the expectations of the most optimistic Republican and the fears of the most pessimistic Democrat. It is not too early to begin inquiry into the reasons for this extraordinary development.

RECENT TRENDS IN SENATE ELECTIONS

Some rather dramatic results have been recorded in Senate elections in recent years. As Senator John Heinz, chairman of the National Republican Senatorial Committee, observed: "Being an incumbent Senator is increasingly hazardous to one's political health." [2] Figure 5-1 shows that normally over 90 percent of those House members seeking reelection are returned. The proportion of Senate incumbents reelected is both lower on the average (just over 75 percent in this period) and more variable from one election to the next (varying from 97 percent in 1960 to 55 percent in 1980). Further, the trend is rather dramatically downward—an average of less than 60 percent reelected in the last three elections. A total of 39 Senate seats switched parties in the last three elections, more than the previous *six* elections.

But there are other important developments in Senate elections, as shown in Figure 5-2. In 1958 the Republicans experienced a devastating defeat. The Democrats won 13 seats previously held by Republicans, defeating 11 incumbent Republican senators in the process. Thus the high turnover in that year favored the Democrats and gave them a commanding 66-34 majority. By 1962 this majority had swelled to 68-32—the lowest point for the Republicans since the years of the Great Depression. Predictions were that it would take decades for the Republicans to win a majority in the Senate. Some recovery was realized in the 1966, 1968, and 1970 elections, but then there were setbacks in 1972 and

Fig. 5-1. Percentage of House and Senate Incumbents Reelected, 1958-1980.

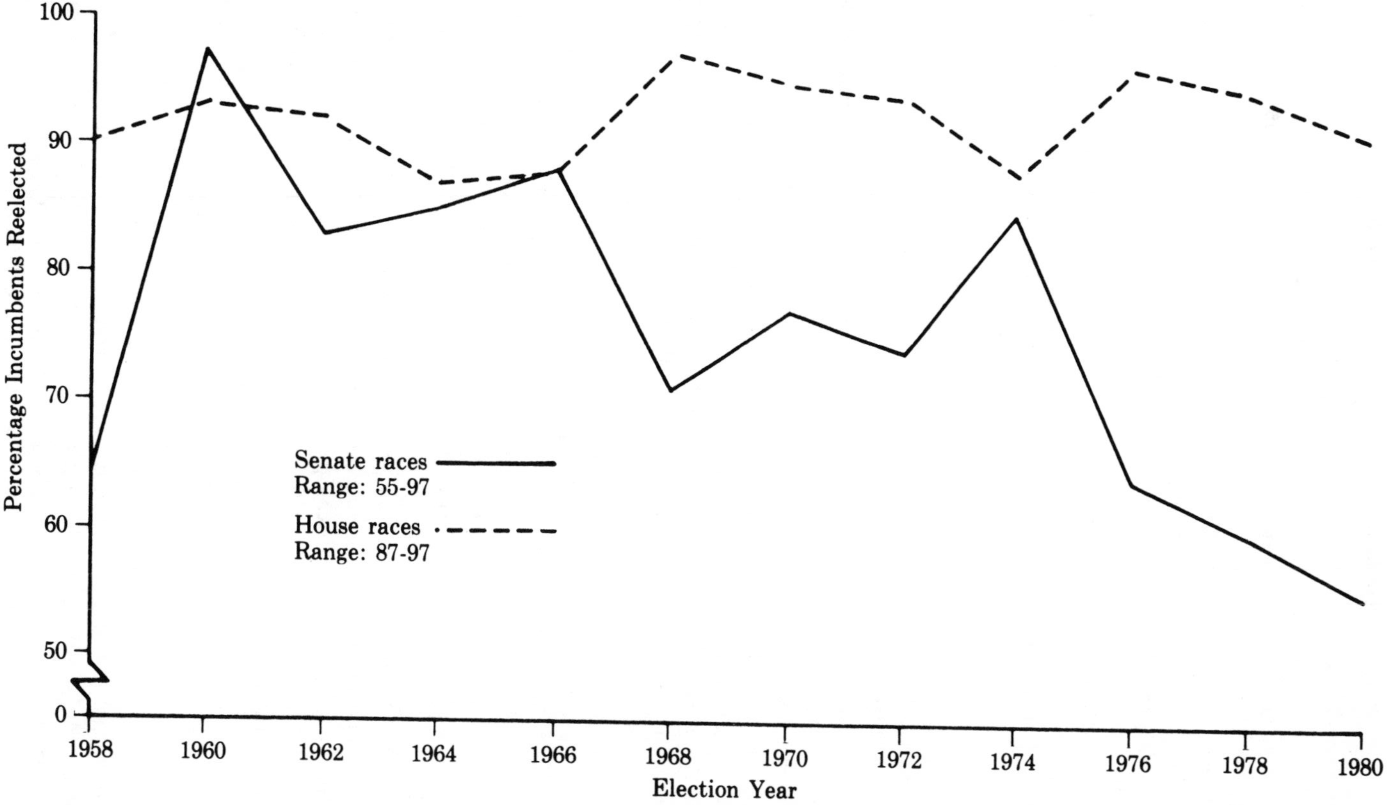

Senate races ——
Range: 55-97

House races ·—·—·—
Range: 87-97

Percentage Incumbents Reelected

100
90
80
70
60
50
0

1958 1960 1962 1964 1966 1968 1970 1972 1974 1976 1978 1980

Election Year

the post-Watergate election of 1974. Senate Republicans held their own in the 1976 elections, in which 14 seats changed parties (seven switches each way). The net gain of 3 seats in the 1978 elections was encouraging to the Republicans, but everyone recognized that 1980 offered a superb opportunity for more gains. Of the 34 seats up for reelection, the Democrats held 24, the Republicans just 10. "Not since the political aftershocks of Watergate almost blew the Republican Party out of Congress six years ago has the GOP seen such a comeback opportunity on Capitol Hill." [3] Still, according to the National Republican Senatorial Committee, a good showing was expected to produce "a net gain of at least three to six Senate seats—and maybe more if Ronald Reagan leads a heavy Republican tide." [4] However, the results nearly matched the Democratic landslide of 1958—a gain of 12 Senate seats for the Republicans and their first Senate majority since the 83rd Congress (1953-1954). [5]

Another interesting factor to consider is the change in the margin of victory in Senate races. A recent study shows that the number of seats won by 60 percent or more has stayed roughly the same since the 1940s— typically about two-fifths of the seats have been won by this margin in any one election. [6] But important regional shifts have occurred. At one time southern Senate seats were won virtually without opposition and northern seats were hotly contested. Between 1974 and 1978, however, the number of southern seats won by 60 percent or more had decreased to 57 percent while the number of northern seats in this category had increased to over 37 percent. The comparable figures for 1980 were 37.5 percent and 27.9 percent, respectively—a dramatic decrease in the number of safe Senate seats. Furthermore, the definition of a safe percentage was revised as a result of the 1980 sweep. Four incumbents who won by over 60 percent of the vote in 1974 *lost* in 1980 (one of the losers in 1980, Herman Talmadge of Georgia, had won by over 70 percent in 1974).

Increased turnover, strengthened Republican position, and dramatic change in the number of safe seats—these are important trends. What explains these developments? Just what is going on in Senate races? And what are the effects for the 97th Congress? We turn now to a consideration of these important questions.

WHY DO SENATORS LOSE?

What has happened to "the most exclusive club in the world?" Why has it not remained a comfortable haven for aging politicians? First it should be noted that "incumbency advantage" dies hard as a major explanatory factor in analyzing Senate election outcomes. It is a convenient reference point in analyzing elections. And even though it

Fig. 5-2. Democratic-Republican Party Split, United States Senate, 1958-1980.

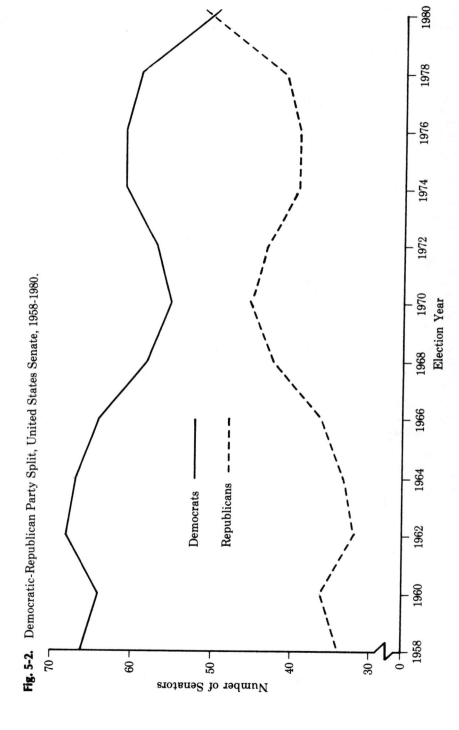

Table 5-1. The Hazards of Calling Senate Races—1980.

	Congressional Quarterly Analysis		Movement Detected	Final Outcome
State	*October 11*	*November 1*	*Detected*	*Outcome*
Alabama	LD	LD	-	R
Alaska	?	?	-	R
Arizona	LR	LR	-	R
Arkansas	SD	SD	-	D
California	DF	SD	D	D
Colorado	LD	?	R	D
Connecticut	LD	DF	D	D
Florida	?	?	-	R
Georgia	SD	SD	-	R
Hawaii	SD	SD	-	D
Idaho	?	?	-	R
Illinois	LD	LD	-	D
Indiana	LD	?	R	R
Iowa	?	?	-	R
Kansas	SR	SR	-	R
Kentucky	SD	SD	-	D
Louisiana	SD	SD	-	D
Maryland	RF	RF	-	R
Missouri	DF	DF	-	D
Nevada	SR	SR	-	R
New Hampshire	?	?	-	R
New York	LD	LD	-	R
North Carolina	LD	LD	-	R
North Dakota	SR	SR	-	R
Ohio	SD	SD	-	D
Oklahoma	LD	?	R	R
Oregon	RF	RF	-	R
Pennsylvania	?	LR	R	R
South Carolina	SD	SD	-	D
South Dakota	?	?	-	R
Utah	SR	SR	-	R
Vermont	DF	LD	R	D
Washington	LD	LD	-	R
Wisconsin	LD	LD	-	R
Totals SD –	7 (6)	8 (7)		22R
DF –	3 (3)	2 (2)		12D
LD –	10 (3)	7 (2)		
? –	7 (7R)	9 (8R)		
LR –	1 (1)	2 (2)		
RF –	1 (2)	2 (2)		
SR –	4 (4)	4 (4)		
	34	34		

(Numbers in parentheses represent the number of correct calls)

Key: SD: Safe Democratic   SR: Safe Republican
       DF: Democratic Favored   RF: Republican Favored
       LD: Leans Democratic   LR: Leans Republican
        ?: No clear favorite

SOURCE: Congressional Quarterly, *Special Report* 38 (October 11, 1980): 2986-3086; Congressional Quarterly, *Weekly Report* 38 (November 1, 1980): 3243-3247.

has never been as reliable in predicting Senate over House elections, most prognosticators have used it more or less as a base point in estimating results.

The Congressional Quarterly *Weekly Report* is one of the few publications to do a race-by-race analysis of congressional elections. The first projections were published on October 11, 1980, and the conclusions were as follows:

> At this point, six of the Democratic seats are in the "no clear favorite" category. Meanwhile, Republicans see only three of their seats in severe jeopardy. . . . This would indicate a reasonable chance of a Republican gain of at least three seats. However, there are eight Democratic seats that only lean in that party's favor. So GOP gains could conceivably go higher.[7]

The second projections were published just before the election on November 1, 1980. At that time, the Congressional Quarterly predicted a "net gain of two or three seats" for the Republicans.

> Although the GOP may narrow the 59-41 margin Democrats now enjoy, it is very unlikely Republicans can take control of the Senate in 1981. To do so, they would need to win all of the close races, plus two of the seven that are currently leaning toward the Democratic candidate.[8]

Table 5-1 shows the Congressional Quarterly analysis for the two periods, along with the final outcome. Note that some movement toward the Republicans was spotted between the two projections. But the final results show Republicans capturing all but one of the "too close to call" seats in the second projection and five of the seven seats that were identified as leaning to the Democrats. The point of this exercise is not to embarrass Congressional Quarterly. Even the Republicans themselves were unaware that they were about to win control of the Senate. Rather, the point is that something is going on in Senate races that is presently not very well understood. There is a natural tendency to rely on the incumbency rule as a base for projections, but one has to reconsider the utility of that rule when it predicts just over half of the races (and only 45 percent of those involving Democratic incumbents).

Republican Senator Paul Laxalt of Nevada commented on the Senate results on the day after the election by saying that "I'm still shellshocked." Former Majority Leader Robert C. Byrd of West Virginia, who lost his Democratic majority, called the election "a healthy shock." [9] And indeed it was. The minority party Republicans had won a landslide election in Congress. The immediate diagnosis was ideological in nature. Columnist William Safire saw it this way:

> Like a great soaking wet shaggy dog, the Silent Majority—banished from the house during the Watergate storms—romped back into the nation's parlor this week and shook itself vigorously.

> In the ensuing carnage ... the Senate of the United States was transformed into the world's greatest deliberately conservative body.[10]

Columnist Anthony Lewis agreed:

> The Senate results make the point even more compelling than Ronald Reagan's electoral vote landslide. What happened in the 1980 election reflected a profound and general turn to conservatism in this country.[11]

And defeated incumbent Senator Frank Church of Idaho said: "The conservatives are in charge now. This is what they wanted and the people have given it to them." [12]

Thus, one explanation for the defeat of particular senators in 1980 may well be that the voters wanted a more conservative government. The results in Table 5-2 would seem to support this view, if it is legitimate to identify the Republican party with conservatism. The Republican candidate gained in percent of the total vote over 1974 (the last election for this class of senators) in all but seven races. Only two incumbent Republican senators suffered a loss in the percent of the total vote they garnered over 1974—Barry Goldwater and Robert Packwood. Four Democratic incumbents—Dale Bumpers, Gary Hart, Daniel Inouye, and Thomas Eagleton—who *won* the election experienced a decline in the percent of vote they received in 1980 as compared to 1974; and, of course, nine Democratic incumbents lost. However one wishes to measure it, the 1980 Senate elections were a triumph for the Republican party. It is true, of course, that 1974 was a particularly bad year for the Republicans—occurring so soon after the resignation of Richard Nixon as president. But the Republicans have suffered serious defeats in the past—such as the one in 1958—without such an impressive recovery. In fact, when the 1958 class of senators was up for reelection in 1964, instead of gaining back seats, the Republicans had a net loss of two additional seats.

We might label this conservative trend explanation for high Senate turnover the "alternative party" or "throw the rascals out" theory of voting behavior. Any such theory is presumably based on the voters' perception of the issues and the record of government performance in Washington. Certainly the theory sounds plausible when one looks at the full set of 1980 election returns—the Reagan victory, the addition of four Republican governorships, a sizable gain of 33 House seats for Republicans, and a large increase in the number of Republican state legislators. But does this explanation work well for other recent Senate elections when incumbents in both parties have been defeated? In other words, is there a more fundamental explanation for the high turnover of Senate seats? To answer that question we turn to an analysis of recent voting behavior.

As is obvious from Figure 5-1, the decline and fall of incumbent senators did not start with the 1980 elections. Those scholars studying

Table 5-2. 1980 Senate Results, with Comparisons to 1974.

State	Winner	% of Vote in 1980* R	D	% GOP Vote in 1974*	% Change, GOP Vote, 1974-1980
Alabama	Jeremiah Denton (R)	51	48	0	+51
Alaska	Frank Murkowski (R)	55	45	42	+13
Arizona	*Barry Goldwater (R)*	50	49	58	− 8
Arkansas	*Dale Bumpers (D)*	41	59	15	+26
California	*Alan Cranston (D)*	39	59	36	− 3
Colorado	Gary Hart (D)	49	51	40	+ 9
Connecticut	Christopher Dodd (D)	43	57	34	+ 9
Florida	Paula Hawkins (R)	51	49	41	+10
Georgia	Mack Mattingly (R)	50	50	28	+22
Hawaii	*Daniel K. Inouye (D)*	18	78	0	+18
Idaho	Steven Symms (R)	50	49	42	+ 8
Illinois	Alan Dixon (D)	43	56	37	+ 6
Indiana	J. Danforth Quayle (R)	54	46	46	+ 8
Iowa	Charles Grassley (R)	54	46	47	+ 7
Kansas	*Robert Dole (R)*	64	36	51	+13
Kentucky	*Wendell Ford (D)*	36	65	44	− 9
Louisiana	*Russell Long (D)*	0	100	0	NC
Maryland	*Charles Mathias (R)*	66	34	57	+ 9
Missouri	*Thomas Eagleton (D)*	48	52	39	+ 9
Nevada	*Paul Laxalt (R)*	58	38	47	+11
New Hampshire	Warren Rudman (R)	52	48	50	+ 2
New York	Alphonse D'Amato (R)	45	44	45	NC
North Carolina	John East (R)	50	50	37	+13
North Dakota	Mark Andrews (R)	71	29	48	+23
Ohio	*John Glenn (D)*	29	71	31	− 2
Oklahoma	Don Nickles (R)	53	43	49	+ 4
Oregon	*Bob Packwood (R)*	52	44	55	− 3
Pennsylvania	Arlen Specter (R)	51	48	53	− 2
South Carolina	*Ernest Hollings (D)*	28	72	29	− 1
South Dakota	James Abnor (R)	58	39	47	+11
Utah	*Jake Garn (R)*	74	26	50	+24
Vermont	*Patrick Leahy (D)*	49	51	46	+ 3
Washington	Slade Gorton (R)	54	46	36	+18
Wisconsin	Robert Kasten (R)	51	49	36	+15

*Represents percent of the total vote in each case.
 Names in italic were incumbents.

SOURCE: The 1980 figures are from *National Journal* 12 (November 8, 1980): 1881, and the Congressional Quarterly *Weekly Report* 38 (November 8, 1980): 3338-3345; the 1974 figures are from Richard M. Scammon, ed., *America Votes 11* (Washington, D.C.: Congressional Quarterly, 1975).

the data from the 1978 national election survey paid particular attention to the differences between the return rate of House and Senate incumbents. Among other things, their analysis concentrates on the differences between the characteristics of senators and representatives and what each represents. House members are typically from a limited area within the state—one which may have been specifically designed to limit competiton (since "gerrymandering" is still practiced, despite the change in rules for drawing district lines). They are successful in developing name recognition among constituents, and recent increases in staff allowances assure even greater personal recognition. Thus, the political world of the House member is typically one which can be managed by the member. It is a comprehensible and a controllable electoral environment. It is also out of the way in the sense that the congressional district is specially created by the state legislature for purposes of representation. It does not have other governmental functions as does a city, county, or state. If anything, its identity is created by the incumbent as that person works his or her way around the district.[13]

Senators, on the other hand, represent sovereign states. There are two from each state; they never have to run for reelection at the same time unless there is a special election for an unexpired term. Their

Table 5-3. Recognition, Rating, and Contact Among Voters in Contested Races, House and Senate, 1978 *(by percent).*

	Recognize and Rate	Positive Rating	Some Type of Contact
House			
Incumbents	93	73	90
	(49)*	(56)	(46)
Challengers	44	17	44
Open seat candidates	72	50	73
Senate			
Incumbents	96	61	94
	(10)	(13)	(12)
Challengers	86	48	82
Open seat candidates	88	58	88

*Numbers in parentheses represent differences in percentage between incumbents and challengers.

SOURCE: 1978 National Election Study, Center for Political Studies, University of Michigan, as reported in Thomas E. Mann and Raymond E. Wolfinger, "Candidates and Parties in Congressional Elections," *American Political Science Review* 74 (September 1980): 623, 624, 627.

election district does not change as a consequence of the census. They are much less in control of their electoral environment. Other elections occur within the state that may affect them; they have little contact with the state government and little or no control over it. And while a House member may have one or two newspapers, a few radio stations, and a television station or two to worry about, a senator must be concerned about the media throughout the state.

Table 5-3 shows dramatic differences between the cozy and highly manageable political world of the House incumbent and the cosmopolitan electoral environment within which senators must live. There are huge differences between the recognition, positive rating, and contact scores of House incumbents and those of challengers. Senate incumbents have high recognition and contact scores—but so do their challengers. House races are between the known and the unknown candidate; Senate races are between the known and slightly better known candidate. Further, though Senate incumbents tend to be better known than House incumbents, they get a less positive rating.

It is clear from the voter contact data that Senate challengers profit greatly from extensive media coverage. As indicated in Table 5-4, even though House incumbents were recognized less than Senate incumbents

Table 5-4. Voter Contact with House and Senate Candidates through the Media, 1978 *(by percent).*

	Type of Media Contact		
	Newspaper, Magazine	*Radio*	*Television*
House			
Incumbents	71	34	50
	(39)*	(19)	(26)
Challengers	32	15	24
Open seat candidates	57	28	48
Senate			
Incumbents	73	45	80
	(10)	(8)	(10)
Challengers	63	37	70
Open seat candidates	78	49	78

*Numbers in parentheses represent differences in percentage between incumbents and challengers.

SOURCE: 1978 National Election Study, Center for Political Studies, University of Michigan, as reported in Thomas E. Mann and Raymond E. Wolfinger, "Candidates and Parties in Congressional Elections," *American Political Science Review* 74 (September 1980): 623, 624, 627.

from media sources (House members tend to rely heavily on mail), still the differences in recognition between incumbents and challengers in House races are much greater. Analysis also shows that television in particular contributed greatly to the positive ratings for Senate challengers.[14]

The end result is that if the voters are in the mood to "throw the rascals out," then it appears that senators are right out front as visible targets for the expression of voter dissatisfaction. Mounds of data exist to show that voters are presently upset with the performance of government. Apparently, they don't connect House members with "the mess in Washington." It seems that political scientist Richard F. Fenno's observation is still correct that "we do not love our Congress," and yet "we do . . . love our congressmen." [15] It is another story for senators, however. According to Alan I. Abramowitz:

> . . . voters may use different criteria to evaluate the performance of senators and representatives. Senators appear to be associated more often with controversial national issues than representatives. . . . Their greater prominence in the media may result in senators having less control than representatives over the information which voters receive about their performance.[16]

Ironically the greater resources available to senators no doubt contribute to more notoriety that, in turn, encourages the voter to identify the incumbent with national politics. The more vulnerable senators become, as a consequence of their being identified with Washington, the more likely they are to receive formidable, well-financed challenges. The natural response of incumbents is to spend more, thus contributing to a cost spiral. As Chapters 4 and 6 explain more fully, the growth of political action committees (PACs) has also contributed to this increase in campaign expenditures and quite possibly to the voter awareness of candidates that appears to contribute to greater Senate turnover.

In conclusion, the reason senators lose sounds very much like what many describe as good old responsible democratic politics. Voters are aware of both candidates, they hold the incumbent accountable for what happens in Congress, and they support the challenger if they are dissatisfied. Meanwhile, House incumbents can count their blessings as they seek to control voter awareness of themselves and their potential challengers. In fact, an understanding by House members of what is happening in the Senate races may reduce the number that resign to run for the Senate.

HOW DID SENATORS LOSE IN 1980?

Now that we have seen why it is that Senate incumbents lose, the success of the Republican strategy in 1980 becomes much clearer. First,

Republicans spent a lot of money; even more money was spent for them by the political action committees. Second, they ran a unified campaign—one in which presidential candidate Ronald Reagan identified himself with all of the Republican candidates. The effect of the money was to insure recognition of the challenging candidates. The effect of party unity was to identify Democratic incumbents with the record of the Carter administration. Though it is too early to have firm evidence on either of these points, it does appear to follow logically from studies of earlier elections that Republicans increased their chances of winning with this two-pronged strategy.

Before discussing money and party unity, we need to distinguish among the various Senate races in 1980. A campaign chairman must determine where to allocate money, and a quick review of Table 5-5 provides important clues as to where this money will go. Open seats— where an incumbent is not running—offer one good possibility. But there are differences among open seats. Those resulting from the resignation of the incumbent may produce highly competitive primary elections, but these contests are not normally as divisive for the party as those in which the incumbent is defeated. Note the difference in results for the two types of open seats. Even in a year of a Republican sweep,

Table 5-5. Types of Senate Races in 1980 and Comparative Results.

Type of Seat	Results	Average GOP Percentage
1. Open seat—resignation		
a. Democrat (Conn., Ill.)	2D	43
b. Republican (N.D., Okla., Pa.)	3R	58
2. Open seat—primary defeat		
a. Democrat (Ala., Alaska, Fla.)	3R	52
b. Republican (N.Y.)	1R	45
3. Safe for Incumbent		
a. Democrat (Ark., Calif., Ga., Hawaii, Ky., La., Ohio, S.C.)	7D, 1R	30
b. Republican (Kan., Nev., Utah)	3R	65
4. Competitive for Incumbent		
a. Democrat (Col., Idaho, Ind., Iowa, Mo., N.H., N.C., S.D., Vt., Wash., Wis.)	3D, 8R	52
b. Republican (Ariz., Md., Ore.)	3R	56

SOURCE: Compiled by author. Election results computed from data in *National Journal* 12 (November 8, 1980): 1881; and Congressional Quarterly *Weekly Report* 38 (November 8, 1980): 3838-3345.

the Democrats were able to hold the two seats where incumbents had resigned; they lost all three seats where incumbents were defeated in bitter primaries. The one Republican seat in which the incumbent suffered a primary defeat was nearly lost to the Democrats (and probably would have been if the incumbent, Jacob Javits, had not run as the Liberal party candidate, thus splitting the Democratic vote in New York).

Other Senate seats were judged as safe for the incumbent and thus not a high priority for allocating campaign funds. Only the Georgia seat among the 11 consensus "safe" seats fell to the opposition party. And there, the incumbent, Herman Talmadge, was forced into a tough run-off primary that no doubt hurt his general election campaign. High priority is naturally given to those seats judged by everyone to be competitive, with funds allocated toward protecting the incumbents of your party and defeating the incumbents from the other party. By mid-summer the Republicans had spotted six of the eleven Democratic seats in this category as deserving special attention—Colorado, Idaho, Indiana, Iowa, New Hampshire, and South Dakota. They won all but one of the six—Colorado was retained by the Democrats by a narrow margin—and, in addition, they gained three others of the remaining five—North Carolina, Washington, and Wisconsin.

The National Republican Senatorial Committee collected more than 10 million dollars by the end of summer 1980, and had by then already spent more on candidates than was spent during the entire campaign in 1978. Money was allocated to challengers based on the vulnerability of the Democratic opponent. A four-point scale was relied on. Thus challenger Steven Symms was a "1" in his promising race against Frank Church of Idaho, whereas Mary Louise Foust was a "4" in her hopeless race against incumbent Wendell Ford of Kentucky. The bulk of the funds were allocated to challengers and to Republican candidates in open races (93 percent of the total funds allocated by September 30, 1980 had gone to these candidates).[17]

The national Republican committees outspent their Democratic counterparts by huge amounts. One report summarized the situation as follows: "Campaign spending by political parties this year is a Republican-dominated extravaganza in which the Democrats are only bit players." [18] Thus, for example, by the crucial last month of the campaign, the Democratic Senatorial Campaign Committee had raised approximately 1/25 as much as its counterpart on the Republican side (less than $500,000).

In addition, spending by PACs increased dramatically in 1980. In the past, these contributions have tended to favor Democrats since many of them have been sponsored by labor unions. The number of business and independent PACs has grown, however, and Republican candidates have been the beneficiaries. Political action committees can contribute up to $5,000 to each candidate for each election (primary and general). But they may also spend unlimited amounts of money on a campaign if they have no contact with the candidate. The National Conservative Political Action Committee (NCPAC) announced that it was targeting six Democratic incumbents for special attention—George McGovern, Birch Bayh, Alan Cranston, John Culver, Frank Church, and Thomas Eagleton. It developed campaign material attacking the record of these senators. In some cases the material proved embarrassing to Republican challengers, and they were forced to make statements disassociating themselves from the NCPAC effort.[19]

Republicans have traditionally outspent Democrats. What was different about 1980? First, the odds favored Republican gains—24 of the 34 seats were held by Democrats. Second, the critical mood of the nation was likely to benefit Republican candidates if they conducted well-financed, highly visible campaigns. And third, the Republicans spent more, or had more spent for them, than ever before.

After the disastrous 1958 election, the Republicans anxiously awaited 1964 so that they might recapture some of the seats they lost. Unfortunately, however, Barry Goldwater was nominated as the Republican presidential candidate, and his candidacy seriously divided the party. Therefore, instead of gaining back the seats lost in 1958, Republicans suffered additional losses. The Republicans also suffered a sizable defeat in the post-Watergate election of 1974—a net loss of four Senate seats. Thus, they were anxious to recoup their losses in 1980. The 1980 Republican presidential nominee, Ronald Reagan, was determined not to make the same mistakes as Barry Goldwater. He stressed party unity throughout his campaign, with special emphasis on this theme after he had become the apparent nominee. He did not oust the party chairman despite pressure from the right to do so; he met with those candidates he had defeated in the primaries; he campaigned with Republican candidates for Congress; and he wooed all wings of the party at the convention. Meanwhile, up to the time of their convention, the Democrats were rather seriously divided between the Carter and Kennedy supporters, and they never fully recovered to run a coordinated campaign.

In emphasizing the role of money and party unity, I do not want to underplay the significance of special factors associated with individual races. Surely the age of incumbent Warren Magnuson, the investigation of Herman Talmadge's financial affairs, the liberal voting records of Birch Bayh, John Culver, Frank Church, and George McGovern—these and other factors were doubtless important contributions to their defeat. But the Republicans were so outstandingly unified and well financed that they were able to capitalize on the special weaknesses of each

Table 5-6. New Senators for Old in 1980.

State	The Exchange	Party Change	Age Change	Ideological Change*
Alabama	Denton for Stewart	R for D	56 for 40	Uncertain—both moderate conservatives
Alaska	Murkowski for Gravel	R for D	47 for 50	Moderate for liberal
Connecticut	Dodd for Ribicoff	D for D	36 for 70	Liberal for liberal
Florida	Hawkins for Stone	R for D	53 for 52	Uncertain—both moderate conservatives
Georgia	Mattingly for Talmadge	R for D	49 for 67	Uncertain—both moderate conservatives
Idaho	Symms for Church	R for D	42 for 56	Conservative for liberal
Illinois	Dixon for Stevenson	D for D	53 for 50	Uncertain—both moderate to liberal
Indiana	Quayle for Bayh	R for D	33 for 52	Conservative for liberal
Iowa	Grassley for Culver	R for D	47 for 48	Conservative for liberal
New Hampshire	Rudman for Durkin	R for D	49 for 44	Moderate for liberal
New York	D'Amato for Javits	R for R	43 for 76	Conservative for liberal
North Carolina	East for Morgan	R for D	49 for 55	Conservative for conservative
North Dakota	Andrews for Young	R for R	54 for 82	Conservative for conservative
Oklahoma	Nickles for Bellmon	R for R	31 for 59	Conservative for conservative
Pennsylvania	Specter for Schweiker	R for R	50 for 54	Uncertain—both moderate conservatives
South Dakota	Abnor for McGovern	R for D	57 for 58	Conservative for liberal
Washington	Gorton for Magnuson	R for D	52 for 75	Moderate for liberal
Wisconsin	Kasten for Nelson	R for D	38 for 64	Conservative for liberal

*Based on Conservative Coalition support scores for outgoing senators and for House members who won as senators. Ideological position of other new senators based on biographical summaries in the Congressional Quarterly *Weekly Report*.

SOURCE: Congressional Quarterly, *Weekly Report* 38 (December 13, 1980): 3556-3565; and 39 (January 10, 1981): 87-89, 93-95.

The
New Look
in Washington:
All Right Wing

Reprinted with permission of King Features Syndicate.

vulnerable Democratic incumbent. These advantages permitted Republican candidates to promote themselves as credible alternatives to Democratic incumbents in a period in which voters were anxiously searching for new faces.

A REPUBLICAN SENATE

What hath the voting public wrought? Has Foley's "new Senate" been made conservative again? Who are the new leaders of the Senate? How may we expect them to work with the Democratic House and the Republican president?

The data in Table 5-6 help to answer the first questions. The large freshman class of 18 senators in the 97th Congress is, of course, dominated by the Republicans—there are only *two* new Democratic faces. The average age is nearly 12 years younger than the group being replaced (46.6 years for the incoming senators; 58.4 years for the outgoing ones). Younger does not mean more liberal, however. In fact, the two youngest freshman senators, Don Nickles of Oklahoma and Dan Quayle of Indiana, have very conservative reputations. In nine cases, a liberal has been replaced by someone less liberal (either a moderate or a conservative). It seems clear that the Senate has been made conservative again; but it is not the same institution that Foley described as preceding his "new Senate." It is a young and lively Senate in which distinctions between junior and senior members remain blurred.

A review of the new Senate standing committee chairmen, as shown in Table 5-7, further confirms that the conservatism of the 97th Congress does not carry with it the style of the so-called "inner club" of the old days. These new chairmen are young; their average age is less than 56—six of them are under 50. Three are still in their first term; six are in their second term. Compare this distribution with that of 20 years ago: in the 87th Congress, the average age of the Senate committee chairmen was 63. Ten chairmen were over 60—three of these were

Table 5-7. Republican Leadership, 97th Congress.

Senate Members	*Age*	*Term*
Party Leaders		
President Pro Tempore: Strom Thurmond, South Carolina	78	5th
Majority Leader: Howard H. Baker, Jr., Tennessee	55	3rd
Majority Whip: Ted Stevens, Alaska	57	3rd
Conference Chairman: James McClure, Idaho	56	2nd
Conference Secretary: Jake Garn, Utah	48	2nd
Republican Senatorial Committee: Bob Packwood, Oregon	48	3rd
Committee Chairmen		
Agriculture, Nutrition and Forestry: Jesse Helms, North Carolina	59	2nd
Appropriations: Mark Hatfield, Oregon	58	3rd
Armed Services: John Tower, Texas	55	4th
Banking, Housing and Urban Affairs: Jake Garn, Utah	48	2nd
Budget: Pete Domenici, New Mexico	48	2nd
Commerce, Science and Transportation: Bob Packwood, Oregon	48	3rd
Energy and Natural Resources: James McClure, Idaho	56	2nd
Environment and Public Works: Robert Stafford, Vermont	67	2nd
Finance: Robert Dole, Kansas	57	3rd
Foreign Relations: Charles Percy, Illinois	61	3rd
Governmental Affairs: William Roth, Delaware	59	2nd
Judiciary: Strom Thurmond, South Carolina	78	5th*
Labor and Human Resources: Orrin Hatch, Utah	46	1st
Rules and Administration: Charles Mathias, Maryland	58	3rd
Veterans' Affairs: Alan Simpson, Wyoming	49	1st
Select Ethics: Malcolm Wallop, Wyoming	47	1st

*Includes eight years of Senate service as a Democrat. Thurmond switched parties in 1964.

SOURCE: Compiled from data in Congressional Quarterly, *Weekly Report* 38 (December 6, 1980): 3481; 38 (December 13, 1980): 3555; 39 (January 10, 1981): 93-95, 102-103.

over 70, one was over 80! The chairman of the powerful Appropriations committee, Carl Hayden of Arizona, had been in the Senate since 1927 and was first elected to the House in 1912. It is interesting to note that had the Democrats been successful in retaining control of the Senate in 1980, the average age of their Senate committee chairmen would have been over 61—not very different from 20 years ago.

The change in Senate party and committee leadership was only the beginning. During the long period in which the Senate Republicans were in the minority (1955-1981), there had been a virtual quantum increase in staff support for committees, party leaders, and individual members. As a consequence, the shift in party control resulted in a massive cleaning of files and packing of bags. It was estimated that the Republicans would gain nearly 500 committee staff positions alone (it would have been even more but a two-to-one split in staff between the majority and minority went into effect in 1981).[20] This bonanza is a mixed blessing, however, as new chairmen and committee staff directors must struggle to find competent and experienced persons to fill important positions (sometimes competing for talent with the new president's personnel directors).

In Chapter 4, it was pointed out that the Democratically-controlled House probably would attempt to cooperate with the Reagan administration. It is much too early to judge, however, just how the new, new Senate will work with the Democratic House of Representatives or the Republican president. The fact is that this particular combination of party control is quite unusual, if not unprecedented. Republican presidents have had to deal with a Republican Senate and a Democratic House in the past (Herbert Hoover, 1931-1932; William Howard Taft, 1911-1912; Benjamin Harrison, 1891-1892; Chester Arthur, 1883-1884; and Rutherford B. Hayes, 1877-1878) but in these previous cases the Republican party was experiencing an electoral downswing. In the first four cases, loss of the majority position in the House came in the midterm elections and a Democrat was subsequently elected president two years later (Franklin D. Roosevelt following Hoover, Woodrow Wilson following Taft, Grover Cleveland following Harrison and also following Arthur). Hayes won a disputed election over Samuel Tilden in 1876, and although the Republicans retained control of the Senate, they had a net loss of seven seats in that election. They subsequently lost control of the Senate in the 1878 midterm elections.

In the present case, Republican control of the Senate is the consequence of a definite upswing in party fortunes. In addition to control of the Senate, Republicans had a net gain of 33 House seats, and Ronald Reagan won in a landslide in the electoral college. There is nowhere to look for clues as to what happens under these conditions. All we can do is speculate, given what we know about the election itself, and how it is interpreted by the relevant politicians.

In the House, Speaker Thomas P. "Tip" O'Neill, Jr. of Massachusetts is unquestionably a liberal, but he faces quite a different postelection Democratic party in the lower chamber. This trend is discussed more completely in Chapter 4, which is devoted to the House of Representatives. Although over 90 percent of the incumbents were reelected, as usual, the Democrats suffered most of the defeats—27 of the 30 incumbents. Among the Democratic incumbents who lost were the party's whip (John Brademas of Indiana), the chairman of the Congressional Campaign Committee (James Corman of California), and four chairmen of standing committees (including Al Ullman of Oregon, chairman of the important committee on Ways and Means). Four other committee chairmen retired in 1980. A number of key subcommittee chairmen also retired or were defeated. Many of those who lost were stalwart liberals. Of the 20 northern Democrats not returning, 11 had conservative coalition support scores *below* that of the average northern Democrat (these support scores represent the percentage of roll calls on which a member voted with a bipartisan conservative coalition). Perhaps even more important, seven of the eight southern Democrats who lost had scores below the average for southern Democrats.[21] Thus, as a liberal himself, O'Neill lost important support in both the North and the South.

Despite their stated intentions of doing so, whether these changes actually will encourage the House leaders to work with the new president and the Senate Republican leadership is uncertain. The House experienced important changes in the 1980 elections despite the fact that the Democrats remained in the majority. In the 96th Congress, the Democrats had a margin of 117 seats—for a margin of 276-159. That margin has been reduced to 51 seats—243-192. Put another way, it required 59 additional votes for the Republicans to win the day in 1980; now it requires 26 additional votes. On conservative issues, it would appear that these votes are easily available among southern Democrats (29 of the returning southern Democrats had conservative support scores of over 75 percent in 1980).

What about relationships with President Reagan? When Dwight D. Eisenhower was inaugurated only 15 House and *no* Senate Republicans had served with a president of their party. As the president reviewed his situation in Congress he observed that: "Another relevant fact was the unfamiliarity of Republicans with either the techniques or the need of cooperating with the Executive."[22] That particular problem does not exist for Reagan. Though only two Senate Republicans (Thurmond, who was then a Democrat, and Goldwater) was there when Eisenhower was elected president, several members were serving in Congress when presidents Nixon and Ford came into office—18 as senators, another 9 as representatives. Thus the "minority party mentality" which characterized the congressional Republican party in earlier periods is much less prevalent today.

It is also relevant that Ronald Reagan ran perhaps the most party-oriented campaign in recent decades. As noted earlier, Reagan stressed party unity throughout his campaign. The Republican nominee even presided at a fund-raising dinner to relieve the debts of his defeated primary opponents—which included the new Senate majority leader, Howard H. Baker, Jr. Further, President Reagan's close relationship with Senator Paul Laxalt of Nevada insures, at a minimum, that the president will be kept informed as to how his proposals are being received in the Senate, and that Republican senators, in turn, will be advised as to presidential priorities. There is no recent precedent that comes to mind for this extraordinary relationship between a president and a senator.[23]

The election itself would appear to have a positive influence on relations between the president and the Senate Republicans. As noted earlier, the ideological shift occurred rather uniformly in one direction— a more conservative president, Senate, and House of Representatives. Whereas presidential coattails are no longer considered to have the influence they once did, still it is instructive to note that Reagan ran well in relationship to Senate Republican candidates. Even with a third candidate in the race—independent John Anderson—Reagan ran ahead of nine of the winning Republicans, on an even par with another five, slightly behind seven, and well behind just one (Mathias of Maryland ran over 20 percentage points ahead of Reagan). This record is substantially different from Carter's. Although these election results do not constitute a major factor in presidential-congressional relations, they do provide evidence, consistent with other factors, to suggest that cooperation may be expected, at least in the early months of the new administration.

CONCLUSION

On the night the ballots were counted, November 4, 1980, experienced observers could sense that the election—described previously as "too close to call"—was turning out to be an electoral vote landslide victory for Ronald Reagan. Based on exit polls and early returns, network commentators began very early to suggest the dimensions of the Reagan victory. President Carter conceded by 10 p.m. (eastern standard time), having called Reagan to congratulate him more than an hour before.

By the time of the Carter concession speech, it was apparent that a second major development was occurring. The first clue appeared quite early in the evening when incumbent Democratic Senator Birch Bayh of Indiana lost his race against his Republican challenger, Dan Quayle. But the full dimensions of what was happening in the Senate were not apparent until much later. When the last Senate race was finally called the next day—that of Barry Goldwater's narrow victory in Arizona—the Republicans had gained majority control of the Senate. The new leaders of the Senate—party leaders and committee chairmen—were absolutely giddy at the prospect of taking charge. Clearly, this second late-night story was the equal of Reagan's victory over an incumbent Democratic president.

The United States Senate has been undergoing important change for some time now. Michael Foley identifies many of the early shifts away from the club-like atmosphere dominated by very senior members. His "new Senate" has undergone even more change since he completed his analysis. Major internal reforms, combined with significant changes in personnel and party control, have given us a "new, new Senate." For the time being, it is younger, more Republican, more conservative, and more aggressive than in the past. Perhaps, more than any other institution in Washington, this fascinating legislative body should command our attention in the future.

NOTES

1. Michael Foley, *The New Senate: Liberal Influence on a Conservative Institution, 1959-1972* (New Haven, Conn.: Yale University Press, 1980), pp. 253, 259.
2. National Republican Senatorial Committee, *1980 Senate Races,* July 11, 1980, p. 2.
3. *The Washington Post,* 4 May 1980.
4. National Republican Senatorial Committee, p. 1.
5. At that time Republicans held a slim eight-seat majority in the House and just a one-seat majority in the Senate.
6. John F. Bibby, et al., *Vital Statistics on Congress, 1980* (Washington, D.C.: American Enterprise Institute, 1980), p. 16.
7. Congressional Quarterly *Special Report: The 1980 Elections* 38 (October 11, 1980): 2984.
8. Christopher Buchanan, "Modest GOP Congressional Gains Expected," Congressional Quarterly *Weekly Report* 38 (November 1, 1980): 3242.
9. Both quotations from *The New York Times,* 6 November 1981, p. A1.
10. *New York Times,* 6 November 1980, p. A35.
11. Ibid.
12. Ibid., p. A29.
13. For a description of how members define their districts see Richard F. Fenno, Jr., *Home Style* (Boston: Little, Brown & Co., 1978).

14. As reported in Alan I. Abramowitz, "A Comparison of Voting for U.S. Senator and Representative in 1978," *American Political Science Review* 74 (September 1980): 637.
15. Richard F. Fenno, Jr., "If, as Ralph Nader Says, Congress is 'the Broken Branch,' How Come We Love Our Congressmen So Much?" in Norman Ornstein, ed., *Congress in Change* (New York: Praeger Publishers, 1975), p. 278.
16. Abramowitz, "A Comparision of Voting," p. 633.
17. Larry Light, "Republican Groups Dominate in Party Campaign Spending," Congressional Quarterly *Weekly Report* 38 (November 1, 1980): 3238.
18. Ibid., p. 3234.
19. For details on this part of the campaign see Larry Light, "Democrats May Lose Edge in Contributions from PACs," Congressional Quarterly *Weekly Report* 38 (November 22, 1980): 3405-3409. See also Richard E. Cohen, "Big Spenders," *National Journal* 12 (November 1, 1980): 1851.
20. William J. Lanouette, "Changing of the Guard: Senate Braces for Massive Shuffling of Its Staff," *National Journal* 12 (November 29, 1980): 2025.
21. Conservative coalition support scores are reported in Congressional Quarterly, *Weekly Report* 39 (January 10, 1981): 84-89.
22. Dwight D. Eisenhower, *Mandate for Change* (Garden City, N.Y.: Doubleday & Co. 1963), p. 192.
23. Of course, four recent presidents have had Senate experience themselves: Harry S Truman, John Kennedy, Lyndon Johnson, and Richard Nixon. Their styles of working with Congress varied considerably. Johnson had the closest working contact with the Senate.

6

The De-Institutionalization of Electoral Politics

Clifton McCleskey

In order to understand the course of the Reagan administration and of public policy generally in the 1980s, we need to take into account what has been happening on the electoral side of the political process. The principal argument of this essay is that the present crisis of American politics is ultimately rooted in our failure to maintain an institutional framework capable of mobilizing voters and public opinion, of channeling and aggregating group interests, of synthesizing and transmitting the will of the people. Our problem, in a word, is the de-institutionalization of the demand side of politics, the side that in democratic theory drives the machinery of government.

Social commentators have long understood the importance of institutionalization. "Institutions," said Walton Hamilton in an elegant essay on that topic in the first edition of the *Encyclopedia of the Social Sciences,* "fix the confines of and impose form upon the activities of human beings." They regulate our activities in patterned ways, and those ways are "enforced" by various norms and their derived sanctions. Churches, labor unions, and fraternal orders are institutions; so are baseball, the Marine Corps, street corner gangs, and neighborhood block parties.

The American electoral process has always involved a great many institutions, some formally organized, some altogether lacking in charters and officers. The dispensing of "walking around" money in Baltimore is an institution; so are the candidates' forums conducted by the League of Women Voters in Seattle. But among all those electoral institutions, one has stood out in this country almost from the beginning of the present constitutional system: the political party. From the 1790s, when the first American party system began to take shape, until the present time, parties have been the most visible—arguably, the most important—institutions connected with the electoral process. And now they are in a state of decline.

The decline of parties is a crucial key to understanding what has happened to American politics, but other factors are also involved, and I have singled out three of them for attention as well: the heightened role of the mass media of communications; the proliferation of special interest groups; and the increase in voter apathy and alienation. These four developments (and no doubt others as well) are slowly but surely removing the old institutional underpinnings of our political processes, and no new ones capable of serving our needs are in sight.

More than any other single factor, the lack of structure, of institutionalization, has brought American politics to its present confused state. Unless the new president and those about him are incredibly skilled (and lucky), the Reagan administration will flounder as badly as the Carter, Ford, and Nixon administrations, for some of the very same reasons.

THE DECLINE OF PARTIES

Though a number of scholars and observers have concluded that party decline is taking place, it is not a readily observable phenomenon. In fact, others deny any such tendency.[1] The difference in interpretation largely grows out of confusion as to which facet of the institution known as the political party is under examination. For quite some time, we have recognized the necessity of distinguishing between the party in the government (e.g. the party caucuses that organize the United States Senate and House of Representatives), the party in the electorate (the attachments and images that voters have of the respective parties), and the party as an organization (the precinct captain, the county party chairmen, the national executive committee members, and so on).

Although I think it mistaken, a plausible argument can be made that no great change in the first two facets has taken place in the last 10 to 20 years. Even with respect to the third, a superficial examination might yield no cause for alarm. The Republican National Committee met regularly in 1980, as did the Democratic National Committee. Both major parties held their 1980 national nominating conventions on schedule, and a full complement of delegates and alternates attended each.

But that picture changes as one looks more closely at the functions traditionally performed by political parties. One of the most insightful, as well as one of the earliest, attempts to portray party functions was made by Charles E. Merriam in his 1922 book, *The American Party System.* According to Merriam, political parties are involved in the selection of public officials, the formulation of public policy, the provision of criticism and opposition, the education of the general public, and serve as intermediaries between those who govern and those who are governed. American political parties have never had a monopoly on those functions, and their performance of any one of them has never been outstanding. But a record that was once merely mediocre has now become distressing. The functions just mentioned—political education and socialization, interest aggregation, and so on—are no longer performed by the parties to any very substantial degree. In effect, parties are slowly but surely losing their reasons for being, and when that happens to any institution, it is in decline.

It is important to see that while the rate of party decline has accelerated in the past 20 years, it began much earlier. One can identify three outstanding contributions to that decline, all of them reflecting to some extent the reforming zeal of the Progressive era. The first, and perhaps the most important, has been the party organizations' loss of power to control access to the ballot through the nominating process. The chief instrument for that change has been the direct primary. It is not just coincidence that the states which resisted the mandatory direct primary the longest (Indiana and Connecticut) also retained viable party organizations the longest. Today to the best of my knowledge, my own state of Virginia is the only one which leaves it up to party leaders to decide how candidates are to be nominated. Not surprisingly, these party leaders have more influence over nominations than most of their counterparts in other states because they more and more choose to nominate by party conventions that heighten the influence of the party cadres.

The reduction of the party organizations' influence over nominations can be readily seen in connection with presidential politics. As a result of greatly increased use of presidential primaries to select delegates to national nominating conventions,[2] and, particularly in the Democratic party, of a series of internal rules changes designed to open up the party, presidential nominations now depend much more on the candidates and on the mass media, and much less on the party organization. This has progressed so far that an incumbent president, even though he usually has the support of his party's organization, may have trouble winning renomination. Thus President Ford in 1976 very nearly lost the Republican nomination to Ronald Reagan, and President Carter in 1980 was strongly challenged for the Democratic nomination by Senator Edward Kennedy. Carter, of course, had won the 1976 Democratic nomination with little help from party regulars, and Senator George McGovern had won it in 1972 despite the two-to-one preference of party cadres for Senator Hubert Humphrey. Organizational control of the party's nominations can be a powerful incentive for officials and prospective candidates to work with and within an organization; conversely, the loss of that control loosens their ties in the organization.

Party cadres might have been able to retain more vitality, even after the direct primary became widespread, had another blow not been inflicted upon them in the form of loss of patronage power (i.e., control of access to public employment). There are many sound reasons why public employees should not be chosen by political organizations, but it is also clear that patronage was a very useful instrument for organizational maintenance, in part because it is the type of incentive that can be used flexibly and withdrawn easily.[3] Today, party-controlled patronage has almost disappeared.

The spread of merit systems for public employment at the national, state, and local level is only part of the explanation. Even those jobs that are still subject to political criteria are typically filled with little or no involvement of the party organization—the appointing official is increasingly free to make his or her choices without consulting party leaders. Thus, in the early months of President Carter's administration, the Democratic National Committee took the extraordinary step of publicly complaining that the president was not consulting state party leaders on federal appointments that were their traditional prerogatives. The Reagan administration appears to be more sensitive to the party in beginning its appointments process, but even so the Republican organization is only one of several sources of names for appointment, and not necessarily the most important one. Most recently, the courts have acted to limit even more the potential for political appointments by a series of decisions sharply restricting the bases for dismissal of public employees. In essence, the Supreme Court has held that a wide range of public employees has a constitutional right not to be dismissed for political reasons, even if the applicable statutes permit such dismissals.[4]

The third calamity to befall political parties was the deliberate decentralization of the organizational structure. Even in their heyday, parties were not nearly so hierarchical as critics supposed, but state laws regulating parties have compounded the problem by requiring the direct election of the lowest levels of party cadres—precinct chairmen or captains—and by making each level of the organization (local, ward, district, state, and national) formally independent of the other levels.

The result in most cases is what Samuel Eldersveld found in Wayne County (Detroit) in the late 1950s, namely, that the parties were in fact as decentralized as he had initially hypothesized:

> The political party is thus to be visualized as a "reciprocal deference structure." Contrary to the bureaucratic and authoritarian models of social organization, the party is not a precisely ordered system of authority and influence from the top down, though as a "paper" structure it may give this appearance. The organization does not function through the issuance of directives from the top which are obeyed without question. Rather, there is a tolerance of autonomy, local initiative, local inertia. The factors contributing to this property of the party are several: sparsity of activists, voluntary nature of recruitment for party work, limited rewards available to activists, and irregularity of their loyalty. But, primarily, this "downward deference" stems from the absence of effective sanctions, the strong drive for votes, the instinctively adaptive tactics of success-minded party leaders, and the need for lower-echelon support. More than any other social organization, the critical action locus of the party structure is at its base.[5]

Activists in many states have attempted to escape the straitjacket imposed upon the formal party organizations by such legal restrictions by forming "extra-legal" organizations. These organizations—such as the California Democratic Clubs and the Republican Party of Wisconsin—attempted to function as parallel but unregulated parties, endorsing candidates in primaries, developing issues, raising funds, and so on.[6] Though some of these organizations have survived, most found it impossible to combat the forces discouraging political organizations.

Each of these three forces working against party organizations—the loss of nominating control, the loss of patronage, the organizational decentralization—has been exerting influence for several decades. Institutions do not change or die overnight, and so parties survived into the 1960s with a still important if diminished role. But in the 1960s and 1970s other forces began operating to limit still more their influence. Today, party cadres have mostly lost their primacy as experts in explaining and interpreting political life, they no longer dominate access to public officials and leaders, they no longer are a major source of political information and judgment, and above all, they have lost most of their capacity to influence the nomination and election of party candidates for public office. Not many people today go to a party leader for a job, for extrication from legal difficulties, for advice on a political career, for information on what the government is doing, or for inside information on elections. The reason is institutional: the parties have lost power and role significance. Party activists today, taken as individuals, are mostly intelligent and hard-working people, more dedicated and better informed than most of us, contributing disproportionately to political life and getting very little in return. But despite increased paid advertising and fundraising for congressional candidates, party *organizations* today resemble nothing so much as toothless old men wheeled out on ceremonial occasions but most of the time left alone with their memories of what was and their dreams about what might have been.

THE HEIGHTENED ROLE OF THE MASS MEDIA

No one familiar with the careers of newspapermen such as Horace Greeley in the nineteenth century or William Randolph Hearst in the early twentieth century would suppose that a political role for the press is a product of our own times. Those who own, manage, or staff the means of communications have been in the political game since the republic was established.

But over the years the relationship between the players has been radically altered. Two of our earliest and best known political editors and journalists were very much the creatures of party leaders Thomas Jefferson and Alexander Hamilton. Thus the Federalist line espoused by the *Gazette of the United States* and its editor, John Fenno, in the early years of the first administration of George Washington led in 1791 to the establishment of the *National Gazette* under the editorship of Philip Freneau. He not only hewed to the party line being developed by Madison and Jefferson but also remained on the latter's payroll as a clerk in the State Department, which his patron then headed. Today, journalists see themselves not as partners or allies of those in party or public office, but as independent forces—in some cases, as adversaries.

Such orientation no doubt has its benefits, and if that were all that had changed, few would complain. A more important change resulting from the altered relationship between the political sector and the mass media lies in the processes of public opinion formation. Until well into the twentieth century—perhaps even into its second half—public opinion on matters of politics as on other matters was mostly formed through the "two-step flow of communications." First sketched in a study of the 1940 election, and subsequently elaborated in other research, the hypothesis proposed that "influences stemming from the mass media first reach 'opinion leaders' who, in turn, pass on what they read and hear to those of their every day associates for whom they are influential." Because most people are influenced by interpersonal contact with their respective opinion leaders (who tend to be of their own class and status), and because opinion leaders tend to draw their information and impressions from a variety of sources, not just the mass media, the conclusion was that the influence of the mass media was modest and indirect.[7]

Furthermore, until recently the media were balanced by a reasonably healthy party organization. Political campaigns were conducted mainly by party workers and volunteers using a variety of tactics designed to take as much advantage as possible of interpersonal communication and influence (door-to-door solicitation, neighborhood gatherings, office and union hall meetings). Even the mass appeals—parades and rallies—tended to be organized affairs. Advertising in the mass media represented a much smaller share of the campaign effort, and campaigns pursued voters directly, rather than being designed to attract the attention of the mass media. Overall, the media exerted only moderate influence on the course of American politics.[8]

Not any more. Today, the two-step flow of communication has shrunk to a trickle; it no longer describes reality. This has happened to some extent because rank-and-file citizens now get more of their cues directly from the mass media than from interpersonal communication with their proximate opinion leaders; but it is also due to the greater dependence of those opinion leaders themselves on the media. The heightened role of the mass media today reflects, in some cases as well, their more aggressive quest or political influence. In the competition for influence over voters, party organizations have simply been overwhelmed.[9] The more successful competitors include candidates who appeal directly and independently to their electorates and interest groups who play on the citizens' specific needs and concerns. But in today's emergent system of political influence, the role played by the mass media is both the most visible and the most worrisome.

Admittedly, part of the concern engendered by the media is misdirected. Some ultraconservatives believe that the electronic and print media are dominated by a liberally-oriented elite that consciously indoctrinates the public. Some liberals and radicals are equally convinced that the opposite is true. One finds Democrats who believe that George McGovern was savaged by the media in 1972; one also finds Republicans who believe that Richard Nixon was maliciously undone by his liberal enemies in the mass media.

By and large such worries about system-wide bias miss the mark. Everyone has his or her favorite examples of the bias displayed by particular reporters, editors, newspapers, or television stations, but it is entirely conceivable that over the nation as a whole a rough equalling out in the biases of the media takes place, at least with respect to partisanship and ideology. My concern is not media bias against a particular party or creed, but the effects of the media on the political process itself, particularly in elections.

The mass media, to my mind, are distorting the democratic political process. The electronic sector carries the greater responsibility, though the print media are guilty as well. No doubt without intending to, the mass media present political affairs in such a way that few citizens would want to become involved in politics. We should note that the responsibility for this state of affairs does not rest solely with the news profession. Public officials often seek to exploit the mass media (as by the staging of "psuedo-events" designed solely to attract news coverage), thus contributing to the damage done to the democratic process. Such an indictment requires clarification and elaboration.

Distortion of the Democratic Process

Media Distortion and Misinterpretation. The excesses such as those of ultraconservative publisher William Loeb in his *Manchester* (New Hampshire) *Union-Leader* and the less-publicized, more subtle, but nevertheless evident bias of the CBS television network in its 1971 documentary, *The Selling of the Pentagon,* are well recognized. That even responsible reporters and editors can be in error has been documented by Edward Jay Epstein in his article demonstrating how they mistakenly accepted radical claims that a war on black activists had resulted in 27 political executions by the police across the nation.[10] Perhaps more pernicious than outright bias or error in reporting is the tendency of the media to look for mistakes, or misconduct, or ulterior motives in almost everything done by public officials.

Such misinterpretations may be due to ignorance on the part of the mass media of the way government and political institutions work or are supposed to work. Typically, most college-educated journalists do not major in political science or even in another social science. Furthermore, the creed of journalists does not call for them to develop substantive knowledge and expertise; their task is to perfect the art of asking the four W's and the one H (Who, What, When, Where, and How).[11] And finally, the inaccuracies and inadequacies in the coverage of public affairs also reflects the way in which the business of newsgathering is organized and administered. These tendencies are most acute at the level of state and local politics, but they exist at the national level as well.

But the problems inherent in the way journalists are trained and socialized and the conditions under which they work are increasingly compounded by arrogance as well. The traditional cynicism of the press is too often accompanied by feelings of superiority over and hostility toward those in the government establishment. Armed with Freedom of Information laws and with judicial decisions that, for all practical purposes, deny those in public life protection from libel and slander, "investigative" reporters combine fact, speculation, and fiction in ingenious mixtures that titillate rather than educate.

The consequences reach both the citizenry and officialdom. Voters are encouraged to see their officials as either fools or knaves, and to feel that no one really cares about them. True, government may not always be performing well, public officials do make mistakes, and a small number of them is corruptible. But the rising dissatisfaction with government discussed below owes something as well to media emphasis on the alleged failures or misbehavior of officials.[12]

Press arrogance also takes its toll on those in public life, for it often operates to deprive such persons of normal private life (difficult enough for them even without mass media intrusion). Officials and political leaders must be prepared to have their marital problems, recreational habits, youthful indiscretions, personal finances, and bedroom performances subjected to public view. It hardly needs to be said that the almost total lack of privacy accompanying elective office today is sometimes an impediment to attracting the best qualified candidates into government service.

The Trivialization of American Politics. In a populous, economically and socially complex system, only a relatively few issues can be given public attention and debate at any given time. The health of any political system depends heavily on how well this public agenda is managed. The mass media of communication have always played a significant role in the determination of the public agenda, but that role has been greatly enhanced by the continued decline of political parties.

Although the print media have often had difficulty in performing satisfactorily the agenda-setting function, the medium of television has found it particularly hard to handle effectively. The point is made well by Patterson and McClure in their study of the impact of television in the 1972 campaign:

> If the mass media's most far-reaching power is its capacity to determine what people will know about and think about—in other words, to set the public agenda—then television network newscasts, during a presidential election, work to the detriment of a rational electorate. The networks do this because they make little effort, and have few available techniques, to distinguish the important from the unimportant and because the most memorable pictures in this visual medium are more frequently associated with trivial stories than with significant events....[13]
>
> THE problem with television's entry into national politics [is] that network news departments and presidential candidates consistently misuse the medium and underrate their audiences. *[Emphasis in original.]*
>
> Primarily because network campaign news contains so little meaningful information, it fails to have any meaningful effect on the viewers' feelings about the candidates and knowledge of the issues. Television's only effect on the American voter is to cheapen his conception of the campaign process and to stuff his head full of nonsense and trivia.
>
> The networks could not maintain this charade without the active cooperation of presidential candidates who tailor their campaigns to every dictate of the television camera.[14]

The villain, say the authors, is the fast-paced format of the regular 30-minute television news program. Each of the 15 to 20 stories covered on such a program is allotted such a small amount of time that it corresponds roughly to the first two paragraphs in a newspaper account. This is too little to enable them to determine its importance. Since the time allotment is the only way television has to indicate relative significance, the events reported tend to become an undifferentiated jumble.

A further disservice to the public comes with the kinds of choices made as to which items will be put on this jumbled agenda. Too often, those choices reflect either ignorance of the political world, or underestimation of what viewers want and need, or both. The tendency is most dramatically revealed when television deals with candidates and their campaigns, for such "news" too frequently tends to neglect substantive problems and concerns. Instead, what dominates the screen is crowds, smiling candidates, motorcades, poll results, handshaking, and solemn discussion of who is ahead or behind; issues and problems are given little attention because they do not lend themselves to quick and easy visual presentation.[15] The inability of television news to sort out the significant from the insignificant was seen clearly on election night 1980. Having decided very early that Reagan and Bush had won, all three television networks thereafter rehashed the campaign, offered instant interpretations, and sought "human interest" angles—giving little attention to, and even less solid information about, the important congressional and state elections still unsettled.

The Exacerbation of Political Conflict. Of all the shortcomings of the mass media, probably the most resented is their focus on deviant political behavior. By holding out the possibility of providing publicity on a scale otherwise impossible, the media encourage people to make outrageous statements, to engage in antisocial or unsanctioned conduct, and to pursue divisive strategies. In this way, the media help to raise political tensions and to create needless antagonisms.

The mass media and the political system have fundamentally different objectives. Democratic politics, after all, is an attempt to manage social and economic conflict, to reduce its level, and to channel it in peaceful and constructive ways. The mass media, on the other hand, have an informational and educational role so defined as to produce a pronounced bias in favor of publicizing conflict—it builds circulation and expands viewing and listening audiences. Individuals and groups, in pursuit of their own narrow interests, try to generate or to stimulate controversy in order to get media coverage, and when there is not enough conflict being generated to satisfy media needs, reporters and editors have been known to stir up more, as when certain reporters at national party conventions stimulate controversy by their questions and comments on the floor. The fault in all this is not the media's alone.

There is in many of us enough longing for fame that we succumb only too readily to the prospect that the media will quote us in print or give us a few moments on television if only we will say or do something sufficiently unusual or controversial. Such instant celebrity usually fades as quickly as it is gained, but for a great many of us it is better than none at all—a point understood only too well by those whose profession is mass communications.

Conclusion

The mass media are an imposing monument to American freedom, and each and every one of us is indebted to them for the contribution they make to our knowledge and understanding of public affairs. But the mass media also contribute importantly to our present difficulties. Their role in the process of nominating candidates for public office and in campaigns and elections has been growing steadily, and more than ever before the media are shaping the public agenda, telling us what is and is not important, and they are altering our perception of reality in the governing process generally.

THE PROLIFERATION OF SPECIAL INTEREST GROUPS

The extent and influence of interest group activity in American politics has been for many years the subject of scholarly and popular comment. In recent years, an even greater concern has been generated by group promotion of so-called "single issue politics." When, in 1978, Democratic Senator Dick Clark of Iowa was defeated for reelection, the mass media reports gave much of the credit to antiabortion forces. By 1980, a number of other groups with a narrow focus on politics were active in primaries and general elections. Most, though not all, of the newcomers were oriented in a conservative or ultraconservative direction, and some were identified with the evangelical Christian lobby. For those reasons—and because of their attention-getting antics and statements—they became the object of considerable attention.

But these "New Right" groups in 1980 also evoke a sense of *déjà vu*. In the 1960s and early 1970s liberal or leftist radical groups also organized on the basis of a narrow perspective and of moral outrage, for the purpose of influencing our involvement in Vietnam, the laws regarding homosexual conduct, access to abortions, or the extension of welfare services. If the groups of the "New Right" in 1980 are judged in terms of their objectives, tactics, bases of support, and political impact (greatly overestimated), they seem not very different from a great many others; their singularity consists primarily of their orientation to the conservative end of the political spectrum. Seen in isolation, the conservative and ultraconservative groups that have so recently sprouted pose no special danger to our political traditions. But such groups do not exist in a vacuum; they are but part of broader forces and trends that are grounds for concern about the health of American politics.

However, if we are to understand the problems posed by interest group activities, we must first clear the air by rejecting certain charges often leveled against them. Pressure groups (here used synonymously with interest groups) do not ordinarily depend on corrupt and illegal practices to influence governmental officials and politicians; they count instead on access and established relationships. They are not exclusively or even principally serving rich and powerful "special interests"; groups representing unionized employees, retired persons, economically disadvantaged minority groups, and environmentalists—to mention only a few—have often been successful in the game of pressure politics. Nor are these groups and their operations antithetical to democracy. In fact, they serve as very important vehicles for the articulation and representation of citizen interests, and their members are exercising one of the fundamental liberties protected by the First Amendment—the right to band together for political purposes.[16]

In what ways then are interest groups likely to contribute to the difficulties faced by President Reagan? The answer lies in part in the incompleteness of the representation provided by interest groups. Data on the significance of group memberships in the political life of citizens are inadequate, but it appears that some have their particular interests much more effectively represented than have others. Undoubtedly, there is some class bias in this, with those of lower socioeconomic status tending to have less group representation. However, one is likely to find persons at all levels who, for one reason or another, are not effectively linked to group political activity. Thus, very real needs and concerns of some may not be adequately represented anywhere in the present pattern of pressure group politics.

A second aspect of the representational shortcoming of groups involves the relationship between group leaders and rank-and-file members. In some cases, the leaders fail to do a satisfactory job of articulating the concerns of members. It is easy and sometimes tempting to overestimate the frequency with which this occurs (group members, after all, do have ways of getting the attention of their leadership, including disaffiliation from the group), but it certainly cannot be dismissed as of no importance.

But, paradoxically enough, the central problem of interest group politics is made more acute by the trend over the past 15 to 20 years toward the emergence of more and more groups representing more and more people with greater and greater effectiveness. No comprehensive data on the number of interest groups are available, but they clearly have been increasing at a rapid rate. Groups are better organized and better led, and they have more resources than ever before. The trend reflects the increased need felt by citizens for group formation growing out of the expanded role of government, the affluence of the past two decades—which has made it possible to sustain and strengthen an imposing array of interest groups—and the entrepreneurial skill of those who lead them.

The principal problem posed by heightened interest group activity is the increased need for political aggregation—the melding of smaller, narrower interests into larger and more comprehensive ones, the compromising of varying objectives, and the building of more coherent blocs of supporters. Congress has never been able to perform more than a part of such tasks, and as interests have proliferated, the legislature's aggregative capacity has fallen steadily, despite vastly expanded staff and sharply increased numbers of subcommittees. Partially for that reason, President Carter midway in his term broadened the assignment of the Office of Public Liaison in the White House to make it responsible for involving appropriate group leaders in the development of his legislative proposals on an issue-by-issue basis.[17] This action undoubtedly contributed to the better reception given Carter's later legislative proposals by Congress, and President Reagan may well find it necessary to adopt the same approach.

But whether undertaken by legislators or chief executives, this strategy of building a fresh coalition for each issue results in an impossible drain on officials' time and energy and also creates incentives for still more groups to join the struggle. It is simply not possible to aggregate and reconcile vast numbers of interests at the highest levels of government effectively. No matter how hard they try, Congress and the president cannot do justice to all the demands being pressed upon them; far too much grist is being brought to their mill. Somehow, somewhere, the political needs and concerns of literally thousands of interested groups must be subjected to preliminary processing, to the winnowing and merging that will reduce in number the issues requiring attention of legislators and chief executives.

Incentives on the part of the groups themselves to do such screening have long existed, and certain more broadly oriented organizations such as the AFL-CIO, the National Chamber of Commerce, the National Municipal League, and the American Farm Bureau Federation, have attempted to carry out some of the aggregative functions being described. But these organizations are themselves being crowded out of the picture; they do not loom as large on the national stage today as they did 20 years ago. This is not because they are less skilled politically, but because too many other groups now insist upon sharing that stage. In politics, organization is crucial to achievement, and that lesson has been taken to heart by more and more persons with shared interests. Like shipwrecked mariners, who in desperation overcrowd and sink the one remaining lifeboat, this gaggle of interests threatens to submerge us all by its insistence upon a direct role in the shaping of public policy.

INCREASED VOTER APATHY AND ALIENATION

The fourth development bearing on the present and future course of American politics is increased voter apathy and alienation, of which the most obvious and familiar measure is declining voter turnout. From a turnout of 64 percent of the population of voting age in the 1960 presidential election, a post-World War II high, we have dropped to a level of 53.9 percent in 1980. The decline is all the more remarkable when one considers the liberalization of suffrage and registration requirements in the intervening 20 years, most notably in the South but in other areas as well. It is estimated that only 29.1 percent of blacks were registered in the South in 1960, compared with 63.1 percent in 1976. Residence requirements for voting have everywhere been loosened; today 30 to 60 days residence is usually all that is necessary. Literacy tests have been largely eliminated, and voter registration procedures simplified or eliminated altogether. Competition, long regarded as a stimulus to voting, is more widespread today than in 1960, measured in terms of numbers of offices contested and the winning candidates' share of the

Copyright 1980, *Washington Star.* Reprinted with permission of Universal Press Syndicate. All rights reserved.

vote. Levels of education, another correlate of high turnout, similarly have risen sharply in the nation as a whole over the past two decades.

Admittedly, some demographic changes have operated in the opposite direction. For example, the average age of voters today is lower than in 1960, and younger people have poorer turnout records. Similarly, geographical mobility has continued to increase, and frequent moves from one community to another, and from one state to another, tend to depress voter participation. On the whole, however, one would expect an increase rather than a decrease in turnout at the polls over the past two decades.

Though political alienation is not as easily measured as voter turnout, it too appears to have changed for the worse in recent years. Data from nationwide surveys leave no doubt on that score.[18] From 1964 to 1978, the proportion of people who felt that they could trust the government to do what is right most of the time or always dropped from 76 percent to only 29 percent of the total. The number who said that the government is pretty much run by a few big interests looking out for themselves rose from 24 percent of the total in 1964 to 65 percent in 1978. The proportion who agreed that people like themselves have little say about what the government does rose from 29 percent in 1964 to 45 percent in 1978. Interestingly, the least change occurred in attitude regarding the honesty of government officials; 66 percent in 1964 thought hardly any or not many of the people running the government were a little crooked, compared to 53 percent in 1978. The conclusion that political alienation has increased sharply is not based on the responses to these kinds of questions alone. Alienation is a multifaceted concept, and scholars have developed several different approaches to measurement. They consistently point in the direction just indicated.

Levels of voter turnout and of alienation are the product of many and complex forces. I submit, however, that one of those forces is so obvious that we have overlooked it altogether: the change in the process of political mobilization, particularly in the electoral arena. Increasingly over the past 20 years, political campaigning has shifted from interpersonal to impersonal methods, from face-to-face to mass media communications. No matter how cleverly done, television or newspaper efforts cannot motivate some people to take the time and trouble to vote, especially if the polling place is unfamiliar territory and the people who manage it are total strangers. It is much harder to shirk one's civic duty when pulled toward it by friends and neighbors.

The importance of peer reinforcement for voting was understood by every political machine that ever existed; its energies were ultimately expended at the neighborhood level where friendship, camaraderie, and obligation could do their work. Consider, for example, Plunkitt's style in the turn of the century Tammany Hall machine:

> I know every man, woman, and child in the Fifteenth District. . . . I
> know what they like and what they don't like, what they are strong at
> and what they are weak at, and I reach them by approaching the right
> side.
> I hear of a young feller that's proud of his voice . . . I ask him to
> come around to Washington Hall and join our Glee Club. . . . Another
> young feller gains a reputation as a baseball player in a vacant lot. I
> bring him into our baseball club. . . . I rope them all in by givin' them
> opportunities to show themselves off. I don't trouble with political
> arguments. I just study human nature and act accordin'.[19]

Such an approach to politics was never the exclusive province of
political machines; they merely applied the principle more vigorously
and more selfishly. Today, one can still find hard-working political
activists, unconnected to any machine, who tend their flocks of voters
with similar skills and effectiveness. Unfortunately one cannot find very
many of them.

But does awareness of the virtual disappearance of face-to-face
politics contribute as well to our understanding of political alienation?
Perhaps the connection is not as clear and direct, but I believe it is
there. It is a misconception to suppose that alienation is brought about
by the failure of government to meet the particular needs or demands of
the individuals involved. Most persons are realistic and intelligent
enough to know that they cannot expect their particular views to prevail
on policy issues, that the concerns of others have to be taken into
account. Their disaffection arises not because they cannot get their own
way in policy matters but because they feel that "their way" is not even
being heard. They feel unconsulted and unrepresented, and part of the
reason is because they are not part of any system of communication
oriented to leaders and policymakers.

In one sense, those leaders and policymakers are not to blame,
because the expansion of government's role and the increase in population in districts and states make it impossible for most of them to know
and to communicate directly with their constituents. Elected officials do
strive valiantly to keep in touch, and their inability to do so is due in
substantial measure to the overloaded agenda and to the sheer number
of people involved.

But in another sense elected officials *are* responsible for constituents who feel that no one is listening to them; officials increasingly
depend on the mass media (or computerized mailing lists and the like)
and on organized interest groups to communicate with their constituents. The more experienced officials, of course, have a network of friends
and supporters who channel information to them, but that network
seldom attempts to listen and sympathize with citizens, nor are its
members organized and in communication with one another, nor are
they visible to the general public. And even if a rank-and-file citizen's

interest in conservation, the right to life, or job discrimination is being advanced by a special interest group whose leaders communicate directly with elected officials, the rank-and-file citizen is not really part of that communication process, and knows it. Ordinary citizens feel that no one is listening to them for the simple reason that altogether too often no one is. Public opinion polling and other techniques may enable officials to know what their constituents are thinking, but that is not all there is to political representation. It may well be that more political organization and integration and more interpersonal communications would not change public policy very much, but it might do a great deal to help reduce the growing discontent with the political process.

THE CONSEQUENCES OF DE-INSTITUTIONALIZED POLITICS

I began this essay by stressing the decline of party organizations in American politics. That decline accounts for a substantial part of the growing instability, ineffectiveness, and confusion characteristic of the last 15 years. In effect, we have cast our citizenry adrift on the open seas of politics by abandoning—for all practical purposes—an approach to the mobilization of popular political support based on interpersonal communications and relations. By so doing, we have turned our backs on our most unique institutional contribution to the concept of democratic self-government, the political party.

The de-institutionalization of American electoral politics brought about by the decline of parties and the concomitant rise of the mass media, of interest groups, and of political apathy and alienation ultimately affects the governing process in a variety of ways. I want to turn now to a consideration of some of these consequences for the administration of President Reagan.

The Reagan administration, I submit, will not be able to carry out its mandate because it does not have one. It is a mistake to interpret the 1980 elections as the electoral equivalent of a tidal wave for conservative principles and policies. Reagan's margin of victory, though certainly impressive, does not sustain such an interpretation, as responsible observers have noted all along.[20] This topic is given more consideration in Chapter 2. True, Ronald Reagan won the presidential nomination because of the support of a staunchly conservative following built up over a 16 year courtship by him. That cadre of support almost enabled him to take the 1976 Republican nomination away from the incumbent president, Gerald Ford, and in 1980 it gave Reagan a considerable headstart over other Republicans seeking the presidential nomination. Still, the support given in some areas in 1980 to less conservative candidates such as George Bush, John Anderson (before he switched to independent candidacy), and Howard Baker demonstrates that the Republican Party is not monolithic in its conservatism.

The general election results lend even less support to the notion that the electorate moved en masse to embrace Reagan's brand of conservatism. Though the Republican ticket won overwhelmingly in the electoral college (489 to Carter's 49), it had only 51 percent of the popular vote nationwide, compared to 41 percent for Carter. Most of the remaining vote went to independent John Anderson (7 percent), whose stand on issues was calculated to appeal to moderate Republicans and to disgruntled liberal Democrats. Considering that part of Reagan's 51 percent of the vote included a good many cast as a rejection of the Carter administration, I conclude that Ronald Reagan won in 1980 *in spite of* his strongly conservative stands, not because of them. It is quite possible that a more moderate Republican would have done at least as well as Reagan, and perhaps better.

Nor should too much be made of the defeat of liberal senators such as Frank Church, George McGovern, Birch Bayh, and John Culver; the interesting question is how they managed to get elected and (except for Culver) reelected as long as they did, given the nature of their constituencies. Significantly, most of the losing Democratic senators ran well ahead—sometimes far ahead—of the presidential ticket. For example, liberal loser Frank Church polled 49 percent of the senatorial vote in Idaho, while President Carter polled 25 percent in the presidential race. No one can doubt that a shift to the right was continued in 1980, but it was not the massive realignment suggested by some commentators.

It is important to see not only that Reagan lacks a mandate for a conservative revolution but also that political conditions today make it unlikely that any president will come to power with a mandate of any sort. A mandate implies that a broad consensus on a general course of public policy has been developed among a majority of the voters. Furthermore, that constituency must be firm and stable before it can confer a mandate. In that sense one can speak accurately of a mandate for Franklin Roosevelt in the 1930s or for Lyndon Johnson in the mid-1960s. But President Reagan cannot claim that sort of mandate. He indeed has a solidified (and conservative) constituency, but it is still very much a minority in the electorate (Carter, on the other hand, was elected with a temporary majority but never developed a firm constituency). The poor prospects for an electoral mandate reflect to some extent the loss of consensus in recent years in our society. Even so, a mandate might still be managed were it not for the lack of an institutional arrangement by which the mushiness of ordinary public opinion can be converted into solid and continuing support.

Although no mandate for a conservative revolution was given by the voters in 1980, is it not possible that President Reagan will be able quickly build to the support necessary among other government officials to bring about the far-reaching policy changes contemplated? I think not. Democratic party leaders and some of his own party members in the House and Senate will resist any major new departures in policy, as will some administrators in the executive branch. The president may, through skillful politicking, induce such persons to cooperate with him on a limited number of specific measures, but he will not be able to convert them to his conservative faith.

It is not likely that President Reagan can quickly consolidate and stabilize enough support among voters to give him the mandate in office that he failed to receive as a candidate. The reason for this emerges from consideration of the only four means of communication available to a political leader seeking to mobilize popular support: face-to-face inter-action, interest groups, the mass media, and political organizations designed for that purpose. Face-to-face interaction between the political leader and his or her constituents is surely the most desirable arrange-ment, but for presidents and members of Congress, as for most public officials except those in very small jurisdictions, personal communica-tion with constituents can never involve more than a tiny, tiny part of the whole. Just how ineffective this approach can be is illustrated by President Carter's experience. By all accounts, he was very effective in dealing with people individually, or in small groups, but the ability to communicate in that fashion did not help him at all in the larger arenas of public opinion.

A second possible avenue for political mobilization is through organized interest groups. The value of support from group leaders for getting a president's legislative program through Congress is very substantial, as was indicated in the discussion above of President Carter's use of them. However, interest groups do not serve nearly so well as a channel by which political leaders can reach and influence rank-and-file members; by their very nature, such groups are unreliable and unmanageable aids in the business of trying to build popular support. In somewhat oversimplified terms, the problem is this: If group leaders have influence over their members, they will use it to advance the group's (or the leader's) particularistic aims instead of broader ones; if the leaders have little influence over rank-and-file members, they cannot be of much help to public officials seeking to mobilize popular support. Either way, interest group leaders can be expected to guard carefully the organization's internal communications channels to mem-bers.

It is very unlikely that President Reagan can overcome these barriers to the use of interest groups as effective means for communicat-ing with and for mobilizing support from rank-and-file citizens. The interest groups that have patiently labored for years—for decades, in some cases—to carve out their policy niches are unlikely to acquiesce quietly in the wholesale undoing of their handiwork. *The Washington Post,* one day after it announced the plans of the Reagan administration to bring about a "revolution" in public policy, carried a front page report emphasizing the determination of affected interest groups to give battle all the way. And, a few days after that, the administration announced that seven programs originally on its "hit" list were being exempted from proposed budget cuts.[21]

A third possible approach for political leaders is to use the mass media for communications and mobilization, either by purchasing space or air time, or by making themselves the subject of news coverage. As my earlier discussion emphasized, the most obvious drawback is that the mass media offer only a one-way form of communication; but the lack of feedback is not the sole problem. As with interest group leaders, those in the mass media have goals and priorities which more often than not differ from the objectives of political leaders. Furthermore, not everyone targeted for messages is willing to stay in the reading, viewing, and listening audience, and those who do stay have perceptual screens that greatly affect the message actually received. When the communication is intended to help build political support, an additional problem arises from the passive and disconnected state of the recipients. Even if members of the mass audience correctly perceive and favorably react to the message sent via television, newspapers, or radio, they are still isolated individuals, with no immediate means of linking forces with like-minded people—they are not in any significant way mobilized for taking action of any sort.

Given these considerations, it is futile to suppose that the Reagan administration will be able promptly to mobilize public opinion via the mass media. The president is indeed skilled in his dealings with and use of the mass media,[22] but that skill will not prevent him from being undercut by the media once the novelty of a new administration begins to wear off.[23] In my judgment, the mass media today constitute an irresponsible "shadow government"—to borrow a term used in British politics to identify the Opposition leaders—one free to criticize incumbent officials without ever running the risk of having to take public office. Furthermore, even the most skillful use of the media, and even their neutrality or support, would not be enough to reshape public opinion within a short period of time. Before the media and their users can have much impact, persons exposed to them must be ready and in a receptive mood. To bring about that state of mind is a very difficult and time-consuming task. Those incautious souls who compare Ronald Reagan's bid to install a conservative revolution to Franklin Roosevelt's development of the New Deal overlook the unplanned character of the early New Deal and forget how long it took before the now-familiar

"New Deal Coalition" actually took shape. (The nature of that coalition is analyzed more fully in Chapter 2.) Furthermore, Franklin Roosevelt was helped along by an economic crisis of epic proportions, by substantial Democratic majorities in Congress (almost four to one, in 1937), and by the fact that as his program took shape, it promised to extend governmental benefits to more people, not to take away or reduce them.

Finally, a leader can attempt to communicate and to mobilize support through political organizations created for that purpose. Leaving aside the very temporary organizations created by candidates for their campaigns, two principal types of political organizations fit that description. One is the ideological political action group, exemplified by Americans for Democratic Action (ADA) and Americans for Constitutional Action (ACA). Though such groups have important roles in American politics, it cannot be said that the mobilization of broad and continuing popular support is one of them. The second type of organization under consideration is the political party.

But, for reasons already discussed, neither of the existing major parties is able today to function very well as an independent communications network, nor as a vehicle for mobilizing rank-and-file citizens. Admittedly, the Republican party is in somewhat better shape organizationally than is the Democratic party, but even so President Reagan cannot realistically expect his party's apparatus, in its shrunken post-election condition, to do what it could not do during its expanded campaign phase, namely, to gather a firm and stable majority for the president's program. In 1980 only about 24 percent of the electorate identified itself with the Republican party, compared to 41 percent for the Democrats; the remaining 35 percent considered itself "independent." These identifications, remarkably stable from one year to another, are grim reminders of the difficult task ahead for the Republicans.

My assumption is that the Reagan administration cannot solve in an immediate and substantial way our major foreign and domestic problems. As the discussion in Chapter 8 emphasizes, many foreign policy problems have no short-term solutions. For many of our domestic problems—such as the economic issues discussed in Chapter 7—solutions can be found, but we lack the political will to act, as MIT economist Lester Thurow has recently argued.[24] To make such an assertion is not to call for more machismo in the White House, though people there sometimes think so. Rather, in this context "lack of will" refers not to emotional but to organizational conditions, as when we say of a disorganized and dispirited army that it lacks the will to act. That is precisely what immobilizes today's national government (and many of our state and local ones as well). The "will" needed to deal at all successfully with our many pressing problems has to be rooted in the knowledge and security of broad popular support of a continuing sort.

But that kind of grass-roots mobilization increasingly is blocked by the forces outlined in the first parts of this essay.

What then *do* those forces permit a new president to do? In my judgment, only two things are possible for Ronald Reagan. One is to accept the fact that the national government and its role cannot be remade overnight, or even in one administration. By incremental changes here and there, by picking off an occasional easy target, by skillful politicking with congressional, administrative, and group leaders, by trade-offs and compromises, the Reagan administration, like its predecessors, may be able to bring about some marginal improvements in certain policies. Such improvements could be substantial enough to make Reagan supporters feel that their efforts were not wasted, but not so far-reaching as to outrage or threaten those who did not support him.

The only other thing that the Reagan administration can do to promote its conservative goals is to begin a long-range building program to bring about the broadened popular support it needs. That cannot be done by television appeals, no matter how expertly tailored, nor by direct mail solicitations, no matter how wisely targeted; nor can it be done by proxy groups, such as the National Conservative Political Action Committee or the Moral Majority. Such efforts are no doubt helpful, but the basic requirements are a continuing political organization whose field representatives have the time and motivation to talk to, listen to, and politick with friends and neighbors—individually and in small groups—on a frequent basis. These party workers should be geographically based, in order to facilitate informal neighborhood interaction and to avoid the barriers to communication posed by strangers and outsiders, or by persons with too great a difference in social status. It is crucial that the members of the organization be rewarded for their efforts with either material or nonmaterial benefits. At the least, they should have a measure of power, or access to those who have it, commensurate with their place in the organization.

What is being described, of course, is the outline of a territorially based political party. When functioning properly, it is our single best instrument for mobilizing mass political support, for socializing citizens into the roles of democratic politics, for giving form and coherence to public opinion, and for aggregating interests into governing coalitions. If President Reagan wants to make a really important contribution to American politics, he can set to work to make his party a more effective instrument for the discharge of its functions.

But could he—or anyone else—really do anything to promote party revitalization? Though probably not written with Ronald Reagan in mind, the comments of a well-known historian and political commentator, Arthur Schlesinger, Jr., suggest that it is possible:

Two things alone can give these decrepit parties a lease on life: the incubation of ideas that give promise of meeting the hard questions of our age, especially inflation and energy; and the election of competent presidents who will thereafter act to revitalize their parties in the presidential interest. The best hope for the party is as an instrument of presidents who need to overcome the separation of powers and to mobilize mass support in order to put new programs into effect.[25]

I think the first part of that prescription is mistaken and irrelevant; we need, not so much new ideas (compare the argument of Chapter 3), as better institutions for making and implementing choices from among those available. However, I do share the author's premise that leadership could indeed improve the present condition of the party system.

To accomplish that, one does not need exotic or strained prescriptions. The starting point is an understanding of the principal forces that have put parties into decline.[26] If my beginning argument is correct—that these forces are the loss of control of nominations, the overregulation of party structure and function, and the withdrawal of incentives for grass-roots party activity—then the logical starting point is to cut back sharply on the use of the direct primary (including presidential primaries), to deregulate substantially state party organizations, and to find some acceptable way of rewarding party workers for their year-round activity.

So far as the first two steps are concerned, a few states have already shown the way. Connecticut and several western states have devised variations on the "challenge primary" that give the party organization primacy in the nominating process most of the time but provide for resort to direct primaries when intraparty conflict reaches certain levels. In Virginia, the state statutes covering parties are models of brevity and simplicity; mostly the laws confirm the parties' rights to make their own rules for self-government. The third step—rewarding party workers—is undoubtedly the most difficult to solve. I have no simple solution to offer, but think it possible that ways can be found to provide incentives for grass-roots political activity without returning to the old patronage basis of operation (now mostly unconstitutional, in any event).

But these changes will not take place without vigorous leadership. No president can spare the time and attention from the duties of his office to direct personally a party revitalization campaign, but he could commit himself to the search for and support of the contemporary equivalent of such political engineers as Martin VanBuren, Mark Hanna, and James A. Farley. In the meantime, President Reagan can and should begin a long-range program to nurture and sustain the Republican party organization by using it as a communications network, by consulting it on appointments, by helping with its funding and staffing, and generally, by treating it as the important institution that it is.

There is no guarantee that such an effort would yield the kind of conservative mandate desired by the new administration, for it goes against deeply held principles and considerable self-interest on the part of large numbers of citizens. It does appear, however, that enough American voters are now willing to consider an alternative to the liberalism of the 1970s to bring a conservative mandate within the realm of possibility. But I stress that there can be no such mandate without institutionalized support, no institutionalized support without party, no party without a cadre, no cadre without significant functions, no functions without personal ties to the rank-and-file citizen.

NOTES

1. Among those advancing the party decline thesis are Everett C. Ladd, *Where Have All the Voters Gone: The Fracturing of American Political Parties* (New York: W. W. Norton & Co., 1978); Walter Dean Burnham, "American Politics in the 1970s: Beyond Party?" in *The American Party System: Stages of Party Development,* 2d ed., William Chambers and Walter Dean Burnham, eds. (New York: Oxford University Press, 1975); and Frank Sorauf, *Party Politics in America,* 4th ed. (Boston: Little, Brown & Co., 1980), pp. 404-408. For a denial of party decline, see John Kessel, *Presidential Campaign Politics: Coalition Strategies and Citizen Response* (Homewood, Ill.: Dorsey Press, 1980), pp. 245-246.
2. In 1968, only 17 states required delegates to national nominating conventions to be chosen in presidential primaries. Delegates so chosen accounted for only about 40 percent of the total number in each party. The remaining delegates were chosen by other procedures—usually a series of caucuses and conventions—that gave party cadres a larger role than in primaries. By 1980, presidential primaries of one type or another were used in 35 states, Puerto Rico, and the District of Columbia; 72 percent of the Democratic delegates and 76 perent of the Republican delegates were chosen in them.
3. For a brief but authoritative review of patronage and other incentives for party activity, see Sorauf, *Party Politics in America,* pp. 82-91.
4. Branti v. Finkel, 445 U.S. 507 (1980); Elrod v. Burns, 427 U.S. 347 (1976).
5. Samuel Eldersveld, *Political Parties: A Behavioral Analysis* (Chicago: Rand McNally & Co., 1964), pp. 9-10.
6. James Q. Wilson, *The Amateur Democrat* (Chicago: University of Chicago Press, 1962); and Frank Sorauf, "Extra-Legal Parties in Wisconsin," 48 *American Political Science Review* 692 (September 1954).
7. Elihu Katz, "The Two-Step Flow of Communications: An Up-to-Date Report on an Hypothesis," 21 *Public Opinion Quarterly* 61 (Spring 1957).
8. For a review of the role of the mass media in one city in the 1948 presidential campaign, see Bernard Berelson, Paul Lazarsfeld, and William McPhee, *Voting: A Study of Opinion Formation in a Presidential Campaign* (Chicago: University of Chicago Press, 1954), pp. 234-252.
9. One close observer argues that the press "seeks to amass, husband, and use power" in local elections and government. It opposes strong party organizations in part because it sees them (correctly) as a rival communications system that will limit the influence of the press. David L. Rosenbloom, "The Press and the Local Candidate," in *Role of the Mass Media in American*

Politics, Vol. 427 of the Annals of the American Academy of Political and Social Science (September 1976), pp. 12-22.

10. Edward Jay Epstein, "The Panthers and the Police: A Pattern of Genocide?" *The New Yorker Magazine* (February 13, 1971), p. 45. For a broader perspective on the problem with television news, see Edward Jay Epstein, *News from Nowhere* (New York: Random House, 1973).

11. On the educational background of journalists, see John W. C. Johnstone, Edward Slawski, and William W. Bowman, *The News People: A Sociological Portrait of American Journalists and Their Work* (Urbana, Ill.: University of Illinois Press, 1976). On the journalist's creed and its consequences, see Bernard Roshko, *Newsmaking* (Chicago: University of Chicago Press, 1975), particularly p. 42; Leon Sigal, *Reporters and Officials* (Lexington, Mass.: Lexington Books, 1973), particularly Chapter 4.

12. Michael Robinson makes much the same point when he concludes that "television has been, for more than a decade, at the core of our growing political malaise." He argues that events are conveyed by television news in such a way as to inject a "negativistic, contentious, or anti-institutional bias" that evokes "images of American politics and social life which are inordinately sinister and despairing." Inadvertent viewers, distressed by these manifestations of evil and decay, may then reject the groups seen as responsible, or the institutions involved, or even themselves (out of feelings of inadequacy). Michael J. Robinson, "Public Affairs Television and the Growth of Political Malaise: The Case of 'The Selling of the Pentagon,' " *American Political Science Review* 70 (June 1976): 425, 430.

13. Thomas E. Patterson and Robert D. McClure, *The Unseeing Eye: The Myth of Television Power in National Elections* (New York: G. P. Putnam's Sons, 1976), p. 82.

14. Ibid., p. 144.

15. Ibid., pp. 21-22; 82-90. Such criticism does not come solely from unsympathetic scholars. Fred Friendly, former president of NBC News, was recently quoted in a UPI (United Press International) interview as saying that television is "a billion-dollar penny arcade. Its capability in the news area has never been greater. Its performance has never been worse...," *Charlottesville* (Va.) *Daily Progress,* 7 February 1981.

16. S. J. Makielski, Jr., *Pressure Politics in America* (Lanham, Md.: University Press of America, 1980), pp. 3-6.

17. For details on the Carter administration's efforts, see *National Journal* 11 (January 13, 1979): 54-57; and *National Journal* 11 (September 8, 1979): 1476-1479. Contact between White House staff and interest group representatives certainly did not originate in the Carter administration, but it apparently was the first to attempt systematically to conduct an outreach program for groups and to build them into the planning and preparation of its legislative programs.

18. David B. Hill and Norman R. Luttbeg, *Trends in American Electoral Behavior* (Itasca, Ill.: F. E. Peacock Publishers, 1980), pp. 109-149.

19. William Riordan, *Plunkitt of Tammany Hall* (New York: E. P. Dutton, 1963), pp. 25-26.

20. Rhodes Cook, "National Mood for Change Boosted Republican Ticket," *Congressional Quarterly Weekly Report* 38 (November 15, 1980): 3370-3371.

21. An account of proposed budget cuts was carried in *The Washington Post,* 8 February 1981. The February 9 issue carried a follow-up story, the thrust of which is indicated by the captions: "Education, Development Aid Defended: Agencies Have Powerful Friends; School, Rights Groups Vow

Fight." The Reagan administration's decision not to pursue certain proposals for cuts in highly sensitive programs was reported in the 11 February 1981
issue.

22. President Reagan's televised address to the nation on our economic problems on February 5, 1981 was by all accounts perceived as well done, as an
example of effective communication. But such perceptions are heavily
influenced by the tendency for most presidents to start their terms with an
appreciative—even indulgent—public. Thus, any pleasure generated for the
Reagan administration by the early Harris poll showing that 77 percent of
adult Americans gave him positive ratings on "inspiring confidence in the
White House" should be tempered by the realization that presidents Carter
and Ford each began his administration with a similar 75 percent rating. By
the end of their respective administrations, Carter's rating had fallen to 34
percent and Ford's rating had fallen to 46 percent. *Washington Post,* 12
February 1981.

23. Top members of the Carter administration have repeatedly expressed
frustration over their inability to get across to the general public an accurate
view of what they were doing and why, and put much of the blame for this
on the mass media of communication. Other presidential administrations—
including particularly those of Richard Nixon and Lyndon Johnson—have
had the same problem. I see no reason to suppose that Ronald Reagan's
experience will be very different.

24. Lester Thurow, "There are Solutions to Our Economic Problems," *New
York Times Magazine* (August 10, 1980), pp. 30.

25. *Wall Street Journal,* 10 May 1980, p. 30; and *Wall Street Journal,* 14 May
1980, p. 20.

26. The importance of understanding the causes of party decline, as distinct
from the symptoms, is illustrated nicely by the report of President Carter's
Commission for a National Agenda for the Eighties. The commission, having
recognized the decline of parties and the fragmentation of interests, offered
three recommendations (pp. 96-97) for improvement: public financing of
congressional campaigns (with a portion of the funds allocated by party
national committees to the individual candidates); retaining presidential
primaries but holding them in four monthly stages organized by time zones;
and giving one-third to one-fifth of delegate positions at presidential
nominating conventions to the party's elected officials, recent candidates,
and party officials. Such proposals amount to offering Band-Aids to control
arterial bleeding; they would help very little and might in some ways add to
the problem.

7

Economic Issues
in the Campaign

Stephen L. McDonald

Although there were many factors, a major reason for the defeat of Jimmy Carter in the 1980 presidential election was the unsatisfactory state of the economy, particularly during the last two years of his term in office. Toward the end of the campaign Ronald Reagan began asking his audiences, "Are you better off now than you were four years ago?" To this question the invariable reply was a resounding "No!" Reagan's audiences were partisan, of course, and they knew the answer expected of them, but the answer would not have been far wrong for the average American. This fact, combined with the fresh appeal of Reagan's economic program, was perhaps critical to the outcome of the election.

During the Carter administration, the economy was plagued by three interrelated problems. The first of these was inflation, which accelerated every year after 1976 and reached near-record levels in 1980. Inflation has been a problem since the mid-1960s, but it has seemed to grow progressively worse, and its cumulative effect has been distressing to most Americans. The second problem was the stagnation of real output in 1979 and the sharp recession of 1980, with an accompanying rise in unemployment. This problem no doubt turned away from Carter many of the votes he normally would have received from industrial workers. The third problem was the slow growth of per capita real income, which turned into actual decline in 1979-1980—almost, but not quite, justifying the belief that the standard of living had deteriorated under Carter.

As indicated, these problems are interrelated. Sharp oil price increases by the Organization of Petroleum Exporting Countries (OPEC), for instance, have simultaneously accelerated inflation, contributed to recession, and slowed the growth of worker productivity and per capita real income. The recession of 1980, although an extension of the 1979 stagnation, was immediately triggered by restrictive monetary measures designed to slow accelerating inflation. The decline in worker productivity and per capita real income in 1979-1980 was largely a product of stagnation and recession in the same period. The slow growth of productivity during most of the Carter administration fed the inflation rate, given monetary and fiscal policies. Inflation itself, by increasing investor uncertainty, may have contributed to stagnation and low worker productivity. So the three problems add up to one big problem for the policymaker, and Carter failed to convince the voters that he had the solution.

We shall examine Reagan's proposed solutions later in this chapter; first, let us look at the statistical evidence of the problems and briefly discuss their causes.

THE STATISTICAL EVIDENCE

Table 7-1 provides some key economic statistics for the period 1972-1980 in the United States. The period 1972-1976, spanning the reelection of Richard Nixon and the Nixon-Ford term, is included to put the Carter years into perspective. The years 1979-1980 are broken down into quarters to provide more detail for the critical period just preceding the election. (The third quarter of 1980 is the most recent period for which data are available as this is written.)

The first column shows that nominal Gross National Product (GNP), in billions of current dollars, grew consistently throughout the period covered by the table. But the next two columns indicate that much of this growth was pure inflation. Thus, as the second column shows, the GNP deflator, the most broadly based index of prices we have, grew about 80 percent from the middle of 1972 to the middle of 1980. When this index is used to *deflate* nominal GNP we have the third column, GNP expressed in (1972) dollars of constant purchasing power, or *real* GNP. Real GNP grew much more slowly than nominal GNP over the period as a whole, and recessions came in 1973-1975 and again in the second quarters of 1979 and 1980. The unemployment rate, as a percentage of the labor force, behaved consistently, rising in 1973-1975

Table 7-1. Some Key U.S. Economic Statistics, 1972-1980.

Year	Nominal GNP (billion $)	GNP deflator (1972=100)	Real GNP billions (1972 $)	Unem- ployment rate (percent)	Real per capita dis. pers. income (1972 $)
1972	1171	100.0	1171	5.6	3837
1973	1306	105.8	1235	4.9	4062
1974	1413	116.0	1218	5.6	3973
1975	1529	127.2	1202	8.5	4025
1976	1702	133.7	1273	7.7	4136
1977	1899	141.7	1341	7.0	4271
1978	2127	152.1	1399	6.0	4418
1979	2368	165.5	1431	5.8	4512
1979Q1	2292	160.2	1431	5.7	4536
1979Q2	2330	163.8	1422	5.8	4510
1979Q3	2397	167.2	1433	5.8	4501
1979Q4	2457	170.6	1440	5.9	4502
1980Q1	2521	174.5	1445	6.1	4502
1980Q2	2521	179.0	1409	7.5	4423
1980Q3	2583	183.0	1412	7.6	4447

SOURCE: U.S., Department of Commerce, *Business Conditions Digest.*

and throughout 1979-1980. The rate declined under Carter in 1976-1979, but never got as low as it was in 1973.

The final column gives per capita disposable personal income in constant (1972) dollars. It shows growth for the period as a whole and during the Carter years up to 1979, but declines in the 1973-1974 and 1979-1980 periods. In terms of after-tax real personal income, the average American was better off in 1980 than in 1976, but less well off in the third quarter of 1980 than in the first quarter of 1979. In general, the economic record of the Carter administration is as good as that of the Nixon-Ford term, but it deteriorated in the critical period just before the 1980 election. ("What have you done for/to me lately, Mr. Carter?")

Table 7-2 gives percentage rates of change for the data contained in Table 7-1. The upper panel provides annual rates of change; the lower panel, quarterly rates of change. Here growth and fluctuations are brought out clearly. Even the nominal GNP series, while growing about 10 percent per year, shows the effects of the recessions of 1973-1975 and 1979-1980. The GNP deflator grew every year, but grew most rapidly in these recession years, which followed or coincided with large increases in OPEC prices. The data further show that inflation fell to 5.1 percent per

Table 7-2.   Rates of Change Some Key U.S. Economic Statistics 1972-1980.

Year	Nominal GNP	GNP Deflator	Real GNP	Unem- ployment rate	Real per capita dis. pers. income
Percentage Change from Previous Year					
1973	11.5	5.8	5.5	−12.5	5.8
1974	8.2	9.6	−1.4	14.3	−2.2
1975	8.2	9.7	−1.3	51.8	1.3
1976	11.3	5.1	5.9	− 9.5	2.8
1977	11.6	6.0	5.3	− 9.1	3.3
1978	12.0	7.3	4.3	−14.3	3.4
1979	11.3	8.8	2.3	− 3.3	2.1
1980Q3	7.7	9.4	−1.5	31.0	−1.2
Percentage Change from Previous Quarter					
1979Q2	1.7	2.2	−0.6	1.8	−0.6
1979Q3	2.9	2.1	0.8	0.0	−0.2
1979Q4	2.5	2.0	0.5	1.7	0.0
1980Q1	2.6	2.3	0.3	3.4	0.0
1980Q2	0.0	2.6	−2.5	23.0	−1.8
1980Q3	2.5	2.2	0.2	1.3	0.5

SOURCE: Calculated from Table 7-1.

year in the last year of the Ford administration, but rose steadily to 9.4 percent in the year preceding the election of 1980. As shown in the third column, real GNP declined in the two recessions. Perhaps more significantly, the rate of growth in real GNP declined from 5.3 percent in 1977, Carter's first year, to −1.5 percent in the year just preceding the 1980 election. Change in the unemployment rate behaved predictably. Real per capita disposable personal income declined 2.2 percent in 1973-1974 and 1.2 percent from the third quarter of 1979 to the same quarter of 1980. Again, there was deterioration during the Carter term as the rate of growth of real per capita disposable personal income declined from 3.4 percent in 1978 to −1.2 percent in 1980.

This statistical review confirms the existence of the three problems identified above; it further shows that the rate of economic improvement under Carter declined almost throughout his term, culminating in retrogression in the last year before the election. It is not surprising, then, that the economic issues hurt Carter's candidacy—and helped Reagan's to the extent that the electorate could believe in the efficacy of his proposals.

Fig. 7-1. Inflation with Rising Output.

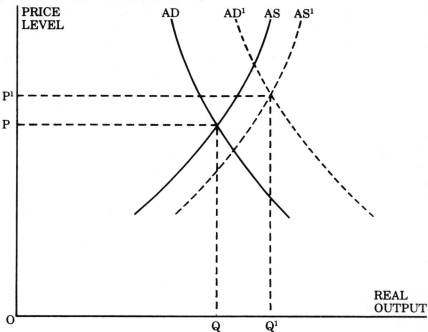

Before turning to the Reagan proposals, it will be helpful to discuss briefly the causes of the problems that dogged Carter. Understanding causes is essential to evaluating proposed cures.

SOME ELEMENTARY MACROECONOMICS

The simplest way to explain inflation and real economic growth (or lack of it) is with the aid of the concepts of aggregate supply and aggregate demand. These two concepts are depicted graphically in Figure 7-1, where the general price level (P) is on the vertical scale and real output (Q) is on the horizontal scale. The aggregate supply function (AS) is upward sloping; the higher the general price level the greater the amount of output forthcoming, given the quantity and quality of productive resources (labor) and their prices (nominal wages). The aggregate demand function (AD) is downward sloping; the higher the general price level the smaller the real quantity demanded, given the propensities to spend and the nominal money supply. Where the two functions intersect we have the "equilibrium" price level and quantity of output for the given conditions.

Normally, both aggregate supply and aggregate demand grow from year to year; that is, the functions shift to the right, as indicated by the dashed curves in Figure 7-1. It is readily apparent that if aggregate demand grows faster than aggregate supply the price level will rise in association with rising output. It is also apparent that if aggregate supply actually falls (the curve shifts left) the price level will rise in association with falling output. Thus we may have inflation with either falling or rising output. If output falls or rises less than proportionately to population we may have inflation with declining real output per capita.

What underlies relative shifts in aggregate demand and aggregate supply? Aggregate demand tends to grow when the propensity to spend grows, given the money supply; or when the money supply grows, given the propensity to spend. As for the propensity to spend, it grows when prospective investment profits rise relative to interest rates, when households wish to save a smaller proportion of their income, when governments increase outlays relative to tax receipts, or when exports rise relative to imports. The money supply is increased when the Federal Reserve system (the Fed) provides more reserves to the banking system, thereby enabling an expansion of bank credit and deposits, our principal form of money. Aggregate supply grows when there is an increase in the quantity of productive resources (land, labor, and capital) or an increase in their productivity.

Fig. 7-2. Inflation with Falling Output.

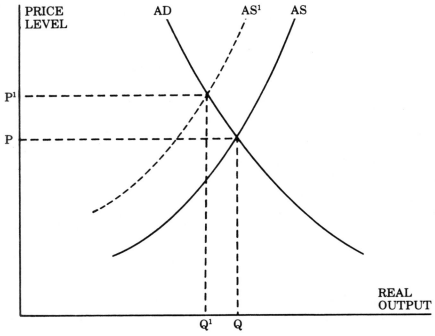

Aggregate supply tends to contract when there is an increase in the price of productive resources (nominal wages), a decrease in productivity (including a crop failure), or an increase in the price of imported raw materials (OPEC petroleum). When inflation is confidently *expected,* nominal wages tend to rise faster than productivity by the rate of expected inflation, and aggregate supply tends to contract (the curve shifts left) or to grow at a slower rate. Large oil price increases by OPEC have similar effects. When either of these events occurs, aggregate supply is reduced (the supply curve shifts left) and, in association with stagnation or modest increase in aggregate demand, the result is an inflationary recession, as depicted in Figure 7-2.

We can now interpret the economic record of the recent past. Generally, since the mid-1960s aggregate demand has tended to grow at a faster rate than aggregate supply as the Fed has increased the money supply at a rate two or three times as great as the normal rate of growth of resource supplies and productivity,[1] and as governments have tended to increase spending relative to tax receipts at high employment levels. The predictable result has been inflation, with the rate accelerating to keep pace with faster and faster growth of money. Accompanying inflation is the expectation of further inflation, so wages have tended to rise at three or four times the rate of growth of productivity.[2] With aggregate supply tending to shift left relatively, it takes larger increases in aggregate demand (or shifts to the right) to raise output per capita. Hence the wage-price spiral. When we have checked the growth of the money supply and therefore the shift to the right of aggregate demand, as in 1966, 1969, and 1980 notably, aggregate supply has shifted left relative to aggregate demand and an inflationary recession has resulted. The Federal Reserve System has never held down the growth of money long enough to halt inflation and reduce expected inflation to zero. So each recovery has been accompanied by a continuation of inflation.

The recession of 1973-1975 and the stagnation of 1979 are associated with large increases in oil prices by OPEC. Particularly with expected inflation, such increases shift the aggregate supply function to the left relative to aggregate demand, as shown in Figure 7-2, and the result is a fall in output and rising prices. The sharp recession in the spring of 1980 is largely a monetary phenomenon, as earlier explained.

This analysis suggests that to solve the problems of inflation, unemployment, and slow growth of real output we must limit the growth of the money supply to about 2 percent to 3 percent per year and decrease government spending relative to tax receipts: this policy must also be continued long enough to eliminate inflation, and therefore the expectation of it. It further suggests, however, that an abrupt change to a more restrictive monetary policy will produce a recession, more unemployment, and low growth of real output per person. A more gradual change of policy will give better long-term results but will allow inflation to continue (at a declining rate) for several years more. The analysis also suggests that so long as we are dependent upon OPEC for a substantial portion of our oil imports, our economy will be subject to shocks leading to inflationary recessions with every large increase in oil prices.

Let us now consider the proposals of the Reagan administration.

THE REAGAN PROPOSALS

A key element of the Reagan economic program is a 10 percent, across-the-board decrease in personal income taxes in each of three years from 1981 to 1983.[3] If enacted, the supposed short-run effect of such a tax reduction would be to increase aggregate demand and raise output and employment. The supposed long-run effect would be to increase personal saving, leading to lower interest rates, more capital formation, and a faster rate of growth of aggregate supply. It is this last supposed effect that Reagan and his followers emphasize. It is recognized that such a tax reduction is likely to increase the federal budget deficit immediately, but the expected higher rate of growth of GNP is supposed to raise revenues and balance the budget within two or three years.

Reagan also proposed to reduce taxes on business income by more generous depreciation allowances.[4] One of the side effects of

Copyright 1980 Cincinnati Enquirer, permission granted by King Features Syndicate, Inc.

inflation is to overstate business income and raise effective tax rates above nominal ones. This is because depreciation allowances for tax purposes are based on historical costs, which due to inflation are lower than replacement costs. If depreciation allowances were based on replacement costs, stated income would be lower and the fraction of actual income taxed away would be lower. Accelerated depreciation produces similar effects by shifting tax liabilities from early years to later asset life. The present value of tax payments is reduced and the expected rate of return on investment is increased. Thus the proposal is based not so much on equity as on the aim to increase capital formation, improve productivity, and cause aggregate supply to grow at a faster rate.

Before his actual economic message to Congress on February 18, 1981, Reagan's thinking on tax and budget proposals was billed as "supply-side economics," designed primarily to increase aggregate supply in the long run. The text of this speech is set out in the Presidential Messages appendix. Although his message did emphasize this approach, there were signs of a subtle shift in the administration's economic thinking that suggested economists of other persuasions were being listened to. For example, the personal income tax cut Reagan proposed would not go into effect until July 1, 1981, rather than January 1, thus lessening federal budget deficit problems. In addition, his message did not call for automatic adjustment of tax rates to offset inflation, as he had at one time been expected to propose. He also acknowledged the importance of monetary policy and the role of the Federal Reserve System in attacking economic problems.

The other side of Reagan's proposed *fiscal* policy is a reduction in government spending. More precisely, as discussed at greater length in Chapter 8, it is proposed that *defense* outlays be increased substantially, so it is nondefense spending that must be drastically reduced if total spending is to fall. Such a reduction is likely to come slowly and painfully, with the long-run aim of balancing the budget within the next few years. In his February 18, 1981 speech, President Reagan proposed to decrease budgeted spending by $41 billion and unbudgeted items by another $8 billion in fiscal year 1982. Defense spending for 1982 would be increased by about $4 billion over the Carter proposal. Additional increases in defense spending are to come in 1983 and 1984.

A $49.1 billion cut in the 1982 federal budget proposed by the new administration in its early months in office would be a very substantial start, indeed. In any case, a reduction in federal spending is seen partly as a means of reducing or eliminating the inflationary impact of tax reductions and partly as a way of freeing productive resources for use in the private sector. The latter use will include capital formation, leading to faster growth of aggregate supply.

With regard to *monetary* policy, Reagan had little to say during the campaign. However, in his February 18 message, and in supporting documents released to reporters, Reagan acknowledged the crucial role that monetary policy would play. He said the nation needed a monetary policy "which does not allow money growth to increase consistently faster than the growth of goods and services. In order to curb inflation, we need to slow the growth of our money supply." A supporting paper released before the speech recommended that the Federal Reserve cut the growth rate of credit and money in half by 1986.

There are two problems in developing a more restrictive monetary policy. The first problem is that monetary policy is the province of the Federal Reserve System, which is not a part of the executive branch of government and is not responsible to the president. The present chairman of the Board of Governors of the Federal Reserve System, Paul Volcker, will remain chairman until his term expires in 1983. Although Volcker sees the need for a more restrictive monetary policy, he and his fellow Governors may feel constrained by the second problem.

The second problem is the connection between monetary and fiscal policies through interest rates. If, in the short run, the Reagan fiscal policy involves a greater federal deficit, interest rates will tend to rise as the government seeks to market the additional debt. Moral pressure may be brought upon the Board of Governors to moderate this effect by increasing the money supply at a faster rate. If such pressure is successful, the result will be faster inflation. On the other hand, if the Board successfully resists such pressure and follows a restrictive monetary policy in the face of large federal deficits, the rise in interest rates in the short run will be even greater, with adverse effects on the demand for capital goods, housing, automobiles, and home appliances. In other words, Reagan's proposed fiscal policy may pose a dilemma for the Federal Reserve System: faster inflation in the short run with greater difficulty in later reducing inflationary expectations, or a relapse into recession.

Rounding out Reagan's economic program is the announced aim of freeing American industry of much uneconomic or otherwise onerous regulation. Two areas deserve special mention. The first is price regulation in the oil and gas industry. Immediately after his inauguration, President Reagan acted to eliminate price ceilings on both oil and gas.[5] This fit in with his belief that higher prices will increase domestic production and also encourage conservation by users, thereby reducing our dependence on foreign oil. The aim will be furthered by a faster rate of leasing of federal lands for oil and gas exploration and by the reduction of environmental restraints on the development of such energy alternatives as shale oil and coal. The second area is environmental regulation generally. President Reagan has said that he believes that many environmental regulations hamper the development of new energy sources, divert capital from more productive uses, and slow growth of real output. Reduction of environmental regulation is more "supply-side economics" designed to speed up growth of supply and reduce inflationary tendencies.

There is more to the Reagan program than we have indicated. But the above proposals seem to be the chief means by which he hopes to deal with the three economic problems we have discussed. The question now is: How effective are the Reagan proposals likely to be?

PREDICTED SUCCESS OF THE REAGAN PROPOSALS

With regard to the important 30 percent reduction in personal income taxes, at least three questions may be posed. Will the reductions be inflationary? Will they provide significant stimulus to the supply side in the longer run? Will they permit the federal budget to be balanced within a few years?

A reduction in personal income taxes is in the first instance an increase in household disposable income. There is a close correlation between disposable personal income and consumption expenditures.[6] Past experience with tax cuts tells us that consumption expenditures are likely to be increased by 93 to 95 percent of the increase in disposable income, probably within one year's time. So the first and predominant effect is to increase aggregate demand relative to aggregate supply. Our earlier supply-demand analysis suggests that the result will be greater output and higher prices than otherwise would prevail. Greater output is all to the good because there was considerable slack in the economy in 1980, except that tighter labor and goods markets, and fuller utilization of plant and equipment capacity, virtually assure rising inflation rates. So the personal tax reduction, taken by itself, is likely to make us better off with regard to employment and output, but worse off with regard to inflation. In addition, more inflation in the short run will make it more difficult to reduce inflationary expectations in the longer run, and thus more difficult to restrain wage inflation.

Will personal tax reductions provide much long-run supply stimulus? There will be two effects. The first effect is to increase personal saving. Some part of the increased disposable income will be saved and the absolute amount of personal saving will rise. Taken by itself, this will increase the supply of capital, lower interest rates, and increase investment. This is the desired supply-side effect. However, what counts for capital formation is not just personal saving but total savings—personal, business, and government—and personal saving is only about one-fourth of the total.[7] Furthermore, there is an inverse correlation between personal saving and government saving. The more the government saves, the less is personal disposable income; the more individuals save, the less is national income and government tax receipts. Thus, even in the long-run we cannot be sure that a personal tax reduction will increase the total supply of capital.

But there is a second effect, an incentive effect. Lower effective marginal tax rates mean that the after-tax rate of return to saving and work is increased, and the proportion of personal disposable income saved may be likewise increased. If so, it is possible that the long-run supply effects will be positive. We cannot be certain about this, however. There is a large element of simple faith in the belief that reduced personal taxes will make aggregate supply grow at a faster rate in the long run.

There is less reason to doubt that it will occur in the case of business tax reductions. Tax reductions increase business net income, some part of which will be retained (saved) by business firms. They also increase the after-tax expected rate of return, which provides a positive incentive to investment. Past experience with business tax reductions, in the forms of rate reductions, accelerated depreciation, or the investment tax credit, gives us good reason to expect capital formation to be increased.

However, capital formation takes time. The first effect of greater investment outlays is to increase the demand for labor, materials, and equipment—increased aggregate demand. Only with the passage of a certain gestation period does new capital become available for productive use and increase aggregate supply. The gestation period may be from a few months to several years. So the short-run effects of business tax reductions, like personal tax reductions, tend to be inflationary. In the longer run, aggregate supply is increased, with anti-inflationary effects.

To summarize the tax reduction proposals considered alone, they are likely to be inflationary in the short run—the first two years. But in the longer run they are likely to increase aggregate supply relative to aggregate demand, increasing productivity and output, and decreasing inflationary pressures.

The tax reductions are to be coupled, however, with a strong effort to reduce government spending. If that effort is successful (and as noted in Chapter 6, several formidable obstacles to that goal exist) aggregate demand need not be increased in the short run, and output and prices need not rise in that period. Nearly all of the consequences might be long-run supply-side effects, with a net gain in output potential and reduced inflation. We might confidently expect this result if it were not for Reagan's determination to increase real defense expenditures. The more they are increased, of course, the more difficult it will be to reduce total government expenditures. And if the total is not reduced, the net tax and expenditure effects will be inflationary in the short run, as we have already indicated.

Will the proposed tax reductions permit the federal budget to be balanced within a few years? The answer to this question will be determined by two separate factors. As previously indicated, it depends in part on the success of the Reagan administration in reducing or holding down the growth of government expenditures. There is considerable doubt about whether the president will be able to reduce total government spending in view of his commitment to increase defense expenditures. The other factor is the extent to which national income tax receipts at the new lower level of rates grow in response to fiscal and monetary policy. We cannot be sure of that, due to uncertainty about incentive effects, but a rough calculation suggests that the budget cannot be balanced by 1983 as hoped without a much higher rate of inflation than desired.

The calculation is as follows. Between 1978 and 1980 each additional dollar of GNP generated approximately 13 cents of additional personal and corporate income tax receipts at the federal level.[8] With a 30 percent reduction in rates over three years that figure would average about 11 cents. The tax reduction itself would result in a loss of revenue of about $100 billion over the three years. Starting with a deficit of about $50 billion, growth must generate $150 billion of revenues if the budget is to be balanced, assuming no change in government expenditures. The required rise in GNP over the period is $1,350 billion (150 ÷ .11). Starting with an assumed GNP of $2,800 billion in 1981, the required rise is 48 percent—15 percent per year. Even if real growth accelerated to 5 percent per year, this figure implies 10 percent inflation per year. If inflation slows down due to a more restrictive monetary policy, it appears unlikely that the budget can be balanced by 1983. (But, of course, if inflation can be slowed sufficiently by means of monetary policy, there is less urgency to balance the budget. This matter will be discussed more completely later in this chapter.)

The deregulation of oil and gas prices will, of course, cause faster inflation in the very short run (in 1981). In the long run, however, it cannot help but stimulate domestic exploration for oil and gas, increase domestic supplies, and reduce domestic demand—thus diminishing our dependence on foreign oil. This, in turn, will reduce the inflationary (and recessionary) shocks to our economy of further increases in the price of OPEC oil, to say nothing of its effects upon national security and freedom of international policy. The proposal to reduce the severity of environmental regulations generally, if carried out, will lower business costs and free capital for other investments, thus tending to lower the rate of inflation in both the short and the long run.[9]

The Reagan proposals, therefore, promise to be somewhat inflationary in the first two or three years but mildly expansive of capacity and deflationary after that. They promise faster growth of capital stock and of labor productivity in the long run, and therefore faster growth of per capita real income than in the recent past. Beyond that, much depends on our further adaptation to a permanently higher real cost of energy, and on the appropriateness of monetary policy. We conclude with a brief discussion of these matters.

ENERGY COSTS AND PRODUCTIVITY

It is obvious that growth of real per capita income depends heavily upon growth of real output per worker. In the United States, the latter fell from an average of 2.1 percent per year in 1950-1973 to an average of .4 percent annually in 1973-1978.[10] There has been much recent discussion of this decline and its causes, and one popular explanation is a decline in the personal saving rate and, by implication, a decline in capital formation. But as explained earlier, personal saving is only about one-fourth of total saving; and total saving (gross) has declined only from an average of 15.4 percent of GNP in 1950-1973 to an average of 14.6 percent of GNP in 1973-1978.[11] This could hardly account for such a sharp drop in the growth of worker productivity. Furthermore, there has been a similar drop in the growth of productivity in all the major industrial nations—including West Germany and Japan—since 1973.[12] The cause appears to be common to all the industrial nations.

It is now recognized in the economics profession that the revolution in energy prices, which began in 1973, has had a profoundly adverse effect on worker productivity. For nearly two centuries the industrial nations have been raising worker productivity by substituting inanimate energy (capital) for human energy. This was induced by a relatively cheap supply of inanimate energy. Since 1973, inanimate energy has become relatively dear, and the capital stock of industrial nations, installed on the basis of cheap energy, has become to a degree obsolete. Managers, now stuck with capital destined to use inanimate energy freely, are seeking to reduce energy input, thus reducing the efficiency of industrial processes. In new investment, they seek machinery and processes that economize on energy rather than labor. In effect, they seek to *substitute labor for energy,* and the inevitable result is lower growth of worker productivity. This effect is common to all the industrial nations, of course. We believe it largely, if not entirely, explains the decline in the growth of labor productivity that is common to all the industrial nations after 1973.

If this analysis is correct, a mere increase in the total saving rate, a major objective of the Reagan proposals, will only slightly stimulate the growth of real output per capita. What is required is a technological revolution corresponding to the energy price revolution that will generate machines and processes that economize on energy and labor simultaneously. Such a revolution may require years of research and development in industry, universities, and government agencies. Perhaps the most useful change in tax policy would be to encourage research and development in industry by allowing the immediate expensing of research and development expenditures—super-accelerated depreciation of basic technological capital.

THE IMPORTANCE OF MONETARY POLICY

In most political discussions of the problem of inflation, emphasis has been placed on fiscal policy—on balancing the budget at the federal level. It is important to move from a large deficit toward a balanced budget as a way to halt inflation, but that will not be sufficient to stop inflation of the magnitude experienced recently in the United States. There are two general reasons for this assertion. First, fiscal policy is a relatively *weak* means of increasing or decreasing aggregate expenditure (demand). Second, monetary policy is a *strong* and independent means of affecting aggregate demand.

To decrease aggregate demand by means of fiscal policy requires a decrease in government spending relative to tax receipts. This means the government runs a smaller deficit or a larger surplus. In either case the government pays out to income recipients (suppliers, employees, and Social Security beneficiaries) relatively less than it takes away from income recipients in the form of taxes. The private sector then has less to spend. But the smaller deficit or the larger surplus means that the government must borrow less or may repay more debt. In either case the government leaves more purchasing power in the hands of the private sector. This effect exactly matches the disposable income effect, so there is no net drain of purchasing power from the private sector.

If we stop here it appears that fiscal policy has no net effect on total aggregate demand, but merely diverts spending from consumption primarily to investment primarily. But we cannot stop there. The decreased need of the government to borrow lowers interest rates in capital markets. With lower interest rates, the wealthy will choose to hold larger money balances rather than securities. So additional lending will not be quite as large as the reduction of consumption. Fiscal policy "works" only because some funds become idled with lower interest rates. This effect is believed to be quite small; hence the conclusion that fiscal policy is relatively weak. It can be strong only if there are secondary effects, such as a fall in the expected rate of return on capital due to the decline in consumption.

But monetary policy is strong. In an inflationary situation a reduction in the rate of growth of the stock of money tends to have a more than proportionate effect on aggregate demand. If people choose to hold the same cash balances relative to income, so that the rate of turnover of money is constant, a reduction in the rate of growth of money reduces aggregate demand proportionately. This tends to reduce the rate of inflation, as aggregate demand grows more slowly relative to aggregate supply, and in time people will come to *expect* a lower rate of inflation. The effect of lower expected inflation is to slow down the rate of turnover of money (the inflation "tax" on money balances is lower), so aggregate demand growth is further reduced. Hence the more than proportionate effect of monetary restraint. This analysis suggests that a slow-down in the growth of money in the United States is both more efficient and necessary if we are to halt inflation through public policy.

Table 7-3. Growth of Money and the Rate of Inflation, United States, 1960-1979.

Year	% Change in Money	Rate of Inflation*	Year	% Change in Money	Rate of Inflation*
1960	0.0	1.8	1970	3.7	5.4
1961	2.1	0.8	1971	6.7	5.0
1962	2.4	1.8	1972	7.1	4.2
1963	3.1	1.4	1973	7.3	5.8
1964	3.9	1.5	1974	4.9	9.4
1965	4.2	2.2	1975	4.6	9.5
1966	4.6	3.4	1976	5.5	5.1
1967	4.0	2.9	1977	7.5	6.0
1968	7.0	4.6	1978	8.2	7.3
1969	6.0	5.0	1979	7.9	8.9

*Percentage change, Gross National Product deflator
SOURCE: U.S., Department of Commerce, *Business Conditions Digest.*

The relation of money growth to inflation is not merely speculative. As Table 7-3 shows, there is a correlation between the rate of growth of money and the rate of inflation in recent years in the United States. As the growth of money has accelerated, so has the rate of inflation. During the period covered by Table 7-3 the rate of turnover of money has risen at about the same rate as real output, due at least partly to inflationary output, so the rate of price increase is very similar to the rate of growth of the stock of money.

There is a popular notion that in an immediate sense inflation is caused by excessive monetary growth, but that the latter is due to fiscal deficits; hence, deficits are the more fundamental cause. This notion is based on the belief that the Federal Reserve System (the Fed) largely or wholly finances the government's deficits, thereby supplying reserves to the banking system that proportionately increase the supply of money. It is true that in a normal year the Federal Reserve System is a

Table 7-4. Change in Net Federal Debt and Government Security Purchases by the Federal Reserve System in the United States, 1960-1979.

(1)	(2)	(3)	(4)
		Federal Reserve	
	Change in net	*System purchases*	
Year	*debt (billions)*	*(billions)*	*(3) as % of (2)*
1960	0.7	0.5	71.4
1961	1.8	0.8	44.4
1962	8.3	2.4	28.9
1963	6.0	2.3	38.3
1964	2.5	2.8	112.0
1965	3.1	4.3	138.7
1966	−0.7	3.1	NC*
1967	−0.9	4.5	NC*
1968	18.0	5.5	30.6
1969	−0.1	1.9	NC*
1970	6.9	3.6	52.2
1971	19.6	7.8	39.8
1972	20.5	5.9	28.8
1973	18.3	3.6	19.7
1974	2.6	4.5	173.0
1975	51.6	4.2	8.1
1976	83.0	9.7	11.7
1977	72.5	10.3	14.2
1978	59.8	10.1	16.9
1979	54.9	7.9	14.3

*Not calculable.
SOURCE: Tax Foundation, Inc., *Facts and Figures on Government Finance.*

net buyer of government securities. This is the Fed's chief means of making the money supply grow. But as Table 7-4 shows, there is no necessary relationship between Fed purchases and concurrent deficits. It is entirely possible to slow down the rate of growth of money to zero or negative values, regardless of the state of the federal government's budget.

It is to be hoped that the Federal Reserve System will exercise more restraint in future. It is doubtful that, in view of the short-run inflationary effect of the Reagan proposals, inflation can be significantly reduced without it.

NOTES

1. The average rate of increase in the money supply was 5.6 percent per year during the Nixon-Ford term and 6.9 percent per year during the Carter administration. The "normal" rate of increase in real GNP is about 3 percent per year.
2. The average rate of increase in nominal wages was 7.1 percent per year during the Nixon-Ford term and 8.2 percent per year during the Carter term. The "normal" rate of increase in output per worker hour is about 2 percent per year.
3. In his speech to the Congress of February 18, 1981, President Reagan proposed that the effective date of the personal tax reduction be July 1, 1981. The indicated reduction for fiscal 1982 would be $44 billion. See Presidential Messages appendix for text of President Reagan's economic messages.
4. The business tax reductions would be retroactive to January 1, 1981. The reduction for fiscal year 1982 would be $9.7 billion, according to Reagan's February 18, 1981 speech.
5. In one of his first acts as president, Reagan abolished price controls on oil. A speed-up of gas decontrol will require congressional action.
6. Robert J. Gordon, Macroeconomics, 2d ed. (Boston: Little, Brown & Co., 1980), p. 63.
7. U.S., Department of Commerce, *Business Conditions Digest,* October 1980.
8. Tax Foundation, Inc., *Facts and Figures on Government Finance,* 1979, p. 99.
9. It may also increase environmental damage, so that we will have traded off environmental amenities for greater real GNP.
10. Gordon, *Macroeconomics,* p. 559.
11. Tax Foundation, *Government Finance,* p. 72.
12. Gordon, *Macroeconomics,* p. 559.

8

The Reagan Victory: Diplomatic and Strategic Policy Implications

Cecil V. Crabb, Jr.

The national election of 1980, in the words of one of Jimmy Carter's public opinion pollsters, constituted a "referendum of unhappiness" by the American people.[1] Characteristically, for a national election in the United States, such pocketbook issues as inflation, unemployment, high taxes, and government spending were at the forefront of voter concern. Even as the hostage crisis in Iran and the Soviet Union's invasion of Afghanistan dominated the headlines, Americans still ranked foreign policy issues low on the list of the nation's most urgent problems.[2]

Despite the traditional American preoccupation with domestic problems, by the early 1980s citizens perhaps were cognizant, more than ever before, that foreign policy questions increasingly had become pocketbook issues. Few Americans needed to be told that another price increase in oil produced by the Organization of Petroleum Exporting Countries (OPEC) directly affected their economic well-being or that their standard of living was dependent upon Japanese-American trade relations. Studies of public sentiment during the months preceding the national election revealed deep misgivings in the electorate about the recent course of events abroad and their nation's response to them.

MAKING AMERICA GREAT AGAIN

Several disturbing events in the late 1970s—the Iranian revolution and seizure of American hostages; the belated discovery of a large Soviet military presence in Cuba, and their massive invasion of Afghanistan— highlighted two facts about the American position abroad that fueled public discontent. One was the evident decline of American power and influence overseas. The other was the equally evident inability of the Carter administration to reverse that process. As they entered a new decade, most Americans found these developments profoundly disturbing. President Theodore Roosevelt had urged the nation to "speak softly, but carry a big stick." By the early 1980s, however, America's "stick is down to a toothpick," as one citizen expressed it.[3] Few Americans were prepared to accept the fact that the three-fold role of their nation since World War II—"world policeman, world banker, and world manager"— had ended permanently. The United States must once again become "a powerful locomotive force in the international system."[4]

Against this background, Ronald Reagan's pledge to "make America great again" was well received. As much as any national election in the United States can accurately be interpreted as a mandate, Ronald Reagan and his advisers had obtained overwhelming public endorsement of that goal. In carrying out that mandate, the Reagan foreign policy team will encounter several basic policy dilemmas. A number of

Reprinted with permission of Chicago Tribune-New York Daily News Syndicate.

specific ones will be identified at a later stage in this chapter. Meanwhile, we may briefly note several of them, applicable to the broad range of American foreign affairs from relations with the Soviet Union to reviving American influence in Latin America.

CONSTRAINTS ON REPUBLICAN DIPLOMACY

The diplomatic efforts of the Reagan administration will be subject to a number of general constraints, among which five seem fundamental and pervasive. First, Republican policymakers will discover that American power in the external environment has declined, in some respects irreversibly. Regardless of which party controls the White House and Congress, it will be more difficult in the 1980s for the United States to work its will abroad, if for no other reason than that there are now some 150 independent nations whose behavior affects American foreign relations, as opposed to approximately one-third as many at the end of World War II. The Reagan White House will also discover that a multipolar global environment is more turbulent and unstable, and less conducive to rational decisionmaking and to external manipulation, than was true in the early postwar era.

Second, at every turn Republican officials will find that it is extremely difficult to translate political rhetoric and ideological pronouncements into viable external policies that promote the diplomatic and security interests of the United States. The transition, for example, from Democratic leadership under President Truman to Republican leadership under President Eisenhower produced very few fundamental changes in American foreign policy. Richard Nixon's electoral victory in 1968 did little to change the direction of American foreign policy toward most regions and global issues. The most remarkable fact about post-World War II American foreign policy perhaps is its *basic continuity,* irrespective of which political party controls the White House.

A third general constraint upon the diplomacy of the Reagan administration was highlighted by the discussion in Chapter 7: the disparity between its internal and external objectives. How will Reagan's attempt to "make American great again"—requiring, for example, a substantial increase in national defense spending—harmonize with his pledges to reduce government spending, to lower taxes, to balance the budget, and to cure (or at least limit) inflation? Republican officials have offered little more than vague assurances that such contradictions can be resolved, without indicating how they propose to do so. To cite but a single example: soon after Reagan entered the White House, his budget director called for massive reductions in American foreign aid. To foreign leaders, this was not likely to be construed as evidence that America was "great again." [5]

In the fourth place, the Reagan foreign policy team will assuredly discover in the months ahead that its resounding public mandate contains elements of ambiguity, instability, and unpredictability. Ronald Reagan's electoral victory may well have indicated that the American people were more united about their nation's role in global affairs that at any time since the war in Vietnam. In that sense, the long-missing consensus that had been lacking in American public opinion may now be substantially restored. Yet this consensus is fragile and marked by troublesome anomalies. What the American people are *against,* for example—the mistreatment of American hostages in Iran and elsewhere, the Soviet attempt to subjugate Afghanistan, or Castro's efforts to export revolution throughout Latin America—is much clearer than what they are *for* in the diplomatic field. While a majority of citizens wants the Reagan administration to "make America great again," it is doubtful that anything more than a small minority of the people has seriously considered the financial costs of doing so. Nor do most citizens have an overly clear conception of how greatness can be restored in relations with other countries. The Reagan electoral mandate may mean one thing above all: Americans want a different and successful foreign policy, and they will largely leave the responsibility to the president and his advisers for producing it. A certain utopian quality about Reagan's public mandate could prove troublesome in the months ahead, as his administration confronts a number of hard realities abroad.[6]

Finally, as Thomas L. Hughes has cautioned, the Reagan administration must resist the temptation to "mistake a defense buildup for a foreign policy" or to "summon up a national will for imprecise ends." [7] Two elements that are fundamental for diplomatic success are reasonably clear foreign policy goals and sufficient and varied power to achieve them. It would not be unwarranted to say that since the Vietnam War, American foreign policy has been deficient on both of these counts. Republican officials have left no doubt that they intend to enhance U.S. global power, particularly military power. Thus far, they are less clear about the objectives for which this improved power position will be used. President Reagan and his aides have not provided a clear rationale or set of guiding principles governing the application of American power abroad. Until they do, their success in attaining their announced diplomatic objectives is likely to be very limited.

ENDING "THE WAR OF THE STATE DEPARTMENTS"

During a campaign speeches dealing with foreign policy issues, Ronald Reagan declared:

The present Administration has been unable to speak with one voice in foreign policy. This must change. My administration will restore leadership to U.S. foreign policy by organizing it in a more coherent way.[8]

Earlier chief executives have pledged to impose unity upon the foreign policy process and to restore the State Department to a position of primacy in dealing with external issues. Under President Carter, for example, Secretary of State Cyrus Vance believed that he had been designated as the president's chief foreign policy spokesman, but ultimately, Vance resigned following White House failure to consult with him in the ill-fated attempt to rescue the American hostages in Tehran. This was but one dramatic example of what appeared to be a kind of endemic disunity and paralysis in the executive branch, which is discussd more fully in Chapter 3. Vance's problem led Alexander Haig, President Reagan's secretary of state, to say that a leading goal of Republican officials would be "to end the paralyzing conflict between [the State Department] and separate advisers of the White House, all too given in the past to reckless kibitzing, if not sabotage" of the president's announced policies.[9]

Yet even before he had entered the Oval Office, Ronald Reagan discovered that the problem was deep-seated and that its existence could be attributed to something more than President Carter's style as chief executive. The newly appointed secretary of agriculture, John R. Block, stated publicly that the United States should consider using its food surplus as a diplomatic weapon, implying that the United States might make food available to other countries, depending upon their diplomatic behavior.[10] Other Reagan officials, however, quickly explained that Block's viewpoints did not necessarily represent those of the president and his foreign policy advisers. A few weeks later, Secretary Haig also publicly questioned the foreign aid reductions called for by the director of the Office of Management and Budget.

These are merely recent examples of what a former official of the Carter administration called "the war of the State Departments," or the urge of nearly every executive agency to participate in foreign policy decisionmaking, often eclipsing the once preeminent position of the State Department.[11] The problem, which has become increasingly serious since the 1960s, has multiple origins. One of these is the fact that the line between domestic policy and foreign policy has become all but impossible to draw. More than at any time in American history, developments abroad impinge upon the nation's internal well-being and future. Conversely, domestic policy decisions involving levels of taxation, size of the federal deficit, or deregulation of the petroleum industry crucially affect the influence and policies of the United States overseas.

Another factor engendering the war of the State Departments has been the weakening of the presidential office throughout most of the 1970s. As long as fears of the "imperial presidency" dominated public and congressional attitudes, the authority of the chief executive over his own subordinates was weakened; and executive officials were often encouraged by their allies on Capitol Hill to adopt positions different from those of the White House.

We have already alluded to another condition fostering disunity within the executive branch: the lack of a public consensus on foreign policy objectives since the war in Vietnam. In some measure, the dissonance coming from the executive branch in recent years was merely reflective of a much deeper underlying public confusion and uncertainty about the nation's proper role in international affairs after the trauma of Vietnam. Until that war, a public consensus served as the foundation for American foreign policy. Substantial agreement existed among the American people and their leaders concerning two pivotal aspects of the dominant challenge facing the United States abroad: the nature and source of the threat to the United States overseas, in the form of expansive communism; and the nature of the U.S. response, in the form of the containment strategy. If the election of Ronald Reagan, accompanied by Republican control of the Senate, signified that once again Americans were deeply concerned about the Soviet threat, considerable uncertainty still existed in the public mind about how it could most effectively be met and about America's responsibility for doing so.[12]

REVIVING THE CONCEPT OF BIPARTISANSHIP

A different, but no less troublesome, development engendering disunity within the foreign policy process has been the conflict between the executive and legislative branches in dealing with external problems. During the 1970s, that problem became more acute than at any time since World War II. Jimmy Carter's apparent inability to manage Congress, and to work effectively with it, significantly eroded public confidence in his leadership ability. By contrast, Ronald Reagan and his supporters have called for the revival of a bipartisanship approach to foreign policy; and they have promised to consult regularly with legislative leaders on major diplomatic issues.[13]

The concept that "politics stops at the water's edge" is an emotive and almost universally popular idea. In Chapter 4, for example, it was pointed out that Democrats most likely will seek to cooperate with the White House in solving many national problems. Yet as postwar diplomatic experience has repeatedly demonstrated, the principle of bipartisanship is easier to assert than to apply in a manner acceptable to the principal executive and legislative agencies involved in foreign policy decisionmaking. The complexities of the problem are highlighted by the demand, expressed repeatedly on Capitol Hill, that Congress be treated as a partner in the foreign policy process.

Yet under the American constitutional system, this demand creates genuine dilemmas for the president, no matter how much the White House may desire bipartisanship in the foreign policy sphere. If the demand is acceded to, for example, the chief executive in effect risks turning over the responsibility for the management of foreign relations to Congress, thereby making the U.S. government a modified parliamentary system, in which the executive derives its support and authority from the legislature. Moreover, if the experience of the 1970s is indicative, Congress never has been more disunified internally, less subject to party leadership, and less prepared to speak with a clear and coherent voice in foreign policy than it is today. Among the three principal branches of the American government, Congress continues to rank lowest in public confidence and esteem.[14] Many of the causes of this disunity within Congress are identified more fully in Chapters 4 and 5.

On the other hand, if the Reagan White House does not consult Congress in key foreign policy decisions, it will assuredly be accused of a hypocritical and merely rhetorical dedication to bipartisanship. Democrats, accompanied perhaps by some members of Reagan's own party, can be counted on to join in the complaint.

The Reagan administration's approach to this problem is likely to emphasize two main elements. First, it will try to work more effectively with Congress than did the Carter administration. Second, it will adhere to the principle that the chief executive has ultimate responsibility under the Constitution for decisions in the diplomatic field.

IMPROVING THE AMERICAN DEFENSE POSTURE

During his presidential campaign, Ronald Reagan reiterated his conviction that the United States could only achieve "peace through strength." In his view:

> Peace is *made* by the fact of strength, economic, military and strategic. Peace is *lost* when such strength disappears, or just as bad, is seen by an adversary as disappearing.[15]

A major goal of the Reagan administration, therefore, was the creation of a strong America and a strong military.

Reagan's view on the necessity of improving the American military position derived from a two-fold conviction that the power of the United States vis-a-vis the Soviet Union had deteriorated significantly since the war in Vietnam, and that this tendency could and must be reversed. Ronald Reagan and his supporters thus rejected the notion that the decline of American power was inevitable or irreversible. Nor did they believe that Soviet superiority in some categories of armed strength had to be accepted as a permanent phenomenon. Indeed, by his decision to cut real defense spending, his unwillingness to develop new weapons such as the B-1 Bomber or the neutron bomb, and his uncritical endorsement of détente, President Carter had contributed to the military imbalance of the 1980s. In Reagan's view, the SALT II arms limitation agreements, withdrawn from Senate consideration by Jimmy Carter in the face of mounting opposition, merely perpetuated the Soviet military advantage.

For Republican officials, another aspect of the Soviet-American military rivalry had profoundly disturbing implications The Reagan foreign policy team did not believe, as President Carter had suggested early in his term, that Americans had an unwarranted or an "inordinate fear of Communism." To the contrary, events during the late 1970s indicated that the apprehensions of the American people about Soviet expansionism and interventionism were amply justified by actual or potential Soviet moves. In the Persian Gulf area, Poland, Latin America, and other settings, the Kremlin demonstrated its readiness to use its military arsenal.

Nor were President Reagan and his foreign policy advisers optimistic about the future of Soviet-American relations. An earlier period of Russian history was known as the "time of troubles," and in the view of many competent authorities, Soviet-American relations will almost certainly enter a new troubled period in the years ahead. As the Communist hierarchy encounters mounting internal problems, such as continuing food deficits, lack of high-technology equipment, increasingly acute energy and labor shortages, and ongoing political dissidence, many commentators believe that Soviet diplomatic behavior will become more externally aggressive and unpredictable than in the recent past. Under these conditions, America must be unusually vigilant, since "the bear strikes hardest when it is wounded." [16]

Republican officials were also genuinely concerned about another aspect of America's power: a pervasive belief outside the United States that American power had declined, and that during the 1980s the disparity would continue to widen in Moscow's favor. Several Asian leaders, for example, urged Washington to redress the military balance, before a number of smaller countries concluded that a *Pax Sovietica* was inevitable and adjusted their policies accordingly. For many purposes, the objective facts about the Soviet-American military equation were less important than existing perceptions about them; and countries throughout the world saw Soviet power rapidly eclipsing American power.[17]

These impressions, of course, were not unrelated to facts about the Soviet-American arms equation. By the end of 1980, for example, the Soviet Union and its Warsaw Pact allies were superior to the United States and its partners in the North Atlantic Treaty Organization (NATO) in several key categories of armed strength—such as long-range and intermediate-range missiles, military manpower, combat-ready and reserve divisions, tanks and artillery, and nuclear-missile submarines. (In certain other categories—such as the number of nuclear warheads in their arsenals, strategic bombers, combat aircraft, aircraft carriers, and destroyers—the Western powers either possessed superiority over, or equality with, their Communist adversaries.) For Western defense strategists, however, perhaps the most disturbing tendency during the past decade or so has been the steady increase in Soviet defense spending.[18] Even after the increases in the national defense budget recommended by the Carter administration during its closing weeks in office, as a percentage of America's Gross National Product (GNP), the rate of defense spending in the United States remained only approximately half of that in the Soviet Union.[19]

Republican officials were determined, therefore, to narrow the military gap between the United States and the Soviet Union and to convince the Kremlin that it could not gain a position of permanent military superiority. In effect, Moscow would be presented with a painful choice: either settle for a condition of approximate military parity with the United States (ratified in a new series of strategic arms control agreements acceptable to both sides), or engage in a new round of military competition with the United States that, Republican officials were convinced, Moscow could not possibly win.

To enhance the American military position, Republican officials would depend upon several specific measures. President Carter recommended during his last weeks in office that national defense spending be raised to a level of almost $200 billion for fiscal year 1982, an increase of 14.5 percent over the previous year. The Reagan administration promptly pushed the Pentagon's budget to the $220 billion annual level, and some estimates projected that it could reach $300 to $330 billion by 1985.[20] It also proposed to revive or reactivate certain weapon systems that had been cancelled or postponed by President Carter. These included: a modified MX missile system, a new version of the B-1 Bomber (or perhaps an even more advanced "stealth" bomber capable of eluding enemy radar), and revival of the neutron bomb and its possible integration into NATO defense.

Yet, as American officials were aware, an essential step in strengthening the American military arsenal lay in ending the critical personnel

shortage that existed throughout the armed forces. Solving this problem—without violating his campaign pledges—might prove to be the
most serious challenge to President Reagan's military policy. Ronald
Reagan opposed the system of national registration introduced by his
predecessor; nor did he favor a reintroduction of the draft. In his view,
improved military pay scales, along with liberalized allowances and
benefits, would largely alleviate the problem. Yet it seemed question-
able whether Republican policymakers had fully calculated the costs
this approach would entail and the degree to which this could be
reconciled with their strong determination to reduce overall government
spending.

If a global perception exists that American power declined during
the 1970s, this conviction may have stemmed less from a belief that the
United States lacked adequate power, than from doubts that American
officials would use the power at their disposal for diplomatic ends.
Deterred by the fear of becoming involved in "another Vietnam," and by
popular and congressional suspicions of executive power, Presidents
Nixon, Ford, and Carter were often reluctant to apply American
military force overseas. In some instances—when the Carter administration tried to free the American hostages in Iran, for example—executive
officials never discovered how to use the power of the United States
effectively. The Reagan administration will find this challenge no less
baffling and difficult.

Almost a decade after the war in Vietnam, the parameters of
American policy concerning the use of power (and specifically, armed
force) abroad seems clear enough. In the post-Vietnam era, the American people expect the president to avoid two diplomatic extremes: the
indiscriminate interventionism or "policeman of the world" mentality
that led to the Vietnam quagmire; and the ultracautious, vacillating
restraint—often giving the impression of timidity and weakness—
characteristic of Carter's approach to external problems. Between these
two extremes is a course that might be called "selective interventionism" or "pragmatic interventionism." While this approach avoids the
extremes of isolationism and indiscriminate interventionism, it leaves a
number of fundamental questions unanswered. What criteria or principles, for example, should hereafter govern the extension of American
power to affect the course of events? How will a policy of selective
interventionism enhance the predictability and constancy of American
foreign policy (qualities many critics believed were conspicuously absent
during the Carter administration)? To mention another problem we
shall discuss more fully at a later stage in this chapter, will the NATO
allies have a voice in determining when the United States applies it
power abroad? Thus far, officials for the Reagan administration have
supplied few answers to these questions. Until they furnish a somewhat

more comprehensive and coherent rationale for the use of American power throughout the international system, their efforts to improve the effectiveness of American diplomacy are likely to be only moderately successful.[21]

DÉTENTE IN THE 1980s

For several years, Soviet-American relations have been described by the term détente—a multifaceted concept that continues to elicit sharp disagreement on both sides of the Iron Curtain regarding its essential meaning and major implications.[22] In essence, détente means that in some aspects of their relationship, at least, the super powers can avoid cold war confrontations and that they can cooperate on some issues to their mutual advantage.[23]

The Republican electoral victory of 1980 places the future of détente in greater jeopardy than has been the case for perhaps two decades. Reagan and other Republican officials have contended that the benefits from détente have accrued mainly to the Soviet Union, which has acquired a new and formidable power base from which to launch expansionist moves threatening the security and well-being of the United States and its allies.

Differing American and Soviet conceptions of détente are illustrated by the concept of "linkage," which President Reagan and his advisers have said is an indispensable part of détente. On innumerable occasions, President Reagan, Secretary Haig, and other Republican officials have expressed their conviction that Soviet avowals of devotion to détente must be matched by (or linked with) Soviet actions to promote the cause of global peace and security. In the Republican view, the Kremlin cannot expect Western assistance (in the form of advanced computer technology or modern oil-drilling equipment, for example) in developing its internal resources, while it is jeopardizing the security of the Persian Gulf area or threatening a massive military invasion of Poland. Moscow cannot simultaneously call for a "relaxation of tensions" with the United States, while it is inflaming tensions in East Africa or the Caribbean.[24]

By emphasizing the concept of linkage in détente, the Reagan administration confronts the Kremlin with a painful choice. If the Soviet hierarchy rejects the concept of linkage, as it consistently has done in the past, it may anticipate a serious deterioration in Soviet-American relations, accompaned by an intensive effort to enhance the military power of the United States. By contrast, if it accepts the idea that linkage is vital to the meaning of détente, the United States may count upon less expansive Soviet behavior in the Middle East, East

Africa, and Eastern Europe. This will, in turn, permit a genuine relaxation of Soviet-American tensions, paving the way for a new effort to reduce strategic armaments and to arrive at other forms of cooperation between the super powers.

Which alternative will the Kremlin choose? At this stage, the evidence permits no clear-cut answer. The Reagan administration expects that Soviet officials, in time, will conclude that their best interests are served by acknowledging the legitimacy of linkage, thereby limiting their expansionist impulses in the interests of a more stable international system and of gains on the Soviet home front.

Yet, as we observed earlier, in the years ahead the Communist hierarchy in the U.S.S.R. may become less influenced by such rational policy calculations and more impelled by internal political and economic forces to pursue adventuristic policies abroad than was the case during the 1970s. Most fundamentally, perhaps, Moscow's acceptance of the notion that linkage is crucial to successful détente would require drastic changes in Soviet external behavior in the Persian Gulf area or East Africa. The Kremlin cannot make these changes without incurring dramatic diplomatic reverses and a massive decline in its credibility as a super power. Under these circumstances, the prospects for détente do not appear promising; agreement between Washington and Moscow over its essential meaning appears extremely remote.

UNITY AND DISUNITY IN NATO

Ronald Reagan's appointment of the former NATO commander, General Alexander Haig, as his secretary of state underscores one of the chief elements in the continuity of post-World War II American foreign policy. For the Reagan White House, as for every administration for the past generation, Western Europe continues to serve as what General Haig called the "fulcrum" of American foreign policy. The United States abandoned its isolationism after World War II because of the Communist threat to Western Europe and the adjacent Mediterranean area; today, the security of the United States remains inextricably connected to the destiny of its European allies.[25]

Yet, when Republican policymakers turn their attention to European-American relations, they will confront a familiar phenomenon: "disarray," or a condition of recurrent disunity on important diplomatic issues, continues to weaken the cohesion and influence of Western alliance. Indeed, disarray may be an even more serious problem now than a decade ago, with little hope that its underlying causes can be easily eliminated.

Internal disunity has been a feature of NATO since the alliance was created in 1949. In the intervening years, the member nations of NATO have experienced notable success in substantially reducing two ominous threats to European security and political stability. One of these is the danger of an overt Soviet military threat to the NATO area. That risk seems less menacing today than at any time since World War II—and this fact goes far toward accounting for the internal political disunity characterizing NATO decisionmaking. As has been characteristic of military alliances throughout history, as the perceived danger has receded, the tendency of the NATO partners to exert their diplomatic independence has correspondingly increased. The other risk—that Communist movements within key Western European countries could become the dominant political force—has also substantially diminished over the past decade. Today, European communism no longer causes anxiety to policymakers in Washington. Conversely, Europe's vulnerability from another source—the possibility that the region will be denied access to Middle East oil supplies—has dramatically increased.

A trio of specific problems in European-American relations will preoccupy the Reagan foreign policy team. One is the corollary of a problem we identified earlier: the military imbalance between the American and the Soviet alliance systems.[26] On the European front, the Warsaw Pact nations have improved their military capabilities vis-à-vis the NATO forces, and at the level of defense spending existing at the end of the 1970s, this disparity was expected to widen in Moscow's favor. For several years, American officials have been concerned about the implications of this imbalance; they have urged the NATO allies to increase their defense efforts to strengthen NATO's defensive position. Under the Carter administration, for example, Secretary of Defense Harold Brown asked the NATO partners "to behave as if their military security is as important to them as it is to us." [27] Republican leaders have been no less pointed in urging the allies to expand their contribution to the common defense effort. By the beginning of the 1980s, as the Warsaw Pact forces threatened to invade Poland early in 1981, the disparity between the military strength of the Western and Communist positions in Europe continued to engender deep concern in Western capitals.

Yet prospects of a substantial increase in defense expenditures by the NATO countries do not appear encouraging. In the allied view, the European members of NATO increased the level of their defense spending during the 1970s more rapidly than the United States. Nearly all the members of NATO are experiencing internal economic problems and dislocations. Great Britain is gripped by perhaps the most acute economic crisis in its modern history. West Germany fears the implications of an expanded defense budget, both upon its own financial stability and upon the continuation of détente between the United States and the Soviet Union.

The Reagan administration also confronts the question of extending the orbit of NATO outside Europe, specifically to the vulnerable Persian Gulf area. This is essentially a new version of an old problem engendering disunity within the Western alliance. Washington has experienced minimal success in persuading its allies to support its policies in Southeast Asia and the Middle East. The Carter administration, for example, was unable to muster unified NATO support for its effort to implement the "Carter Doctrine," directed at preserving the security of the Persian Gulf area after the Soviet invasion of Afghanistan. On these and other issues in the Middle East—such as the resolution of the Arab-Israeli conflict and the war between Iran and Iraq—it has proved virtually impossible to formulate a common NATO strategy. Nor is it likely that a unified NATO approach to such questions will be found in the near future. Recent discussions among France, Germany, and the Soviet Union on the future of détente underscored Europe's diplomatic restiveness and tendency toward greater independence from its powerful American ally.[28]

In the view of the NATO partners, Washington's failure to consult with them in formulating policy is at the root of the ongoing disarray within NATO. The Reagan administration must deal with this complaint, if it is to impart greater cohesion to the Western alliance. Since 1949, the NATO allies repeatedly have complained that they were expected to approve and support diplomatic decisions—subsequently viewed in Washington as NATO policies—when they had no voice in the determination of these policies. Many European leaders believe that this problem reveals a deep-seated ambivalence in the United States about the role and utility of the Western alliance. The United States routinely seeks the support of its allies, most recently for its strategy in the Persian Gulf area. At the same time, however, it has been consistently unwilling to treat its European allies as partners by soliciting their viewpoints in advance and by giving them a meaningful role in formulating policy on questions directly affecting their interests.

Consulting with the members of NATO, however, may prove more difficult for the Reagan administration than for its predecessors. One reason is that intra-European differences in point of view are becoming sharper. Since the first Arab oil boycott in 1967, for example, the Western allies have disagreed among themselves about the best response. Thus far, the existence of supranational institutions, such as the European Economic Community, has done little to mitigate these differences. Although American foreign policy under the Reagan-Haig team no doubt will continue to be strongly Europe-oriented, the paramount reality that has impeded consultation among the allies in the past will remain. For the reality is that, in terms of the military contribution of its members, NATO has always been, and it remains today, an inherently unequal partnership. If most of the planned expansion in American military power envisioned by the Reagan administration is carried out, NATO is likely to become an even more unequal military coalition in the future than it was in the past.

THE MIDDLE EASTERN VORTEX

One of the most dramatic and far-reaching changes in American foreign policy since World War II has been the emergence of the United States as a Middle Eastern power. Until the Battle of North Africa during World War II, most Americans neither knew nor cared about developments in that region. Yet when, on January 24, 1980, President Jimmy Carter declared the preservation of the security of the Persian Gulf area to be a vital interest of the United States, few Americans needed reminding that their economic well-being and their military security were directly affected by the events in that oil-rich, if politically unstable, area. Remarkably, less than a decade after America's traumatic involvement in the war in Vietnam, Carter's statement—followed by the creation of a Rapid Deployment Force and other measures to implement it—caused hardly a ripple of public or congressional opposition.[29] The reason was perhaps evident: by the 1980s, millions of Americans knew that their welfare was involved in the security of the Persian Gulf region in a way they had never discerned in their earlier involvement in Southeast Asia.

Through a series of major and minor steps—from pressuring Moscow to withdraw its forces from Iran and to bolstering the security of Turkey in the early postwar era, to the shuttle diplomacy of Henry Kissinger and the Camp David peace agreements of Jimmy Carter—the United States has expanded its involvement and presence in Middle Eastern affairs. It would be no exaggeration to say that today both its friends and its adversaries in the area have now accepted this fact and derive certain benefits from it. For countries such as Israel, Egypt, Jordan, and Saudi Arabia, the United States remains an important source of military, economic, and diplomatic support and an essential counterweight to Soviet influence. Even for vocally anti-American countries, however, an active American role in the Middle East is not without advantages—if only because it supplies them with a visible external threat (called "the Great Satan" by the Ayatollah Khomeini's regime in Iran) that is useful in promoting internal unity and national cohesion.

The Reagan administration will almost certainly preserve the basic continuity of American foreign policy in the Middle East and significantly expand American involvement there. President Reagan and his advisers have repeatedly indicated their firm support for Israel and their intention of preserving America's traditionally close ties with it. They have also endorsed the recently concluded peace agreements between Israel and Egypt and called for a renewal of efforts to seek a negotiated settlement of the unresolved controversies dividing Israel and its Arab neighbors.[30]

Republican policymakers have been outspokenly critical of Soviet expansionism in Afghanistan, and they have cautioned Moscow against new attempts to penetrate the Persian Gulf area. Under Reagan's leadership, the Rapid Deployment Force is being equipped and trained for possible use in the area, a move that requires the United States to acquire supply and base facilities in the Persian Gulf region. Reagan administration officials have echoed President Carter's insistence that the allies join the United States in preserving the security of this vulnerable region. If they do not sufficiently understand the fact already, Soviet officials have been reminded that the United States has vital interests in the Middle East—particularly in the Persian Gulf area—that it can and will defend.

Difficult as it was, Jimmy Carter's determined and prolonged effort to conclude an Israeli and Egyptian peace settlement was easier than the challenge now facing Republican officials. The Middle East never before has been as fragmented and torn by mutual suspicions and antagonisms as it is today. One regional conflict (such as that between Iran and Iraq) engenders new hostilities (such as acute tensions between Jordan and Syria). Proponents of the same political movement—the Ba'ath party in Iraq and Syria—remain mortal enemies. Saudi Arabia, Kuwait, and the smaller Persian Gulf states fear both the continuation and the outcome of the Iraqi-Iranian war. The Palestine Liberation Organization, which comprises several more or less autonomous organizations, continues to rely upon terrorism in opposing the Zionist enemy, along with several Arab governments deemed friendly to it.

In this highly unstable and dangerous environment, the Reagan administration will need to exhibit a high degree of diplomatic skill, discrimination, and patience. After the release of the American hostages held in Tehran, the new era in Iranian-American relations can only prove a demanding test of diplomatic acumen. No doubt for a period of several months, in the "cooling off period," relations between the two countries will be conditioned by mutual recriminations and grievances. The Reagan administration generally has indicated that it intends to honor the agreements negotiated by Carter in obtaining the freedom of the hostages. Given the recent history of Iranian-American relations, perhaps the most crucial understanding contained in them—a pledge by the United States not to intervene in the Iranian political process—is one that the Reagan administration will be strongly inclined to observe.

In view of its poor showing in the war against the Iraqi invader, and of its deteriorating economic conditions, in the not too distant future Iran almost certainly will seek to normalize its relations with the United States. Without assistance and trade from the United States and other Western nations, Tehran faces a humiliating military defeat and internal collapse. Without help from the United States or other sources, the Iranian oil industry will remain in a state of devastation.

In this new phase of Iranian-American relations, two possible pitfalls lie in the path of the Reagan administration. One pitfall is the danger of once again becoming responsible for the success or failure of the Iranian government. For even with possible assistance from the United States, Iran's future is uncertain, at best. The other pitfall is that the Reagan administration's failure to be at least minimally receptive to Iran's needs would have ominous consequences—such as triggering a new anti-American eruption within Iran and among supporters of its revolution; weakening of the regime of the Ayatollah Khomeini, perhaps fatally; hastening the internal disintegration of Iran; and possibly opening the door to enhanced Soviet influence.

Elsewhere in the Persian Gulf, efforts to bolster the security of adjacent states—by acquiring bases and depots for the Rapid Deployment Force and by augmenting American naval power in the area—will also have significant political consequences. Even friendly governments, such as President Sadat's regime in Egypt, are clearly uneasy about jeopardizing their position of nonalignment and aggravating intraregional tensions through overt military collaboration with the United States. The American military buildup in the Persian Gulf also poses difficult choices for Saudi Arabia, where the long-dominant position of the ruling Saudi family has become increasingly precarious. Overly close identification with the United States might create new political turbulence within that key Middle Eastern country.[31]

In actively attempting to contain Soviet expansionism on the eastern flank of the Persian Gulf, the Reagan administration will encounter the same opposition from Pakistan that the Carter White House had faced. The Reagan administration is unlikely to expand aid to Pakistan significantly. At the same time, Republican policymakers probably will be less restrained than their Democratic predecessors in increasing covert American assistance to the Afghan rebels, possibly through third parties such as the People's Republic of China.

"LOW PROFILE" IN SUB-SAHARAN AFRICA

Since the late 1950s—when most of the nations of black Africa acquired their independence—American policy toward the region has been governed by the principle of "low profile." That reality is not likely to change during the Reagan administration. To African leaders, America's limited involvement in the affairs of that continent suggested indifference and neglect by Washington toward their pressing internal problems.[32] The Carter administration's highly publicized efforts to identify with the aspirations of these nations produced no fundamental changes in African attitudes toward the United States. Indeed, since its diplomatic rhetoric was seldom matched by decisive policies, the influence of the United States in the region may have been impaired.

A graphic illustration of Africa's relatively low priority on the American diplomatic scale was provided in 1975, when Congress prohibited the Ford administration from intervening to prevent a Communist takeover (or de facto control) of Angola. Despite this fact, in the years that followed, Soviet and Cuban officials experienced considerable difficulty manipulating African nationalist groups for their own ends. The Soviet-Cuban venture into Angola has not paid the dividends that Moscow and Havana have expected; in this setting and elsewhere on the continent, African opposition to external Communist intervention has often been intense.[33]

Two potential areas of conflict are likely to be at the forefront of the Reagan administration's African diplomacy. First, strife continues in East Africa, centering upon Ethiopia, whose Soviet-backed government confronts an insurgency in its Ogaden province and conflict waged by Somalian rebels in the south. Supported by its Soviet and Cuban allies, the Ethiopian government thus far has been unable to impose its authority effectively upon its rebellious provinces. The strategic importance of East Africa for the United States and its allies, however, has been enhanced by the Soviet invasion of Afghanistan, along with the Iraqi-Iranian war. The Carter administration negotiated an agreement with Somalia permitting American use of the key port of Berbera, which was greatly expanded and modernized during an early stage of Soviet friendship with Somalia. In return, Washington promised to increase moderately American assistance to Somalia, whose officials will undoubtedly renew their requests for military assistance to the Reagan White House. Republican policymakers will remain wary of efforts to draw the United States more deeply into the East African quagmire, regardless of their desire to contain Communist influence there.[34]

The other dominant African question has been, and remains, one of the most difficult and frustrating problems confronting the United States abroad. Yet it is also the test by which black African states measure the interest of other countries in their problems and their future. This is the racial conflict in southern Africa epitomized by the apartheid system in South Africa. Despite efforts by black nationalist groups, often with the support of the United States and other foreign countries, no appreciable change has occurred in the apartheid regime of South Africa. Some commentators believe that, if anything, it has become more oppressive and less susceptible to change with the passage of time.

More than any other single foreign policy issue, perhaps, the racial question in southern Africa will highlight a crucial difference between the diplomatic styles of Carter and Reagan. Africans, for example, widely anticipate that the Reagan White House will abandon America's commitment to the cause of international human rights, subordinating this ideal to strategic and other American objectives.[35] The campaign statements of Ronald Reagan and other Republican candidates on the subject of international human rights lend considerable credence to this belief. At the same time, Reagan and his supporters contend that their position on the human rights question is often misunderstood and misrepresented. Their doubts on the subject stem not from a lack of commitment to the ideal, either for Americans or other peoples. Rather, they stem from skepticism about whether it actually lies within the power of the United States to promote the cause of human rights in foreign countries—and, if not, whether the attempt to do so would have more negative than positive results. Moreover, Republicans believe that pro-human rights groups display an unjustifiable ambivalence in their approach to the subject. They direct accusations of human rights violations against right-wing regimes while ignoring violations committed by left-wing governments and revolutionary groups. Moreover, as our subsequent discussion of Latin America will indicate, experience has shown that an American-supported crusade for international human rights sometimes has effects totally contrary to the diplomatic interests of the United States and counterproductive to the cause of human rights. The United States, as Alexander Haig declared before the election, should not engage in conduct under the rubric of human rights that, in effect, drives "authoritarian regimes, traditionally friendly to the West, into totalitarian models where they will remain in a state of permanent animosity to the American people and our interests."[36]

In the setting of southern Africa, President Reagan and his foreign policy aides will have basically the same options that have been available to American officials for the past generation. They can ignore the racial conflict in Africa—perhaps on the grounds that apartheid is not properly a matter of international concern, or because it does not lie within the power of the United States to change the system fundamentally. If they adopt this course, the results will be predictable: United States influence on the African scene will continue to decline and Soviet and Cuban forces will spearhead the liberation of Africa from racial oppression.

Alternatively, the Reagan White House may take the course long urged by black African governments, African nationalist movements, and their supporters. The United States can lead an international campaign to confront the government of South Africa, in an effort to compel changes in its oppressive apartheid system. In the short run, more than any other course, this decision would win immediate good will for the United States throughout black Africa; it would undermine the appeal of communism within the region.

Other considerations, however, make this course less attractive. The ideological propensities of most Republican policymakers are strongly contrary to this approach. Moreover, to be successful, such a campaign would require a series of highly coordinated measures—ranging from moral censure, to economic boycotts, to the possible use of military forces against South Africa—designed to alter the fundamental nature of South African society. Such actions would introduce a new source of disunity within the NATO alliance and seriously weaken America's ability to defend the strategic Persian Gulf area. Most crucially perhaps, there is no guarantee that the goal would be achieved. If that campaign failed (or if, after a prolonged period, it were abandoned because of a lack of public support within the United States), the results would predictably be widespread African disillusionment toward the United States and pervasive doubt about the credibility of American foreign policy.

Not infrequently, foreign policy is an exercise in choosing the least unpalatable alternative. That principle is likely to govern the Reagan administration's approach to the African racial issue. Under Republican management the United States is likely to adopt a middle-of-the-road approach to the problem, consisting of several elements: American ideological support for the principle of racial equality in Africa and other regions; reliance upon persuasion and diplomacy directed at inducing changes in South African society acceptable to whites, blacks, and other ethnic minorities; and efforts to persuade anti-South African groups to moderate their demands in the interest of an enduring resolution of the problem.

Although conditions in the two societies are admittedly different, Republican policy toward South Africa is likely to emphasize the same principle that finally produced a new black government in Zimbabwe (formerly Southern Rhodesia): any agreement reached producing change in South Africa must be at least minimally acceptable to all parties to the controversy. This approach will not win plaudits for the United States among black African societies. But it will likely appeal to the Reagan administration for the compelling reason that it offers fewer drawbacks for American policy in Africa than any available alternative.[37]

THE CHANGING AMERICAN POSITION IN ASIA

Despite widespread expectations to the contrary, the United States did not withdraw from Asia after the war in Vietnam. As in the past, it remained keenly interested in Asian developments; and the security and diplomatic interests of the United States were directly affected by them. According to some views, the Carter administration's most outstanding diplomatic achievement was the restoration of normal relations between the United States and the People's Republic of China (PRC). This laid the basis for a new, and perhaps even stronger, American position in Asia.

Initiated by the Nixon administration, the rapprochement between the United States and mainland China was an historic turning point in post-World War II American diplomacy. Among its many far-reaching implications, it was a major diplomatic setback for the Soviet Union. The Soviet hierarchy now was forced to consider the ominous possibility that in any future conflict with the United States, Moscow would be compeled to fight a "two-front war" against NATO in the west and China in the east. Some authorities, such as George F. Kennan, have said that these and other anxieties about the security of Soviet borders accounted for the incursion into Afghanistan and for the ongoing Soviet military buildup.[38]

By the early 1980s relations between the United States and the PRC were more cordial and constructive than any time since 1949 when the Communists first came to power in mainland China. Peking looked to Washington as a major source of assistance in carrying out its "four modernizations," designed to improve conditions in what was still one of the world's poorest societies. Business groups within the United States eagerly anticipated the opportunities awaiting them in "the China market." With the Chinese population approximating one billion people, the sale of one bottle of Coca-Cola or one package of American cigarettes to every Chinese adult would yield substantial profits to American entrepreneurs. Yet, as in the past, Americans underestimated the barriers in the path of a vastly expanded Sino-American trade. Unless the United States and other countries provided extensive credits to Peking—or unless the PRC was willing to finance foreign purchases with its expanding petroleum output—China would be hard-pressed to acquire the foreign exchange needed to increase its imports significantly.[39]

Presidential candidate Ronald Reagan and other Republicans did not conceal their opposition to American recognition of the People's Republic of China, accompanied (they charged) by the nation's abandonment of Nationalist China (Taiwan). Yet despite their long-standing emotional ties to the nationalist regime, Republican policymakers are unlikely to reverse the recent course of Sino-American relations. Indeed, they probably will forge new links in the chain of Sino-American collaboration. The Carter White House had authorized a joint Sino-American intelligence project and had agreed to furnish certain nonlethal military equipment to the People's Republic of China. Peking certainly will renew its requests for other kinds of American military hardware in the years ahead.

In responding to these overtures, President Reagan and his aides will be mindful of certain realities inhibiting closer Sino-American relations. Republican officials, for example, are aware that China is not a military ally of the United States; that profound ideological differences still exist between the two countries; and that, ambiguous as the concept may be, some semblance of détente must be preserved with the Soviet Union. The Republican administration, Alexander Haig declared, does not advocate a policy of "poking sticks in the polar bear's cage." Most crucially perhaps, the Reagan White House is aware that China has now acquired "an American card." If, when, and under what circumstances, it is played is a decision for Chinese policymakers to make, primarily in the light of their own country's domestic and foreign interests.[40]

The withdrawal of American power from Southeast Asia enhanced the importance of the Japanese-American alliance and compelled officials in both capitals to reexamine their relationship. Two other recent developments have accelerated this tendency. One is the ongoing buildup of Soviet power in Asia during the 1970s, particularly naval forces, accompanied by rising tensions between the U.S.S.R. and Japan. As an island kingdom, Japan is acutely conscious of its vulnerability to this Soviet threat. By contrast, during the 1970s the American military position in East Asia deteriorated markedly, partly as a result of the need to strengthen American forces in the Persian Gulf area.[41]

To redress the widening military imbalance in Asia, the Reagan White House will almost certainly maintain pressure upon Tokyo to increase its contribution to regional defense, consonant with Japan's enormous economic and financial power. Although the government of Prime Minister Zenko Suzuki was committed to a 7 percent increase in Japanese defense spending, Japan's level of defense expenditures was approximately half the rate of the NATO allies.[42]

A number of obstacles lay in the path of a significantly expanded Japanese contribution to regional security and to a more dynamic Japanese diplomatic role in Asian and global affairs. Public opinion in Japan, for example, remained opposed to any radical change in the nation's foreign and defense policies. The provisions of the Japanese constitution—inserted largely at the instigation of the United States itself during its period of occupation—prohibited Japan from maintaining a large national defense establishment. A resurgent Japan would also create anxieties among the smaller nations of Asia, some of which were subject to Japanese hegemony. Moreover, few Americans have really grasped the consequences of a rearmed and diplomatically independent Japan. As one commentator has observed, it would inevitably produce "a more independent Japanese foreign policy that occasionally will lead Japan to take positions . . . that are not consistent with those of the United States." [43]

As businessmen and workers in the American automobile and electronics industries have become painfully aware, the dominant issue in Japanese-American relations is commercial policy. The aggressive and often ingenious trade practices of what is sometimes called "Japan, Inc." have given Tokyo a $10 billion foreign trade surplus—almost eight times larger than when the Nixon administration complained about Japan's unfair trade policies. Japan has now become the world's largest manufacturer of automobiles, and its net earnings from sales in the American market have increased over 300 percent since the Vietnam War.[44]

Like the Carter administration before them, Republican policymakers will encounter a mounting chorus demanding protectionist measures against this growing stream of Japanese imports. On the basis of the ideology and historical orientation of their party, Republicans may prove more receptive to such pleas than their Democratic predecessors, who have long been identified with the principle of reciprocal trade.

Yet two realities are likely to limit any Republican inclination to rely primarily upon protectionist measures in resolving the Japanese-American trade controversy. One is the massive dependency of American agriculture—still the most productive sector of the American economy—upon sales to Japan. In turn, this presupposes that Tokyo has acquired dollar balances with which to buy American commodities and products. The other constraint is the need to reverse the marked decline in American productivity in recent years.[45] This decline, as officials in Washington know, is at the root of the inability of the United States to compete successfully against Japanese imports. In the long run, reversing this decline—along with renewed efforts to expand American sales within the Japanese home market—offers greater promise of restoring America's competitive position than reliance upon tariff barriers and other protectionist steps to restrict Japanese imports. Achieving this objective will depend directly upon the Reagan administration's domestic efforts to curb inflation, reduce government spending, and take other steps designed to stabilize and revitalize the American economy, as described more fully in Chapter 7.

The Reagan administration is likely to preserve the basic continuity of American foreign policy toward two other key Asian countries—South

Korea and the Philippines. America's commitment to the defense of South Korea will unquestionably be maintained, with little prospect of a substantial reduction in United States forces stationed in that country.[46] Close defense and economic ties also will continue to exist between the United States and the Philippines; and these may even be strengthened, as part of Washington's effort to bolster the security of the Persian Gulf and Indian Ocean areas. Americans will be distressed by violations of human rights in both South Korea and the Philippines. However, Washington has had minimum success in protecting human rights in either country, and the Reagan administration may be less disposed than its predecessor to make the effort.[47]

REVOLUTION AND DICTATORSHIP IN LATIN AMERICA

Several days before his inauguration, Ronald Reagan met with Mexican President José López Portillo. The meeting underscored two aspects of current United States-Latin American relations: the considerable anxiety in Mexico concerning the election of Ronald Reagan, and the low ebb in the influence of the United States throughout the inter-American system.

Two perennial issues, both becoming more urgent and difficult with the passage of time, head the list of problems confronting the Reagan administration in Latin America: (1) the old problem of dictatorships (usually military juntas) throughout the region, and (2) the problem of violence and radical change, symbolized by the revolutionary turmoil currently sweeping Central America. In some respects, the prospects for stable democratic governments within the inter-American system appear less favorable today than when the Alliance for Progress was launched by President Kennedy in the early 1960s. In one Latin American nation after another, the political process follows a familiar cycle. After a prolonged period of ineffectual civilian rule, a military junta seizes power, ostensibly to correct the mistakes of civilian leaders; constitutional guarantees and laws are suspended, and the military elite rules by decree; revolutionary and violent opposition erupts against the junta's authority, and this evokes growing reliance by the government upon coercive methods. On the basis of recent experience, one of two results can usually be expected. Either the military government, in time, succeeds in largely suppressing opposition to its rule; or the society is plunged into a condition of ongoing internal political ferment and recurring violence.

The former outcome is illustrated by recent events in the two most influential Latin American countries—Brazil and Argentina. Since 1964, Brazil has been governed by military elements devoted to maintaining internal order and to achieving rapid national development. It is determined to become the most influential nation in Latin America and ultimately to emerge as a global power. Brazil's acquisition of a nuclear potential—in the face of Washington's evident disapproval—provides eloquent testimony to its foreign policy ambitions and its emergence as a regional force.[48]

Although only one-third as large as Brazil, Argentina has comparable aspirations. Following a short rule by Isabel Péron, the government came under military control early in 1976. In the years that followed, its military elite largely was successful in bringing about an end to anarchy and armed opposition. In recent years, it has achieved considerable success in solving Argentina's grave internal problems.[49]

In formulating and administering a consistent policy toward Latin American military juntas, the Reagan administration will face vexing policy dilemmas. From the experience of the Carter administration, Republican officials are aware that placing the theme of human rights at the forefront of their Latin American policy is likely to achieve few tangible results, other than alienating leaders in Brazil, Argentina, and other Latin American states. No convincing evidence exists that in the recent past Washington has actually been able to protect the rights of Latin Americans against right-wing or left-wing extremists. Yet if Washington ignores the violence endemic in most Latin American societies, it inevitably will be accused of supporting dictatorships and neglecting the cause of freedom in the western hemisphere.

For both ideological and pragmatic policy considerations, the Reagan administration can be expected to reopen the dialogue with Latin American states governed by right-wing regimes. Conservatives nearly always prefer order to either liberty or equality. More accurately, they believe order is a prerequisite for the exercise of other freedoms. And Republican policymakers are also aware that, whatever the drawbacks of this course, it is not likely to damage the image and influence of the United States within the inter-American system, and there is a fair prospect that it will enhance it.

Contemporary Central America exemplifies the second political pattern, of internal political ferment and recurring violence. In that region, violence precipitated by both right-wing and left-wing groups has become endemic. Throughout Central America, the influence of the United States has declined sharply, and the government of Mexico is deeply concerned that the revolutionary tide will sweep northward. Central American societies suffer acutely from the bedrock problems engendering political turbulence and polarization throughout Latin America—widespread poverty; high unemployment; inadequate health, educational, and housing facilities; and above all perhaps, inexorable population expansion.

In this region also, the Reagan administration will find itself faced with the same dilemma that has confronted the United States during most of the twentieth century, arising out of the problem of intervention by the United States in the affairs of its neighbors. On the one hand, Republican officials are aware of Latin America's universal opposition to intervention and dictation by the United States. They know that the Nixon administration's overt attempt to overthrow the Marxist-oriented Allende government of Chile in 1973 won little goodwill for the United States. Nor have attempts by the United States to isolate Castro's Cuba elicited enthusiastic support from other Latin American republics.

Yet for many years, American officials have also been cognizant of a deep ambivalence in Latin America about interventionism by the United States. Nearly every political group within Latin America seeks Washington's support in its effort to acquire or maintain political power and to defeat its political opponents. Almost all governments within the region want large-scale U.S. assistance in meeting their critical internal needs, even while they resist efforts by Washington to instigate the domestic reforms needed to make such aid effective. Similarly, the United States is accused of indifference to conditions within the western hemisphere, for its refusal to become deeply involved in developments there.

In the existing Central American context, the Reagan administration will confront such dilemmas at every turn; and Republican policymakers will be extremely hard-pressed to resolve them satisfactorily. Guatemala serves as a case in point. In 1954, President Eisenhower intervened openly in the country's politics and prevented a threatened Communist takeover of the government. Such intervention, however, did little to solve the country's deep-seated economic and social problems. Today the conflict between the ruling military junta and its left-wing opponents has turned the country into what has been called "Fortress Guatemala," and political stability remains as elusive as ever.[50]

Tiny El Salvador is engulfed in ongoing political violence. Land reform and other measures sponsored by the government, with Washington's encouragement, have thus far done little to improve the lives of its impoverished citizens; nor have they deterred efforts by indigenous and foreign-backed revolutionary groups to overthrow the government. In this violence-prone environment, moderate political groups have found their position increasingly precarious.[51]

In Panama, despite the successful resolution of the Panama Canal controversy by President Carter, the military government of General Omar Torrijos Herrera continues to rely upon the army to enforce its authority. The promises of General Torrijos to "democratize" Panama have not materialized; critics inside and outside the country clamor against his dictatorial rule, and Panamanian revolutionary groups are active within the country and in neighboring Central American countries. Although Reagan and other Republicans were highly critical of the new Panama Canal treaties, it seems doubtful that his administration will seek to modify them, if for no other reason than that an attempt to do so inevitably would trigger a new wave of anti-American sentiment throughout the western hemisphere.[52]

Many of the policy dilemmas we have identified will come into sharp focus when Republican officials endeavor to formulate an effective response to the situation in Nicaragua. In July 1979, the long reign of the Somoza dynasty, closely linked with and supported by the United States, came to a violent end. After a prolonged revolutionary struggle, leaving some 30,000 people dead, the left-wing Sandinista movement gained control of the government. Espousing a Marxist program and overtly supported by Castro's Cuba (and indirectly perhaps by the Soviet Union), the Sandinistas called for radical changes in Nicaraguan life. While officials in Washington long had feared the emergence of another Cuba within the inter-American system, in time they also became aware of a painful reality: the Sandinista movement was the dominant political force in Nicaragua. Failure to engage in at least limited collaboration with it would plunge the country into revolutionary upheaval and pervasive violence again, and almost certainly it would strengthen the Communist appeal throughout the region. The Sandinista movement did not export revolution to surrounding construction, and the Carter administration decided to provide economic assistance for that purpose. Yet before he left office, President Carter suspended economic aid to Nicaragua on the grounds that military weapons going to left-wing rebel groups in El Salvador were being supplied by the Sandinistas.[53]

Under the Reagan administration, the future course of Nicaraguan-American relations is uncertain. If the Sandinista-controlled government of Nicaragua satisfied two criteria—the government preserved its independence from Cuban, Soviet, or other external control, and the Sandinistia movement did not export revolution to surrounding countries—then relations with the United States, in time, might resemble the ties that Washington has maintained for many years with Yugoslavia and Poland. If the Sandinista regime fails one or both of these tests, Nicaragua's relations with the United States can only deteriorate. At a minimum, under these conditions the Reagan administration will be tempted to divorce itself from any responsibility for Nicaragua's internal problems and will withhold assistance in solving them. It may well be attracted to this course because of the recent experience of Jamaica, where a Marxist-oriented regime totally failed to solve the country's critical internal problems, after which the voters chose a new, procapitalist government. Alternatively, if the Sandinista-controlled government of Nicaragua in fact becomes another Cuba—if it actively sponsors revolutionary activities in neighboring countries—that fact might induce officials in Washington to intervene against it, just as Eisenhower intervened in Guatemala earlier or Nixon supported opposition movements against the pro-Marxist Allende regime in Chile.

THE DIPLOMATIC ROAD AHEAD

Our analysis of specific diplomatic issues confronting the Reagan administration permits certain brief conclusions about the prospect for American foreign policy under Republican management. President Reagan's general goal—to "make America great again"—faces a multitude of obstacles arising from the domestic and foreign environment. As he and his supporters have acknowledged, reviving the power and influence of the United States abroad will likely require many years.

As our earlier treatment emphasized, the success of Reagan's diplomacy will be massively conditioned by Republican success in solving pressing domestic problems, particularly efforts to promote economic stability and to increase American productivity. Among students of international relations, it long has been axiomatic that the power of a nation in foreign affairs depends perhaps most crucially upon the strength of its economic base.

In this and earlier chapters, the point has been made that the national consensus reflected in the Republican electoral landslide of 1980 is extremely fragile and marked by numerous contradictions and inconsistencies. Some of the contributors in this text are dubious that a national consensus even exists. If that is true, its absence could seriously impede Republican efforts to undertake "a new beginning" in foreign and domestic affairs. In the foreign policy realm, the American people have shown a high degree of unity concerning the kind of inconsistent, indecisive, and ineffectual diplomacy they did not like about the Carter administration's record. Considerably less unity exists, however, among the American people on two other crucial aspects of foreign affairs: the means available to the Regan administration to pursue the objectives of the nation abroad, and the costs the American people are willing to incur—not only financial outlays, but time, energy, and psychological enervation as well—to achieve the objective.

Our discussion has highlighted the fact that numerous major and minor obstacles confront the Reagan White House in the external milieu. A leading obstacle is the likely intensification of Soviet adventurism and intervention in selected areas, such as the Persian Gulf region and Latin America. As the specific case of Nicaragua illustrates, the Reagan administration will be severely challenged to discriminate among several varieties of communism in terms of how they affect American foreign policy interests. President Reagan will be required to differentiate carefully among them and to tailor American policies accordingly.

Political turmoil and upheaval throughout the Third World is not likely to abate, and may well accelerate in the 1980s. In many cases, this fact will severely limit the ability of both the United States and the Soviet Union to achieve their diplomatic purposes in the less developed countries. For many of these countries—and the list gets longer every year—their internal needs are becoming increasingly urgent, although their ability to utilize external assistance effectively is declining. In turn, this reality sharply limits America's ability to respond to their needs effectively; it also reduces the incentive in Washington to make the effort.

As has been true since World War II, however, the pivotal issue in United States foreign policy has been, and unquestionably it will remain, Soviet-American relations. Our discussion has called attention to the fact that prospects for more constructive relations between Washington and Moscow appear to be remote. If this development does not necessarily decree an increase in the danger of nuclear war, it virtually guarantees that below the nuclear threshold relations between the super powers will remain tense, competitive, and mutually suspicious.

Finally, in view of these realities, another urgent requirement of contemporary American diplomacy, identified earlier, is worth reiterating here. Assuming that the Reagan administration is successful in building a stronger power base to support its external policies, its diplomatic record will depend heavily upon successfully meeting another challenge. This is its ability to formulate—and to gain public, legislative, and allied support for—a clear rationale for the application of American military power overseas. In some respects, this could prove to be Ronald Reagan's most difficult diplomatic task. But unless a rationale for the use of American power abroad is forthcoming, many of the diverse diplomatic activities and programs envisioned by Republican officials will make little positive contribution to the success of the United States in foreign affairs.

NOTES

1. *New York Times*, 5 November 1980.
2. Ibid. In the words of another analyst, the American people's "discontent" with the Carter administration "focused on the economy." See the report of Adam Clymer in *New York Times*, 5 November 1980.

3. *New York Times,* 5 November 1980; and *New York Times,* 9 November 1980. An extended discussion of public attitudes on the eve of the national election may be found in Steven V. Roberts, "The Year of the Hostage," *New York Times Magazine,* 2 November 1980, pp. 26, 30, 61-74. See also the analysis of the election results in *U.S. News and World Report* 89 (November 17, 1980): 26-30.

4. Charles William Maynes and Richard H. Ullman, "Ten Years of Foreign Policy," *Foreign Policy* 40 (Fall 1980): 2-6.

5. *Newsweek* 97 (February 9, 1981): 45-46.

6. An example of such anomalies in public expectations about the Reagan administration was revealed in a national public opinion poll taken early in 1981. According to its results, the people interviewed showed greater confidence in Reagan's leadership to accomplish foreign policy than domestic objectives. Thus, some 87 percent of the sample believed that the Reagan White House would see to it that the United States was respected by other nations. Yet only 58 percent believed it would succeed in reducing the size of the federal government; 37 percent believed he would be able to balance the federal budget; and 25 percent believed it would be able to halt inflation. In general, the survey showed less confidence in Reagan's ability to accomplish his goals than the average president. See the *New York Times*/CBS poll in *The New York Times,* 3 February 1981. Utopian expectations by Americans toward the presidency are analyzed more fully in Chapter 3.

7. Thomas L. Hughes, "The Crack-Up," *Foreign Policy* 40 (Fall 1980): 35.

8. See the text of Reagan's speech in *New York Times,* 20 October 1980.

9. Marvin Stone in *U.S. News and World Report* 90 (January 12, 1981); 76.

10. *New York Times,* 24 December 1980.

11. See the views of former Assistant Secretary of State Hodding Carter on foreign policy decisionmaking within the executive branch in *New York Times,* 31 December 1980, and *New York Times,* 5 January 1981.

12. Cecil V. Crabb, Jr., *Policy-Makers and Critics: Conflicting Theories of American Foreign Policy* (New York: Praeger Publishers, 1976). Several diverse approaches to American foreign policy since World War II are identified and analyzed in this text. The problem of a declining public consensus about the nation's foreign policy goals and behavior is dealt with in James Chace, "Is a Foreign Policy Consensus Possible?" *Foreign Affairs* 57 (Fall 1978): 1-17; and George Quester, "Consensus Lost," *Foreign Policy* 40 (Fall 1980): 18-33.

13. *New York Times,* 4 January 1981; and see the views of Max L. Friedersdorf, Reagan's chief liaison officer for legislative relations in the *New York Times,* 6 January 1981.

14. Demands during and after the Vietnam War that Congress be treated as a full partner in the foreign policy process—along with leading examples of congressional initiatives in the diplomatic field—are discussed more fully in Cecil V. Crabb, Jr. and Pat M. Holt, *Invitation to Struggle: Congress, the President and Foreign Policy* (Washington, D.C.: Congressional Quarterly Press, 1980).

15. *New York Times,* 20 October 1980; see also the discussion of the Republican ticket's foreign policy goals in *U.S. News and World Report* 89 (November 17, 1980): 22-23.

16. President Carter's ambassador to Moscow, Thomas J. Watson, Jr., for example, is convinced that Soviet-American relations are entering a very

"dangerous" period in the years ahead, as presaged by the Soviet invasion of Afghanistan. See *U.S. News and World Report* 90 (January 19, 1981): 35, 38. See also the more extended analysis of recent and future Soviet external behavior in Craig R. Whitney, "The View from the Kremlin," *New York Times Magazine,* 20 April 1980, pp. 31-33, 92; and Donald Zagoria, "Into the Breach: New Soviet Alliances in the Third World," *Foreign Affairs* 57 (Spring 1979): 733-754.

17. *Baton Rouge Morning Advocate,* 27 November 1980; *New York Times,* 16 November 1980
18. A detailed study of the American military posture in the opening of the 1980s is *U.S. Defense Policy: Weapons, Strategy, and Commitments,* 2d ed. (Washington, D.C.: Congressional Quarterly, 1980). Comparisons of American and Soviet military forces in the major categories of armed strength are available in the Defense Department's *Annual Report: Fiscal Year 1980* (Washington, D.C.: Government Printing Office, 1979) and in subsequent volumes of this series. See also Major Tyrus W. Cobb, "Military Imbalance: Soviet Expansion During Détente," *Military Review* 57 (March 1977): 79-86.
19. Comparisons of national power—even when confined to the single dimension of military power—are, of course, always crude approximations that may leave a misleading impression. Some American officials conceded that the Soviet military advantage might be more apparent than real—when it was considered that in any future global conflict Moscow might have to wage a two-front war, against the North Atantic Treaty Organization (NATO) in the west and against the People's Republic of China in the east. Moreover, on the NATO front alone, the Communist edge could be largely illusory: according to orthodox military doctrine, an attacking force would need a 3- to a 5-1 military advantage over defending NATO forces to achieve their objectives.
20. *New York Times,* 11 January 1981; and *Newsweek* 97 (January 19, 1981): 22.
21. One commentator on Ronald Reagan's thought states that he has "sometimes exhibited [former Secretary of State John Foster] Dulles' readiness to go to the brink of conflict with the Russians over what he saw . . . as crucial issues." The problem with this kind of selective reliance upon military force, however, is that it leaves the definition of "crucial issues" to momentary and pragmatic considerations; this, in turn, does little to enhance the predictability of American foreign policy. See Hedrick Smith, "Reagan: What Kind of World Leader?" *New York Times Magazine,* 16 November 1980, pp. 47, 161-177. Reagan's designated secretary of defense offered another set of criteria for governing American interventionism. He told the Senate Armed Services Committee that the United States should fight wars only if they were vital to national survival, if the American people understood and supported America's involvement in them, and if the United States fully intended to win. See *New York Times,* 7 January 1981.
22. Relations between the United States and the Soviet Union may be thought of as entailing four possible conditions or stages: global or limited war, cold war, détente, and cooperative relations (or entente). Détente thus represents an evolution in their relationship, away from war and violence and toward more normal and peaceful contacts. Yet in the Soviet interpretation, détente also permits the Kremlin to support "wars of national liberation" throughout the Third World and to engage in other behavior that Washington has deemed inimical to peaceful and cooperative relations.

23. More detailed examination of the concept of détente—focusing upon diverse Soviet and American conceptions of it—may be found in Coral Bell, *The Diplomacy of Détente: the Kissinger Era* (New York: St. Martin's Press, 1977); and Gerald L. Steibel, *Détente: Promises and Pitfalls* (New York: Crane, Russak & Co., 1975).

24. See the interview with Ronald Reagan in *Time*, 117 (January 5, 1981): 30-31; and the views of Alexander Haig as quoted in *Newsweek* 96 (December 29, 1980): 16.

25. Smith, "Reagan: What Kind of World Leader?" p. 47; and see the statement by Alexander Haig to the Senate Foreign Relations Committee, *New York Times*, 10 January 1981.

26. More detailed information on the NATO-Warsaw Pact military imbalance and discussions of the implications of it may be found in the symposium, "NATO in a Wider World?" *NATO Review* 28 (December 1980): 1-30; a briefer treatment is available in *U.S. News and World Report* 89 (October 6, 1980): 41-43.

27. *New York Times*, 7 December 1980.

28. *New York Times*, 14 December 1980. For an examination of West German viewpoints and policies, see Marion Donhoff, "Bonn/Washington: Strained Relations," *Foreign Affairs* 57 (Summer 1979): 975-987.

29. For the text of the Carter Doctrine, see President Jimmy Carter's "State of the Union Address," January 23, 1980, as distributed by the Department of State, Current Policy No. 132, pp. 1-4.

30. See the interview with Reagan in *Time*, 117 (January 5, 1981): 30-31; Smith, "Reagan: What Kind of World Leader?" p. 174; and the summary of foreign policy issues facing the Reagan administration in *U.S. News and World Report* 89 (January 5, 1981): 45-47.

31. Ramon Knauerhase, "Saudi Arabia's Foreign and Domestic Policy," *Current History* 80 (January 1981): 18-23.

32. Background discussions on the evolution of American foreign policy toward Africa are available in Vernon McKay, *Africa in World Politics* (New York: Harper & Row, 1963): 245-429; and Frederick S. Arkhurst, ed. *U.S. Policy Toward Africa* (New York: Praeger Publishers, 1975).

33. Gerald R. Ford, *A Time to Heal* (New York: Harper & Row, and The Reader's Digest Association, 1979), pp. 345-346, 353, 358-359.

34. Recent American policy toward eastern Africa is discussed in Russell W. Howe, "United States Policy in Africa," *Current History* 76 (March 1979): 99-100, 130.

35. *U.S. News and World Report* 89 (January 5, 1981): 47.

36. See the excerpt from Haig's speech to the Republican Convention in the *New York Times*, 18 December 1980. An incisive critique of President Carter's human rights policy, written from a conservative perspective, is William F. Buckley Jr., "Human Rights and Foreign Policy," *Foreign Affairs* 58 (Spring 1980): 775-797.

37. Background on American postwar policy toward southern Africa is available in Rupert Emerson, *Africa and United States Policy* (Englewood Cliffs, N.J.: Prentice-Hall, 1967), pp. 76-94; more recent discussions of developments in the region and America's response to them are Russell W. Howe, "United States Policy in Africa," *Current History* 76 (March 1979): 97-101; Richard Dale, "South Africa and Namibia: Changing the Guard and Guarded Change," ibid. pp. 101-105; and John Grotpeter, "Changing South Africa," ibid. 78 (March 1980): 119-24.

38. See the interview with George F. Kennan, in *U.S. News and World Report* 88 (March 10, 1980): 33.
39. See the detailed analysis of Sino-American commercial relations in the publication by the Bureau of Public Affairs, Department of State, *Gist* (October 1980) pp. 1-2; and *New York Times,* 10 October 1980.
40. Marshall D. Shulman, a former State Department authority on the Soviet Union under the Carter administration, said that the prospect of Sino-American military collaboration was a "nightmare" for the Kremlin. See *New York Times,* 8 December 1980. Many of the complex issues facing the United States in its relations with China in the years ahead are dealt with in Michel Oksenberg, "China Policy for the 1980s," *Foreign Affairs* 59 (Winter 1980-1981): 304-323. And see the views of Alexander Haig, *New York Times,* 11 January 1981.
41. See, for example, the data on relative American and Soviet military power in Asia in *U.S. News and World Report,* 89 (December 8, 1980): 34-35; and John M. Newman, "Soviet Strategy in Asia, 1977-79," *Asian Affairs* pp. 305-35.
42. See the data on Japanese defense spending in the *New York Times,* 28 December 1980; and *New York Times,* 14 January 1981.
43. Isaac Shapiro, "The Risen Sun: Japanese Gaullism?" *Foreign Policy* 41 (Winter 1980-1981): 61-62.
44. See the data on U.S.-Japanese trade relations in the *New York Times,* 28 December 1980. A more extensive analysis of the problem is available in Saburo Okita, "Japan, China and the United States: Economic Relations," *Foreign Affairs* 57 (Summer 1979): 1090-1111.
45. Thus, during the period 1960-1965, nonfarm productivity in the United States increased by an average of 3.6 percent annually; during 1966-1970, the average growth was 1.5 percent annually; in 1971-1975, the productive gain was 1.4 percent annually; and in 1976 through September 1980, the growth in productivity fell sharply to .2 percent annually. See the data from the Bureau of Labor Statistics, as reproduced in the "National Economic Survey," *New York Times,* 11 January 1981, p. 18. The problem of declining American productivity in recent years is analyzed more fully in Chapter 7.
46. For a discussion of recent developments within South Korea and their implications for American foreign policy, see Fuji Kamiya, "The Korean Peninsula After Park Chung Hee," *Asian Survey* 20 (July 1980): 744-53.
47. The major issues in contemporary Filipino-American relations are identified in Richard H. Kessler, "The Philippines: the Next Iran?" *Asian Affairs* 7 (January/February 1980): 148-61.
48. Recent political and economic developments within Brazil are described in Robert M. Levine, "Brazil: Democracy Without Adjectives," *Current History* 78 (February 1980): 49-53; and see Roger W. Fontaine, "The End of a Beautiful Relationship," *Foreign Policy* 28 (Fall 1977): 166-75.
49. More extended discussion of Argentine-American relations may be found in Peter H. Smith, "Argentina: The Uncertain Warriors," *Current History* 78 (February 1980): 62-65, 85-86.
50. The Eisenhower administration's intervention in Guatemala is described in Dwight D. Eisenhower, *Mandate for Change* (Garden City, N.Y.: Doubleday & Co., 1963), pp. 421-27; for a discussion of recent developments in the country, see Alan Riding, "Guatemala: State of Siege," *New York Times Magazine,* 24 August 1980, pp. 16-29, 65-67.

51. The accelerating political crisis in El Salvador is analyzed more fully in William Leo Grande and Carla Anne Robbins, "Oligarchs and Officers: the Crisis in El Salvador," *Foreign Affairs* 58 (Summer 1980): 1084-1104.

52. Recent developments in Panama are described in the *New York Times,* 28 September 1980.

53. The rationale of the Carter administration's policy toward the Sandinista regime in Nicaragua is explained more fully in the statement by Warren Christopher, "Assistance to the Caribbean, Central America," *Department of State Bulletin* 80 (March 1980): 66-69. The emergence and goals of the Sandinista movement are described in Thomas W. Walker, "The Sandinista Victory in Nicaragua," *Current History* 78 (February 1980): 49-53.

9

Conclusion: Electoral and Policy Realignment or Aberration?

Ellis Sandoz and Cecil V. Crabb, Jr.

The analysis of the 1980 election and its meaning, in the preceding pages, calls attention to a number of important and recurrent problems about the operation and future of the American political system. Before identifying them, however, several admonitions are in order regarding the attempt to draw firm conclusions about the significance of elections so soon after the events themselves.

First, we are aware of risks inherent in making pronouncements about the nature and future of American politics based upon the evidence available from a single national election. Moreover, the essays in this book were written early in 1981, before full election data and detailed scholarly analyses of their meaning and significance were available. As illustrated by the numerous studies that have been offered of the crucial election of 1932, many years may be required before comprehensive data are available for detailed evaluation.

Second, even after statistical and other forms of data about voting patterns in 1980 become available for analysis, a perspective of several years may be required before significant voting patterns can be identified and analyzed. Aside from being well informed about their respective fields, the contributors to this symposium are also interested citizens. As the volume's epigraph from Thucydides eloquently suggests, the authors are members of interest groups, supporters of particular political candidates and organizations, taxpayers, and wage-earners. All of this unquestionably affects their ability as scholars to assess the outcome of the 1980 election impartially and impersonally.

Third, our conclusions are offered with another, more obvious, caveat in mind. Customarily, incoming administrations gain control of the executive branch of the American government with the avowed intention of carrying out a multitude of major and minor campaign promises. It is not necessary to adopt a cynical view of the American political process to believe that party platforms are made primarily "to run on, not to stand on" and to recognize that every new administration in American history has failed to carry out all of its campaign promises or to implement its announced programs. Even after the landmark election of 1932, for example, the New Deal of Franklin Roosevelt was widely at variance with what the American people expected from the national government when they elected a Democratic administration. During the 1930s, however, mounting internal crises and unforeseen problems at home and abroad produced responses from the Roosevelt administration that were designed to solve them effectively. Public opinion polls and the overwhelming reelection of the Democratic ticket in 1936 indicated convincingly that the New Deal had the solid support of the American people. This is but another way of saying that the electorate wanted the Roosevelt administration to respond constructively to existing national problems. Citizens were not unduly concerned about whether the response could be reconciled with planks in the platform of the Democratic party or with the campaign speeches of FDR.

An analogous situation will confront President Reagan and the Republican policymakers in the 1980s. Indeed, it would be surprising if changing circumstances and urgent problems did not compel departures—in some cases, perhaps, radical departures—from the Republican party's announced public policy goals. For more than two centuries, the American people have preferred pragmatic (Do they work?)—not doctrinaire—solutions to the nation's problems. There is little reason to believe this propensity is any less a characteristic of political behavior today than in previous eras of American history.

Fourth, the careful reader will have discerned that it is possible for qualified observers to offer conflicting insights and antithetical conclusions on the basis of the same data. We have made no attempt to impose a predetermined viewpoint upon our several authors, to demand that they adhere to a chosen "party line" in their analyses, or to reconcile the divergent interpretations contained in their essays. As befits a free society that values uninhibited intellectual inquiry and debate, the outcome has been a collection of essays containing diverse—and in some instances, admittedly opposite—judgments concerning the significance of the 1980 national election. As we have indicated, this result may be explained partially by the proximity of the event and by the unavailability of certain relevant data. Yet this is only part of the explanation.

More than a century after the event, contrary interpretations continue to be offered on the meaning and the importance of the election of 1860 that brought the Republican party of Abraham Lincoln to office. If distinguished political historians continue to disagree on this question, and unanimity is unlikely to be achieved in the years ahead, then we confidently can expect that the election of 1980 will continue to evoke widely varying interpretations in the future. Not only, then, is there truly an "iron curtain of the future" (as Arnold Toynbee has said) that clouds our crystal ball, but there is also the honest diversity of opinion about the significance of past events that is a necessary trait of scholarly interpretations.

Finally, whether the obvious Republican electoral landslide of 1980 also inaugurated a new era in American politics remains a question whose answer is much less obvious. The extent to which it may have done so is a matter we shall examine shortly, in the light of evidence accumulated to date. Meanwhile, we would emphasize that more time is required to assess the election's lasting significance, that parallels with earlier national elections may be misleading, and that informed commentators may not yet understand adequately how the new elements of this election will affect the future operation of the American political system.

A "NEW ERA" IN AMERICAN POLITICAL LIFE?

With these admonitions in mind, we now focus upon several leading themes and problems discussed in the preceding chapters. These have been identified by one or more of the contributors as matters significant for an understanding of the American political process and the elections of 1980. Few of them are wholly new problems, although in 1980 they may have taken novel forms. Some are as old as the American Republic and are inherent in the nature of democratic government itself. All of them are important. And we may be certain they will recur in subsequent national elections.

A fascinating question for any informed student of the contemporary political scene is: Did the Republican victory in 1980 inaugurate a "new era" in American political life? Parallels have been widely drawn between it and the election of 1932, which clearly produced a far-reaching political realignment in the United States.

Alternatively, some contributors believe that the electoral outcome in 1980 marked a return to the long period of Republican-controlled government witnessed (with the exceptions of the Grover Cleveland and the Woodrow Wilson administrations) from the Civil War until the defeat of Herbert Hoover in the great Democratic landslide of 1932. According to other interpretations, the election of 1980 was a milestone in the political history of the United States, for it brought an end to the long era of Democratic political dominance that began with the 1932 election of Franklin Roosevelt.

Not unexpectedly, our contributors give differing answers to the question, in part because the idea of a "new era" in American politics after 1980 has several possible connotations. It may mean, for example, that the Republican victory in 1980 was an innovation, primarily because it provided evidence of a fundamental realignment of political parties and organizations in American society. For many years, some political observers and professional organizations have predicted such a realignment, believing it to be both inevitable and highly desirable for the continued good health of the American body politic. Some evidence might be adduced to show that, on the basis of the 1980 election, this realignment has now occurred.

But most of our contributors do not share this interpretation. Neither James Sundquist and Richard Scammon in Chapter 2, nor Clifton McCleskey in Chapter 6, supports this contention. In their view, any interpretation of the electoral results in 1980 that asserts the occurrence of a basic political realignment in the United States is premature and unjustified. In the main, they explain the election of Ronald Reagan and other Republicans on the basis of unique factors and circumstances whose effect leaves the underlying American political structure largely unaltered.

But it is also possible to speak of the realignment of the American political system through the election of 1980 in another sense: as marking the emergence of what is sometimes described as a "New Conservatism" as the dominant political ideology of the country. According to this viewpoint, the outcome of the 1980 election was an epochal event. It witnessed the demise of liberalism as the American people's preferred ideological creed and their dramatic espousal of conservative principles in solving urgent national problems.

Once again, however, our experts hold mixed opinions on this important question. Some of them believe that considerable evidence supports the contention that the "New Conservatism" has become the preferred political creed of the American people. In that sense, Ronald Reagan was elected to the White House—and the Republican party gained control of the Senate and scored significant gains in the House— mainly because the American people agreed with the ideological orientation of leading Republican candidates. Citizens, therefore, expect Republicans elected to office to be guided by conservative precepts in formulating internal and external policies.

In Chapter 6, however, Clifton McCleskey arrives at a strongly contrary conclusion. By his account, the results of the 1980 election are explained mainly by certain unique and nonideological forces that produced the Republican electoral landslide. There was no conservative consensus, hence no mandate; nor could there be one, given the shambles of the American political system by 1980. If this viewpoint is correct, then the basically liberal propensities of the American electorate remain substantially unaltered. The election of 1980 was essentially an aberration, not a realignment; and a return to power of the Democratic party reasonably may then be anticipated in the near future. Moreover, if this analysis is valid, it is logical to expect that Republican control of the national government will be short-lived for another reason. Republican officials will quickly become frustrated, and their regime will be rendered largely ineffectual, when they attempt to apply conservative principles in what remains an essentially liberal political environment. Under these conditions, President Reagan ultimately could prove to be as indecisive, and as incapable of leading the nation in solving pressing domestic and foreign problems, as was his predecessor.

A third perspective on the new era supposedly inaugurated by the election of Ronald Reagan is offered in Chapters 2 and 3, where various concepts of "cycles" in American political life are discussed. According to the views expressed in Chapter 2, the Republican victory in 1980 may be seen as merely a normal and expected phase in the natural rhythm of the American political system. In one form, the cyclical theory explains the 1980 election by reference to periodic swings of the political pendulum between left-wing and right-wing extremes. After remaining on the left side of the political arc for many years, the pendulum returned to the right, bringing Ronald Reagan and his supporters into power. Alternatively, the results in 1980 are explained as a massive protest vote against the party that has long been in power. In due course, if this theory is tenable, a natural political momentum will move the pendulum leftward again, giving the Democrats control of the White House and Congress. This political cycle is what the concept of rotation in office usually means; and the events of 1980 merely signify that the American two-party system is operating normally.

In the somewhat more elaborate and multistage version of the rotation theory offered by Erwin Hargrove and Michaël Nelson in Chapter 3, the outcome of the 1980 election can be understood by reference to a three-stage rhythm in American political life. Presidential administrations thus are classified as representing the preparation, or the reform, or the consolidation stages of the cycle. In the end, the authors remain uncertain about just where Ronald Reagan belongs in their cycle. They call attention to a feature of the Reagan presidency that admittedly makes it difficult to fit the 1980 election into their cyclical scheme. In effect, Reagan and many of his supporters gained office by promising to reform the reformers—that is, by appealing to a return to pre-New Deal principles defining the role and function of government in the American society. As the authors implicitly concede, their cyclical explanation—in which perhaps the pivotal idea is the reform stage—does not easily accommodate a chief executive who advocates a reactive curbing of governmental growth and a return to an earlier vision of American political life. The reforms advocated by Ronald Reagan and his supporters involve curbing the growth of (if not dismantling) much of the New Deal—Fair Deal—Great Society—New Frontier structure accumulated over a half-century, on the theory that private organizations and individual initiative are best able to solve the problems plaguing American society. In this sense, the Reagan presidency does not fit clearly into the three-stage cycle identified from presidential administrations since 1900.

DILEMMAS OF THE MODERN PRESIDENCY

Has the presidential office in the United States become an impossible assignment? As Chapter 3 asks: Do the American people expect omnipotence and benevolence from their chief executive? Do they demand miracles from the president, even when they sometimes deny the White House the means needed to solve urgent problems at home and abroad? Is the recent political fate of Jimmy Carter a prospect that will likely face any occupant of the Oval Office in the years ahead?

Implicitly and explicity, the future of the American presidency is an important, and increasingly urgent, question with which all of the contributors are concerned. As much as any other single factor, the tide of discontent that swept the Carter administration out of office evolved from a pervasive belief among voters that the Carter presidency had failed. To millions of voters, the Carter White House was indecisive, bungling, and inept in responding to a wide range of internal and external problems. Correctly or not, Jimmy Carter gave the impression to the electorate of being overwhelmed by these problems and of having no more insight into how to cope with them than the ordinary citizen. Quite possibly, a fundamental Carter error lay in his undue fear of perpetuating the "imperial presidency" of the Johnson and Nixon years, leading him to avoid at all costs any impression that his own incumbency deserved that label. Carter's mistake may well have cost him the support and respect of a majority of the American people.

For it is not a strong presidency Americans resent or reject but an abusive or a vacillating one. Watergate and other less spectacular examples of the imperial presidency notwithstanding, it is doubtful that the American people fear a vigorous and effective chief executive because he might abuse his vast power. Instances of serious abuse of presidential power have been rare (far rarer, for example, than instances of misuse of power by governors and mayors). Perhaps the outstanding fact about President Nixon's involvement in the Watergate episode for most Americans was that his perversion of the presidential office was dealt with decisively, in accordance with prescribed constitutional procedures. Within a relatively short period of time, a transition was made in the presidency and any threat to the stability of the American system of government was averted.

Fears about the imperial presidency also were an outgrowth of the anguish surrounding the war in Vietnam. But again, as several studies of this conflict have convincingly shown, the groundswell of public opposition against the foreign policies of the Johnson and Nixon administrations did not come about because the chief executive exercised vast power during this conflict. For most citizens, the Johnson administration was discredited by the war chiefly because of LBJ's failure to devise a strategy capable of achieving American objectives in that conflict or, failing that result, to liquidate the American position in Southeast Asia as a lost cause. Thus, President Johnson was not repudiated because he was imperial, but because he failed to resolve an external problem that was draining the resources of the nation and exhausting it psychologically.

The point of this discussion is to emphasize the idea that, as much as at any other time in American history, the people want a president who will be successful in discharging the duties of his office. As pointed out in Chapters 5 and 8, for example, citizens expect the president to address the nation's urgent internal and external concerns and to produce solutions for them. In 1980 the electorate concluded that Jimmy Carter had failed to do this, while Ronald Reagan showed convincing signs that he could succeed in doing so.

As some of the contributors have observed, along with many other students of the modern presidency, public expectations today concerning the presidency verge on becoming a form of modern utopianism. More than any other government leader, the occupant of the Oval Office is expected to demonstrate insights into, and to formulate policies for solving, a vast range of complex domestic and foreign problems. The public expects this at a time when many of these problems are novel, of unprecedented urgency, and baffling even to the best minds. As Stephen McDonald indicates in Chapter 7, for example, this is especially true of the nation's current economic crisis, which President Reagan apparently is expected to solve. Yet economists are sharply divided among themselves concerning the underlying causes of America's economic disabilities; and they are similarly divided into differing schools of thought about the best way that these economic maladies can be cured. A condition of "stagflation"—or "inflationary recession," meaning simultaneous stagnation of production and rising prices worsening inflation—does not fit most contemporary economic models, and many proposed remedies for it may intensify the disease. Yet President Reagan, like President Carter before him, is expected to find a cure; his performance as president will be judged by his ability to prescribe one.

Chapter 8 called attention to comparable utopian demands about problems in the foreign policy sphere. Many Americans appear to be convinced that Ronald Reagan will "make America great again," correct the existing military imbalance between the United States and the Soviet Union, restore the image of the United States in regions such as black Africa and Latin America, safeguard the security of the Persian Gulf area, maintain unity within a NATO alliance that is acutely in disarray (while also convincing the European allies to shoulder a larger share of the Western defense burden), and solve the problem of rising Japanese imports into the United States (without at the same time reducing the volume of American exports). Yet, very few Americans have seriously considered whether some of these problems can be solved in an acceptable manner. Nor have they seriously calculated the financial and other costs involved in their solution.

These examples highlight what has forcefully emerged as a paramount issue confronting the American system of government. It is sometimes described as the crisis of the presidency. As Jimmy Carter's incumbency proved, and as millions of Americans were able to observe during his four years in the White House, the presidential office has become an incredibly demanding, exhausting, and perhaps an inherently impossible job. The more urgent the problems facing the American society become, the more the American people have been inclined to look to the White House for solutions to them. This tendency may express the public's tacit conviction that acceptable solutions are not likely to be forthcoming from either Congress or the judiciary.

It is the judgment of some of our contributors that these utopian conceptions of the presidency not only were present in the 1980 election but played a considerable role in its outcome. If that is true, then Ronald Reagan's determination to reverse the trend toward big government—inevitably involving a retrenchment in the leadership overtly exercised by the president in solving national problems—runs counter to the implicit desires of the American people. Presumably, the electorate will judge the Reagan presidency by the same standard it applied to its predecessor: How successful has the chief executive been in solving, or mitigating, critical national problems? If the electorate's judgment is unfavorable on this score—or if the voters conclude that the president has attempted to avoid his rightful responsibilities by undue reliance on private sector organizations—Republican control of the White House and of the Senate could prove to be only a brief interlude.

Ronald Reagan will attempt to persuade the American people to abandon many of their deeply-held utopian expectations about the presidency and other federal government agencies. On the basis of experience since the New Deal, his chances of succeeding do not appear promising. And if he fails, then the GOP can soon anticipate a return to its normal role of the past half-century: serving as the opposition party in American politics.

PRESSURE GROUPS AND THE CONTEMPORARY POLITICAL SYSTEM

Another question discussed in nearly every chapter of our study is the role and impact of pressure groups within the contemporary American political system. In Chapter 4, for example, interest group activity during the 1980 election was described in detail. Again, as emphasized in Chapters 2 and 6, political amateurism, pressure groups, and political action committees (PACs) were held to have contributed mightily to the "de-institutionalization" of the two-party system in the United States. The reactions of interest groups will be a crucial element in determining whether the Reagan administration is able to formulate and carry out economic and fiscal policies capable of halting the inflationary wage-price spiral and achieving other economic objectives. Chapter 8 called our attention to the fact that pressure group activity has been, and will continue to be, a significant influence in determining American foreign policy toward such issues as racial oppression in Africa and expanding Japanese sales in the American market.

Substantial consensus exists among our contributors concerning salient characteristics of pressure group activity in the United States. First, it is increasing. Attempts by interest groups to influence national policy never have been more intensive, better financed, and more skillfully pursued than they are today. The evidence accumulated in our analysis of the 1980 national election indicates that such intensive interest group activity will continue to be a conspicuous part of the political process.

Second, from the evidence available, executive and legislative policymakers alike appear to be more susceptible and vulnerable to pressure group influence than previously. Within the executive branch, the expanding role of government in American life has produced a corresponding increase in interest group activity directed at the White House and executive agencies.

Within the legislative branch, receptivity to the influence of pressure groups has similarly increased. For reasons explored fully by Neil MacNeil in Chapter 4 and by Charles O. Jones in Chapter 5, the prestige acquired because of seniority and experience, the powers of committee chairmen, and the influence of party leadership in both the House and the Senate have declined. The loyalty of the American people to one of the two established political parties has diminished; larger numbers of voters now regard themselves as independents, affiliated with neither party. Deterioration of the traditional party organizations at all levels—brought about through party reforms intended to produce a more truly democratic and representative mechanism for consensus building, candidate selection, and campaign participation—actually has produced what Chapter 6 labels as the de-institutionalization of the party system. Single-interest pressure groups and political action committees (PACs)—concentrating on controversies over abortion, gun control, or racial questions—have become the hallmark of contemporary politics and now are sufficiently potent to determine political contests.

Such single-interest politics was a noteworthy feature of the 1980 House and Senate races, with talk of "targeted" opponents and "hit lists" of incumbents marked for defeat at the hands of the Moral Majority and related conservative groups. "Nickpack" (the phonetical rendering of the acronym NCPAC or National Conservative Political Action Committee) cheerfully claimed credit for the defeat of liberal Democratic senators Birch Bayh of Indiana, George McGovern of South Dakota, John Culver of Iowa, and Frank Church of Idaho, for example. Lest it be thought that only the ultraconservatives can play political hardball on the latest pattern, early 1981 found a liberal PAC, calling itself the National Committee for an Effective Congress (NCEC), publishing its own list of conservatives targeted for defeat in the 1982 elections. The list included: Republican senators S. I. Hayakawa of California, William Roth of Delaware, Richard Lugar of Indiana, Harrison Schmitt of New Mexico, and Independent Harry Byrd of Virginia. Growth of such political participation can only foster the fragmentation of political processes and make the task of consensus-building increasingly difficult, especially as those tendencies are exacerbated by the decline of party organization and the continued ascendancy of electronic political communication. Under such conditions, interest groups have unique opportunities to influence policy and elections. But they do so with little regard for the requirements of coherence in public policy and of the national interest.

Such changes in the climate of the American political environment will inevitably affect the policies and programs of the Reagan administration and become factors of consequence in determining its course and success. At the outset, the Reagan White House and Republican Senate must attempt to find policy proposals that can survive in a House of Representatives still under Democratic control, even if it is much more conservative than during the 96th Congress. President Reagan simultaneously must try to control and unify an executive branch that is subject to mounting interest group pressures, stirred as never before by a strong retrenchment effort. And administration supporters on Capitol Hill must somehow discover a formula for achieving sufficient unity in Congress in favor of policy initiatives to withstand a broad-spectrum coalition posing stiff opposition to budgetary and program cuts.

Whether or not Reagan and the Republicans have a national mandate, they believe they have one. And the mandate's terms involve enacting a policy package whose primary aim is to reduce the growth of the federal government in the first such sustained counter-move since FDR took office in 1932. That effort will take the Reagan administration squarely into the densest part of the political thicket; it entails a wholesale cutting of funds and eliminating whole herds of "sacred cow" social programs near and dear to the hearts of many members of Congress and their constituents. The resulting pressure-cooker political atmosphere promises to be close to the combustion point by the time midterm elections come up in 1982.

Perhaps more than any contest in recent history, the 1980 election underscored our realization that earlier attempts to police the electoral process and reform it have not succeeded in ending serious abuses. Regulations governing the amount of money pressure groups and committed individuals may expend for political purposes impose few effective restraints. In fact, it would appear that new-style pressure groups, together with the mass communications media, threaten to supplant the two established political parties as the most influential forces channeling power within the American political system.

CAMPAIGN SPENDING AND NATIONAL ELECTIONS

Our contributors have drawn widely varying conclusions on the issue of campaign spending. In Chapter 5, for example, the point is made that substantially greater campaign expenditures by Republican candidates in comparison with their Democratic opponents significantly affected the outcome of several key Senate races. The analysis of the House races in Chapter 4, however, de-emphasizes the significance of the disparity in determining election results there. All agree that Republicans always outspend Democrats. Despite this fact, the Democrats under the leadership of Speaker Thomas P. "Tip" O'Neill, Jr. of

Massachusetts retained control of the House in the first session of the 97th Congress.

Discussion in these two chapters analyzed another interesting aspect of the 1980 contest: the idea that essentially different forces are likely to determine the results of presidential, Senate, and House elections. A higher level of campaign expenditures, for example, may be more crucial in electing senators than in deciding the choices for members of the House. Alternatively, it may be a relatively minor factor in explaining the outcome of the presidential race. Generalizations are hazardous, however. The financial collapse of the Hubert Humphrey Democratic candidacy in the 1968 election is a prominent example of this. If Humphrey had not run out of money during the final days of the campaign, there is a strong probability that Nixon might not have won that close contest.

Most of our contributors would agree that the costs of conducting a national election in the United States have become astronomical and indefensible; these costs show no sign of decreasing. Laws purporting to regulate campaign expenditures are easily evaded and have no evident restraining effect in limiting the total outlay for this purpose. The latest additions to the ranks of influential pressure groups—the political action committees, in some cases organized for the explicit purpose of evading existing regulations governing campaign expenditures—have burgeoned in American politics, as we have seen. They have expended huge sums for the purpose of electing or defeating particular candidates. It is clear that in 1980 there was no really equivalent countervailing power pitted against PACs intent upon getting one candidate elected and another defeated.

The challenge of how to approach regulation of campaign expenditures in the country thus remains on the political agenda as a problem to be addressed. The lesson that emerges from our study is that existing laws and regulations are inadequate to restrain such activities effectively. A totally new approach may be needed to impose ceilings upon campaign expenditures.

THE VULNERABILITY OF INCUMBENTS

One of the striking features of the 1980 election was the vulnerability of the incumbents. From the White House on down, except for the House of Representatives, the tide ran against returning incumbent office-holders to power in the national government. Based upon the election results, the old political adage—that incumbents have a substantial political advantage over their challengers—no longer applies as a certainty to the contemporary American political environment. Jimmy

Carter became one of the few chief executives in American history to be denied reelection, and Democratic incumbents suffered a heavy toll in the Senate. And even though 92 percent of the incumbents who ran were reelected, the Democratic majority in the House was substantially reduced.

The fact that incumbency no longer confers automatic advantages upon candidates for national office can be explained by several factors, some of which have already been identified. For example, there are the utopian and unrealistic expectations of the public surrounding the presidential office—and to a lesser degree, perhaps, the performance of Congress. As was pointed out in Chapter 4, however, a failure by the president to satisfy these demands not only weakens his appeal to the electorate, but it also impairs the political prospects of those congressional candidates seeking to ride the president's coattails. An unsuccessful presidency (as the voters assessed the Carter incumbency) was a "kiss of death" for a number of senators and representatives seeking reelection as well. It was an impediment some of them never were able to overcome.

The growing vulnerability of political incumbents can be attributed to another factor: the declining prestige of the House and the Senate in the public mind. According to public opinion polls in recent years, Congress has ranked well below the presidency and the judiciary in public respect and assessments of their performance in solving pressing national and international problems. Increasingly, the public has become mindful of the double standard frequently employed by the House and Senate toward their own performance and toward the activities of the executive and judicial branches. Legislators, for example—including, in time, nearly all Republicans—were shocked by the misdeeds of President Nixon and his subordinates in the executive branch during the Watergate episode; in time, they moved decisively to compel the resignations of those responsible for this abuse of executive power. Similarly, in recent years legislators have expressed alarm about abuses or misuses of judicial power, about judicial lawmaking that usurps the responsibilities of Congress, and about the failure of judges to deal decisively with the rising national crime rate.

At the same time, Congress has remained remarkably indifferent and unresponsive to its own evident misuses of power, to its poor image in American public opinion, to its consistently mediocre record in dealing effectively with critical problems at home and abroad, and to scandalous and unethical conduct by its own members. This remains true despite the fact that the House of Representatives did expel one of its members for misconduct in 1980—the first such expulsion since 1861—Democratic Representative Michael Myers of Pennsylvania. Additionally, in domestic affairs, many of the causes of stagflation today stem from costly policies and programs adopted by substantial congressional majorities and to a longtime addiction to deficit spending. In foreign affairs, legislative assertiveness during the 1970s imposed restraints upon the power of the president to act abroad, without providing a clear alternative strategy to the White House for responding to external events affecting the diplomatic and strategic interests of the nation. After almost a decade of a strong congressional influence in foreign policy decisionmaking, no evidence exists that the American people prefer it to forceful presidential leadership in that vital realm.

The vulnerability of political incumbents can also be explained by reference to another phenomenon. This is the serious weakening of the American party system. On Capitol Hill, this has led to growing disunity within the House and Senate, to uncoordinated and sometimes contradictory policy proposals from them, to interminable legislative procrastination, and to an overall public impression that indecision and immobilization may be an even more severe problem for Congress than it is for the presidency. Rightly or wrongly, citizens may conclude that in Congress, the problems are institutional and endemic, whereas in the executive branch they stem largely from the failure of an individual president to take charge and to exert his authority effectively.

The heavy toll exacted of political incumbents in the election of 1980 may also be attributed to a growing public disillusionment with the results of a steadily expanding role by the national government in all aspects of American life. By 1980, as Ronald Reagan and his supporters contend, the plight of many incumbents reflected the electorate's justifiable disappointment with their performance in office. As the powers of the national government have reached into all spheres of the American society, many of its problems have become progressively more acute. To millions of voters, that fact dictated giving a new group of executive and legislative officials a chance to reverse this disturbing tendency.

THE MASS MEDIA AND THE POLITICAL PROCESS

Another question, discussed directly or indirectly in almost every chapter of this symposium, is the influence of the mass media upon the American political process. According to most interpretations of the 1980 election, the image conveyed to the electorate by the media—of the decisiveness and confident poise of Ronald Reagan versus the hesitancy and uncertainty of Jimmy Carter—was of great importance in explaining the outcome. Reagan exploited his talent as an actor to maximum advantage to defeat his Democratic opponent, while Carter (in marked contrast to his successful use of the media four years earlier) was consistently handicapped by a negative image sent into every home in the country by television and the press. Other factors, of course, played a part in the Republican electoral sweep of 1980. But few, apart from the economic distress of the nation, were of greater importance than the impact of the media upon the electoral process.

Our authors (see especially Chapter 6) have called attention to other implications of the role of the media in the American political system. A pervasive complaint among the American people today—that the presidential political campaign is entirely too long, too complicated, and too expensive—is an outgrowth in some measure of the media coverage of it. By the time election day has arrived, the American people have become saturated with, and exhausted by, the detailed, repetitious, and often trivializing coverage given to the campaign by the media. A consequence is a buildup of voter apathy and resultant low voter turnout at the polls on election day. Since the GOP traditionally has been the minority party in the United States, voter absenteeism is likely to penalize the Democratic party more than it does the GOP. In a number of key political races, for instance, the Democratic party counted upon a high voter turnout to elect its candidates; in some cases, their defeat could be explained at least partially by the fact that a larger number of voters than was anticipated stayed away from the polls on election day.

The early concession of President Carter over national television, more than two hours before the polls closed on the West Coast—and the even earlier projection of Reagan as the winner by one network—highlight other aspects of the issue. Democratic party candidates and strategists believe that these facts affected the outcome of key elections in the western United States, nearly always in a manner favorable to the Republican party. While it may be doubted that these events affected the ultimate outcome of the presidential race in 1980, in more closely contested races at the presidential or congressional levels in the future, it might have a decisive influence upon the final result. And they did affect some of the 1980 races in the Senate and House of Representatives. The media can hardly be blamed for permitting the president to concede the election, of course. But their coverage of the campaign and the election poses a number of serious questions related to professional ethics, to the definition of what is "news," and to the role of network commentators in what may be called the new politics of the age of mass communication and instant information.

In Chapter 6, considerable responsibility is assigned to the media for the de-institutionalization of the American two-party system. To be sure, this is only one factor among several influential ones. But overly aggressive reporting by TV news commentators—including a tendency to report the news before it happens—contributes significantly to impairing (or enhancing) the image of political leaders, to holding the operation of the political system up to public scorn and ridicule, and to weakening popular confidence in the normal operation of political processes. Although the American press may be the best in the world, it still must be said that a lack of sound understanding of American political culture by network reporters—together with a hunger for a sensational scoop in the name of investigative reporting—brings a focus on the ephemeral and inconsequential at the expense of the more pedestrian, substantive content of events. To be sure, there are many exceptions to this rule. But there is, doubtless, also a problem of large proportions here, with consequences for the health of our politics, the balance of the deliberative processes whereby a free society governs itself, and the effectiveness of the parties whose vitality is essential to orderly governance.

It is not necessary to exaggerate the impact of the public media upon the American political process to realize that it has been profound and far-reaching in its consequences. It is also apparent that any controls that might be devised will have to be self-imposed by members of the news profession. For few rights are more zealously cherished by Americans, or more fundamental to the existence of our democracy, than those guarantees of free expression protected under the Constitution in the First Amendment. Legal or other governmentally-imposed restrictions upon freedom of the press would be—should be—strenuously resisted by everyone.

That said, however, important issues remain. What is meant by a responsible press within the American political environment? How can TV commentators and newscasters report the news while eschewing any intention to affect the outcome of events? How should the professional ethics of journalists be adapted to the electronic era? Is there no limit to the use of highly sophisticated techniques of sampling and projections of winners from computerized data drawn from key precincts in state and national elections? There is awesome power at stake here. What responsibility, if any, should reporters bear for the consequences of concentrating primarily upon what is wrong with American political life and upon the misdeeds of candidates and officials? These hard questions deserve close scrutiny. The answers must lie somewhere between the extremes of prior restraint through governmental censorship and a completely uninhibited adversary relationship of the press versus the politicians. No one believes every such problem is easy to solve, or even that there is one solution; still, the problems remain. The essays contained in this symposium focus attention upon several aspects of them. The matter is becoming more critical with each national election in the United States. And its solution will continue to engage the attention of the nation's best legal minds and of students of American political behavior for many years to come.

INCONCLUSIONS

The 1980 elections are over and the Reagan administration is installed in Washington. Former President Carter has retired from the national scene, at least for awhile, and is drawing the $70,000 annual pension provided to former presidents. Reagan's victory may or may not mark the beginning of an era, whatever else his concerted effort to make "A New Beginning" for America comes to mean. The dual thrust of his policies is: to restore national prestige by strengthening the military power of the United States, and to cure the multiple economic ills of the country by curbing the growth of federal government and expenses, while freeing up private industry and individual initiative. The gist of his intentions is contained in the documents appended to this volume, and the reader may consult them for the details of his political thinking.

No one can doubt that a new direction in American politics has been charted. To what degree it will be followed remains to be seen. The electoral sweep that brought Reagan and the Republicans to office was not unprecedented. Both Franklin Roosevelt in 1936 and Richard Nixon in 1972 amassed even higher numbers of electoral votes and much wider popular majorities than did Reagan in 1980. But election results are not everything. Vision and personality are potent factors, too. The Republican administration and solid Republican majority in the Senate must contend with a 51-vote Democratic majority in the House of Representatives, where the real battles over Reagan's proposals are likely to be waged.

The judiciary, of course, was not directly affected by the ballot box in 1980. And although five of the nine Supreme Court justices were appointed by Republican presidents Nixon and Ford, the remaining four appear to be determined to remain on the bench so that Reagan cannot appoint their successors. The lower levels of the federal judiciary are heavily populated by judges appointed by President Carter and are otherwise of a liberal orientation. The bureaucracy, upon which so much of government utterly depends, is heavily Democratic in orientation and notoriously resistant to outside control—whether from the Congress or from the president and his appointive officials, whatever their party. The federal bureaucracy cannot be expected to be an accomplice in efforts to abolish programs, reduce operating budgets, and eliminate positions.

The lobbyists who populate Washington, seeking to gain advantage in the scramble for money and power, remain a potent force of expert

"LOOK AT THIS! SEVENTEEN MILLION DOLLARS FOR THE 'Federal Fund for the Preservation and Encouragement of Ostrich and Walrus Sports in America'!... NOBODY COULD OBJECT TO CUTTING THAT!"

operatives largely dedicated to keeping in check any ideas the administration may have of revolutionizing policy and government. The mass media are widely conceded to be liberal and Democratic in their hearts, and that assessment influenced the direct-mail campaign techniques so heavily relied on by conservative PACs who thereby circumvented the press to get their messages to the electorate in 1980.

Finally, there is a broad segment of the electorate itself, so poorly mobilized by the Democratic party in 1980 that many of them sat out the election. Many of these voters are apt to be adversely affected by reductions in social services provided through the more than 80 agencies identified for curtailment or elimination by the Reagan administration. The cumulative impact of these plans, if they are implemented— reduced services for the poor, elderly, and racial minority voters, together with a determined policy of tight money (high interest rates), fiscal retrenchment, a probable slow progress in restraining inflation, and only moderate gains in the employment picture—points toward tough sledding for the Republicans in 1982. This will be especially true if one considers that a key factor in the country's economic ills (the cardinal reason for Carter's defeat, by all accounts) is the energy crisis largely caused by American dependence on foreign oil. No solution in the short run—or possibly even in the long run—is in sight. Senator Kennedy and the old Democratic coalition, meanwhile, are rehearsing in the wings, getting ready to take center stage in 1984.

But the other side must also be considered. The resourcefulness of the new Republicans to effect their mandate and achieve a meaningful new beginning cannot be dismissed. Time is of the essence, if the momentum of the election sweep is to carry the administration's ambitious policy programs through Congress before electioneering for 1982 gets seriously under way. That is a prime element in Republican strategy. President Reagan and his advisors also clearly understand that a centrist position is the only one that really succeeds for long in American politics; extremist politics do not work. Conciliation of the liberal wing of the Republican party began overtly with the selection of George Bush as the vice-presidential nominee. The cuts made in Carter's proposed budget for fiscal year 1982 (beginning on October 1, 1981) did not reduce total spending, which grew by over $40 billion above the 1981 level. Social welfare programs were handled with care.

Public relations with every significant constituency are being handled with masterly finesse by President Reagan. The Congress is not regarded as "those clowns on Capitol Hill," as it was in the Nixon White House. Rather it is being thoughtfully and attentively courted and consulted at every turn, its cooperation sought in open-handed cordiality and the evident genuine respect one partner in the process of governing ought properly to accord the other. The contrast with the approach taken by the Carter White House is most favorable, as even Democrats have acknowledged. Moreover, the Republicans appear to be unified as seldom before. And they seem anxious to remove the old stigma that their party is the haven of only the well-to-do. There is a conscious and intelligent effort, reflecting thorough planning, to open the doors of Republicanism to the nation. No one doubts that Reagan himself is an "ace communicator," as his supporters say, and this is no mean asset in the electronic age, or for a public figure in any age.

Can the new strategy work? Can the force of the election triumph be successfully transformed into the power to lead effectively and govern well? Is the vision stirring enough, the personality of the president potent enough? Perhaps so. The test of it all may come in 1982, most certainly in 1984, for the American people tend to demand success of their political leaders. And they resoundingly stamped *Failed* on the Democratic party and President Carter when they handed out report cards on November 4, 1980. The people protested national humiliation in world affairs and personal unhappiness with economic and domestic affairs, in a rising tide of discontent. If the Republicans can pass the test of their own shrewd devising in 1984, a "New Era" may well have begun: "Are you better off today than you were four years ago?" Time will tell, in this land where the people are king.

Presidential Messages

RONALD REAGAN'S
INAUGURAL ADDRESS

Following is the text of President Reagan's inaugural address as delivered from the west front of the U.S. Capitol on January 20, 1981. Immediately before the 12 noon address, the oath of office was administered by Chief Justice Warren E. Burger.

Senator Hatfield, Mr. Chief Justice, Mr. President, Vice President Bush, Vice President Mondale, Senator Baker, Speaker O'Neill, Reverend Moomaw, and my fellow citizens:

To a few of us here today this is a solemn and most momentous occasion. And, yet, in the history of our Nation it is a commonplace occurrence.

The orderly transfer of authority as called for in the Constitution routinely takes place as it has for almost two centuries and few of us stop to think how unique we really are. In the eyes of many in the world, this every-4-year ceremony we accept as normal is nothing less than a miracle.

Mr. President, I want our fellow citizens to know how much you did to carry on this tradition. By your gracious cooperation in the transition process, you have shown a watching world that we are a united people pledged to maintaining a political system which guarantees individual liberty to a greater degree than any other, and I thank you and your people for all your help in maintaining the continuity which is the hallmark of our Republic.

The business of our nation goes forward. These United States are confronted with an economic affliction of great proportions. We suffer from the longest and one of the worst sustained inflations in our national history. It distorts our economic decisions, penalizes thrift, and crushes the struggling young and the fixed-income elderly alike. It threatens to shatter the lives of millions of our people.

Idle industries have cast workers into unemployment, human misery and personal indignity. Those who do work are denied a fair return for their labor by a tax system which penalizes successful achievement and keeps us from maintaining full productivity.

But great as our tax burden is, it has not kept pace with public spending. For decades, we have piled deficit upon deficit, mortgaging our future and our children's future for the temporary convenience of the present. To continue this long trend is to guarantee tremendous social, cultural, political, and economic upheavals.

You and I, as individuals, can, by borrowing, live beyond our means, but for only a limited period of time. Why, then, should we think that collectively, as a nation, we're not bound by that same limitation?

We must act today in order to preserve tomorrow. And let there be no misunderstanding—we are going to begin to act, beginning today.

The economic ills we suffer have come upon us over several decades. They will not go away in days, weeks, or months. But they will go away. They will go away because we as Americans have the capacity now, as we've had in the past, to do whatever needs to be done to preserve this last and greatest bastion of freedom.

In this present crisis, government is not the solution to our problem; government is the problem.

From time to time we've been tempted to believe that society has become too complex to be managed by self-rule, that government by an elite group is superior to government for, by, and of the people. But if no one among us is capable of governing himself, then who among us has the capacity to govern someone else?

All of us together, in and out of government, must bear the burden. The solutions we seek must be equitable, with no one group singled out to pay a higher price.

We hear much of special interest groups. Our concern must be for a special interest group that has been too long neglected. It knows no sectional boundaries or ethnic and racial divisions, and it crosses political party lines. It is made up of men and women who raise our food, patrol our streets, man our mines and factories, teach our children, keep our homes, and heal us when we're sick—professionals, industrialists, shopkeepers, clerks, cabbies and truckdrivers. They are, in short, "We the people," this breed called Americans.

This administration's objective will be a healthy, vigorous, growing economy that provides equal opportunities for all Americans with no barriers born of bigotry or discrimination. Putting America back to work means putting all Americans back to work. Ending inflation means freeing all Americans from the terror of runaway living costs. All must share in the productive work of this "new beginning," and all must share in the bounty of a revived economy. With the idealism and fairplay which are the core of our system and our strength, we can have a strong prosperous America at peace with itself and the world.

Curbing Federal Powers

So, as we begin, let us take inventory. We are a Nation that has a government—not the other way around. And this makes us special among the nations of the Earth. Our Government has no power except that granted it by the people. It is time to check and reverse the growth of Government which shows signs of having grown beyond the consent of the governed.

It is my intention to curb the size and influence of the Federal Establishment and to demand recognition of the distinction between the powers granted to the Federal Government and those reserved to the States or to the people.

All of us need to be reminded that the Federal Government did not create the States; the States created the Federal Government.

So there will be no misunderstanding, it is not my intention to do away with government. It is rather to make it work—work with us, not over us; to stand by our side, not ride on our back. Government can and must provide opportunity, not smother it; foster productivity, not stifle it.

If we look to the answer as to why for so many years we achieved so much, prospered as no other people on earth, it was because here, in this land, we unleashed the energy and individual genius of man to a greater extent than has ever been done before. Freedom and the dignity of the individual have been more available and assured here than in any other place on earth. The price for this freedom at times has been high. But we have never been unwilling to pay that price.

It is no coincidence that our present troubles parallel and are proportionate to the intervention and intrusion in our lives that result from unnecessary and excessive growth of government.

It is time for us to realize that we are too great a nation to limit ourselves to small dreams. We are not, as some would have us believe, doomed to an inevitable decline. I do not believe in a fate that will fall on us no matter what we do. I do believe in a fate that will fall on us if we do nothing.

So, with all the creative energy at our command, let us begin an era of national renewal. Let us renew our determination, our courage, and our strength. And let us renew our faith and our hope. We have every right to dream heroic dreams.

Those who say that we're in a time when there are no heroes, just don't know where to look. You can see heroes every day going in and out of factory gates. Others, a handful in number, produce enough food to feed all of us and much of the world beyond.

You meet heroes across a counter. And they're on both sides of that counter. There are entrepreneurs with faith in themselves and faith in an idea who create new jobs, new wealth and opportunity. They are individuals and families whose taxes support the Government and whose voluntary gifts support church, charity, culture, art, and education. Their patriotism is quiet but deep. Their values sustain our national life.

I have used the words "they" and "their" in speaking of these heroes. I could say "you" and "your" because I am addressing the heroes of whom I speak—you, the citizens of this blessed land. Your dreams, your hopes, your goals, are going to be the dreams, the hopes and the goals of this administration, so help me God.

We shall reflect the compassion that is so much a part of your makeup. How can we love our country and not love our countrymen? And loving them reach out a hand when they fall, heal them when they are sick, and provide opportunities to make them self-sufficient so they will be equal in fact and not just in theory?

Can we solve the problems confronting us? Well, the answer is an unequivocal and emphatic yes. To paraphrase Winston Churchill, I did not take the oath I've just taken with the intention of presiding over the dissolution of the world's strongest economy.

In the days ahead I will propose removing the roadblocks that have slowed our economy and reduced productivity. Steps will be taken aimed at restoring the balance between the various levels of government. Progress may be slow—measured in inches and feet, not miles—but we will progress. It is time to reawaken this industrial giant, to get government back within its means, and to lighten our punitive tax burden. And these will be our first priorities, and on these principles, there will be no compromise.

On the eve of our struggle for independence a man who might have been one of the greatest among the Founding Fathers, Dr. Joseph Warren, president of the Massachusetts Congress, said to his fellow Americans, "Our country is in danger, but not to be despaired of . . . On you depend the fortunes of America. You are to decide the important question upon which rests the happiness and the liberty of millions yet unborn. Act worthy of yourselves."

U.S.: Exemplar of Freedom

Well, I believe we, the Americans of today, are ready to act worthy of ourselves, ready to do what must be done to ensure happiness and liberty for ourselves, our children, and our children's children.

And as we renew ourselves here in our own land, we will be seen as having greater strength throughout the world. We will again be the exemplar of freedom and a beacon of hope for those who do not now have freedom.

To those neighbors and allies who share our freedom, we will strengthen our historic ties and assure them of our support and firm commitment. We will match loyalty with loyalty. We will strive for mutually beneficial relations. We will not use our friendship to impose on their sovereignty, for our own sovereignty is not for sale.

As for the enemies of freedom, those who are potential adversaries, they will be reminded that peace is the highest aspiration of the American people. We will negotiate for it, sacrifice for it; we will not surrender for it now or ever.

Our forebearance *[sic]* should never be misunderstood. Our reluctance for conflict should not be misjudged as a failure of will. When action is required to preserve our national security, we will act. We will maintain sufficient strength to prevail if need be, knowing that if we do so we have the best chance of never having to use that strength.

Above all we must realize that no arsenal or no weapon in the arsenals of the world is so formidable as the will and moral courage of free men and women. It is a weapon our adversaries in today's world do not have. It is a weapon that we as Americans do have. Let that be understood by those who practice terrorism and prey upon their neighbors.

I'm told that tens of thousands of prayer meetings are being held on this day, and for that I am deeply grateful. We are a nation under God, and I believe God intended for us to be free. It would be fitting and good, I think, if on each Inaugural Day in future years it should be declared a day of prayer.

This is the first time in our history that this ceremony has been held, as you've been told, on this West Front of the Capitol. Standing here, one faces a magnificent vista, opening up on this city's special beauty and history. At the end of this open Mall are those shrines to the giants on whose shoulders we stand.

Directly in front of me, the monument to a monumental man, George Washington, Father of our country. A man of humility who came to greatness reluctantly. He led America out of revolutionary victory into infant nationhood.

Off to one side, the stately memorial to Thomas Jefferson. The Declaration of Independence flames with his eloquence.

And then beyond the reflecting pool the dignified columns of the Lincoln Memorial. Whoever would understand in his heart the meaning of America will find it in the life of Abraham Lincoln.

Beyond those monuments to heroism is the Potomac River, and on the far shore the sloping hills of Arlington National Cemetery with its row upon row of simple white markers bearing crosses or Stars of David. They add up to only a tiny fraction of the price that has been paid for our freedom.

Each one of those markers is a monument to the kind of hero I spoke of earlier. Their lives ended in places called Belleau Wood, the Argonne, Omaha Beach, Salerno and halfway around the world on Guadalcanal, Tarawa, Pork Chop Hill, The Chosin Reservoir, and in a hundred rice paddies and jungles of a place called Vietnam.

Under one such a marker lies a young man—Martin Treptow—who left his job in a small town barbershop in 1917 to go to France with the famed Rainbow Division. There, on the Western front, he was killed trying to carry a message between battalions under heavy artillery fire.

We are told that on his body was found a diary. On the flyleaf under the heading, "My Pledge," he had written these words: "America must win this war. Therefore, I will work, I will save, I will sacrifice, I will endure, I will fight cheerfully and do my utmost, as if the issue of the whole struggle depended on me alone."

The crisis we are facing today does not require of us the kind of sacrifice that Martin Treptow and so many thousands of others were called upon to make. It does require, however, our best effort and our willingness to believe in ourselves and to believe in our capacity to perform great deeds; to believe that together, with God's help, we can and will resolve the problems which now confront us.

And, after all, why shouldn't we believe that? We are Americans.

God bless you and thank you.

PRESIDENT REAGAN'S ECONOMIC POLICY ADDRESS

Following is the text of President Reagan's report to the nation on the economy, as broadcast February 5, 1981.

Good evening. I am speaking to you tonight to give you a report on the state of our Nation's economy. I regret to say that we are in the worst economic mess since the Great Depression. A few days ago I was presented with a report I had asked for—a comprehensive audit if you will of our economic condition. You won't like it, I didn't like it, but we have to face the truth and then go to work to turn things around. And make no mistake about it, we can turn them around.

I'm not going to subject you to the jumble of charts, figures, and economic jargon of that audit but rather will try to explain where we are, how we got there, and how we can get back.

First, however, let me just give a few "attention getters" from the audit. The Federal budget is out of control and we face runaway deficits, of almost $80 billion for this budget year that ends September 30. That deficit is larger than the entire Federal budget in 1957 and so is the almost $80 billion we will pay in interest this year on the national debt.

Twenty years ago in 1960 our Federal Government payroll was less than $13 billion. Today it is $75 billion. During these twenty years, our population has only increased by 23.3 percent. The Federal budget has gone up 528 percent.

Now, we've just had two years of back-to-back double digit inflation, 13.3 percent in 1979—12.4 percent last year. The last time this happened was in World War I.

In 1960 mortgage interest rates averaged about 6 percent. They are 2-1/2 times as high now, 15.4 percent. The percentage of your earnings the Federal Government took in taxes in 1960 has almost doubled. And finally there are 7 million Americans caught up in the personal indignity and human tragedy of unemployment. If they stood in a line—allowing 3 feet for each person—the line would reach from the Coast of Maine to California.

Inflation Impact

Well, so much for the audit itself. Let me try to put this in personal terms. Here is a dollar such as you earned, spent, or saved in 1960. Here is a quarter, a dime, and a penny—36¢. That's what this 1960 dollar is worth today. And if the present inflation rate should continue three more years, that dollar of 1960 will be worth a quarter. What initiative is there to save? And if we don't save we are short of the investment capital needed for business and industry expansion. Workers in Japan and West Germany save several times the percentage of their income that Americans do.

What's happened to that American dream of owning a home? Only ten years ago a family could buy a home and the monthly payment averaged little more than a quarter—27¢ out of each dollar earned. Today it takes 42¢ out of every dollar of income. So, fewer than 1 out of 11 families can afford to buy their first new home.

Regulations adopted by government with the best of intentions have added $666 to the cost of an automobile. It is estimated that altogether regulations of every kind, on shopkeepers, farmers, and major industries add $100 billion or more to the cost of the goods and services we buy. And then another $20 billion is spent by government—handling the paperwork created by those regulations.

I'm sure you are getting the idea that the audit presented to me found government policies of the last few decades responsible for our economic troubles. We forgot or just overlooked the fact that government—any government—has a built-in tendency to grow. Now, we all had a hand in looking to government for benefits as if government had some sources of revenue other than our earnings. Many if not most of the things we thought of or that government offered to us seemed attractive.

In the years following the Second World War it was easy (for awhile at least) to overlook the price tag. Our income more than doubled in the 25 years after the War. We increased our take-home pay in those 25 years by more than we had amassed in all the preceding 150 years put together. Yes, there was some inflation, 1 or 1-1/2 percent a year; that didn't bother us. But if we look back at those golden years we recall that even then voices had been raised warning that inflation, like radioactivity, was cumulative and that once started it could get out of control. Some government programs seemed so worthwhile that borrowing to fund them didn't bother us.

By 1960 our national debt stood at $284 billion. Congress in 1971 decided to put a ceiling of $400 billion on our ability to borrow. Today the debt is $934 billion. So-called temporary increases or extensions in the debt ceiling have been allowed 21 times in these 10 years and now I have been forced to ask for another increase in the debt ceiling or the government will be unable to function past the middle of February and I've only been here 16 days. Before we reach the day when we can reduce the debt ceiling we may in spite of our best efforts see a national debt in excess of a trillion dollars. Now this is a figure literally beyond our comprehension.

We know now that inflation results from all that deficit spending. Government has only two ways of getting money other than raising taxes. It can go into the money market and borrow, competing with its own citizens and driving up interest rates, which it has done, or it can print money, and it's done that. Both methods are inflationary.

We're victims of language, the very word "inflation" leads us to think of it as just high prices. Then, of course, we resent the person who puts on the price tags forgetting that he or she is also a victim of inflation. Inflation is not just high prices, it is a reduction in the value of our money. When the money supply is increased but the goods and services available for buying are not, we have too much money chasing too few goods.

Wars are usually accompanied by inflation. Everyone is working or fighting but production is of weapons and munitions not things we can buy and use.

Taxes

One way out would be to raise taxes so that government need not borrow or print money. But in all these years of government growth we've reached—indeed surpassed—the limit of our people's tolerance or ability to bear an increase in the tax burden.

Prior to World War II, taxes were such that on the average we only had to work just a little over one month each year to pay our total Federal, State, and local tax bill. Today we have to work four months to pay that bill.

Some say shift the tax burden to business and industry but business doesn't pay taxes. Oh, don't get the wrong idea, business is being taxed—so much so that we are being priced out of the world market. But business must pass its costs of operation and that includes taxes, onto the customer in the price of the product. Only people pay taxes—all the taxes. Government just uses business in a kind of sneaky way to help collect the taxes. They are hidden in the price and we aren't aware of how much tax we actually pay. Today, this once great industrial giant of ours has the lowest rate of gain in productivity of virtually all the industrial nations with whom we must compete in the world market. We can't even hold our own market here in America against foreign automobiles, steel, and a number of other products.

Japanese production of automobiles is almost twice as great per worker as it is in America. Japanese steel workers out-produce their American counterparts by about 25 percent.

Now this isn't because they are better workers. I'll match the American working man or woman against anyone in the world. But we have to give them the tools and equipment that workers in the other industrial nations have.

We invented the assembly line and mass production, but punitive tax policies and excessive and unnecessary regulations plus government borrowing have stifled our ability to update plant and equipment. When capital investment is made it's too often for some unproductive alterations demanded by government to meet various of its regulations.

Excessive taxation of individuals has robbed us of incentive and made overtime unprofitable.

We once produced about 40 percent of the world's steel. We now produce 19 percent.

We were once the greatest producer of automobiles, producing more than all the rest of the world combined. That is no longer true, and in addition, the big 3, the major auto companies, in our land have sustained tremendous losses in the past year and have been forced to lay off thousands of workers.

All of you who are working know that even with cost-of-living pay raises you can't keep up with inflation. In our progressive tax system as you increase the number of dollars you earn you find yourself moved up into higher tax brackets, paying a higher tax rate just for trying to hold your own. The result? Your standard of living is going down.

Over the past decades we've talked of curtailing government spending so that we can then lower the tax burden. Sometimes we've even taken a run at doing that. But there were always those who told us taxes couldn't be cut until spending was reduced. Well, you know, we can lecture our children about extravagance until we run out of voice and breath. Or we can cure their extravagance by simply reducing their allowance.

Turning Point

It is time to recognize that we have come to a turning point. We are threatened with an economic calamity of tremendous proportions and the old business as usual treatment can't save us.

Together, we must chart a different course. We must increase productivity. That means making it possible for industry to modernize and make use of the technology which we ourselves invented; that means putting Americans back to work. And that means above all bringing government spending back within government revenues which is the only way, together with increased productivity that we can reduce and, yes, eliminate inflation.

In the past we've tried to fight inflation one year and then when unemployment increased turn the next year to fighting unemployment with more deficit spending as a pump primer. So again, up goes inflation. It hasn't worked. We don't have to choose between inflation and unemployment—they go hand in hand. It's time to try something different and that's what we're going to do.

I've already placed a freeze on hiring replacements for those who retire or leave government service. I have ordered a cut in government travel, the number of consultants to the government, and the buying of office equipment and other items. I have put a freeze on pending regulations and set up a task force under Vice President Bush to review regulations with an eye toward getting rid of as many as possible. I have decontrolled oil which should result in more domestic production and less dependence on foreign oil. And I am eliminating that ineffective Council on Wage and Price Stability.

But it will take more, much more and we must realize there is no quick fix. At the same time, however, we cannot delay in implementing an economic program aimed at both reducing tax rates to stimulate productivity and reducing the growth in government spending to reduce unemployment and inflation.

On February 18th, I will present in detail an economic program to Congress embodying the features I have just stated. It will propose budget cuts in virtually every department of government. It is my belief that these actual budget cuts will only be part of the savings. As our Cabinet Secretaries take charge of their departments, they will search out areas of waste, extravagance, and costly administrative overhead which could yield additional and substantial reductions.

Now at the same time we're doing this, we must go forward with a tax relief package. I shall ask for a 10 percent reduction across the board in personal income tax rates for each of the next three years. Proposals will also be submitted for accelerated depreciation allowances for business to provide necessary capital so as to create jobs.

Now, here again, in saying this, I know that language, as I said earlier, can get in the way of a clear understanding of what our program is intended to do. Budget cuts can sound as if we are going to reduce total government spending to a lower level than was spent the year before. This is not the case. The budgets will increase as our population increases and each year we'll see spending increases to match that growth. Government revenues will increase as the economy grows, but the burden will be lighter for each individual because the economic base will have been expanded by reason of the reduced rates.

Balanced Budget

Now let me show you a chart I've had drawn to illustrate how this can be. Here you see two trend lines. The bottom line shows the increase in tax revenues. The red line on top is the increase in government spending. Both lines turn upward reflecting the giant tax increase already built into the system for this year 1981, and the increases in spending built into the '81 and '82 budgets and on into the future.

As you can see, the spending line rises at a steeper slant than the revenue line. And that gap between those lines illustrates the increasing deficits we've been running including this year's $80 billion deficit.

Now, in the second chart, the lines represent the positive effects when Congress accepts our economic program. Both lines continue to rise allowing for necessary growth but the gap narrows as spending cuts continue over the next few years, until finally the two lines come together meaning a balanced budget.

I am confident that my Administration can achieve that. At that point tax revenues in spite of rate reductions will be increasing faster than spending which means we can look forward to further reductions in the tax rates.

Now, in all of this we will of course work closely with the Federal Reserve System toward the objective of a stable monetary policy.

Our spending cuts will not be at the expense of the truly needy. We will, however, seek to eliminate benefits to those who are not really qualified by reason of need.

As I've said before, on February 18th, I will present this economic package of budget reductions and tax reform to a joint session of Congress and to you in full detail.

Our basic system is sound. We can, with compassion, continue to meet our responsibility to those who through no fault of their own need our help. We can meet fully the other legitimate responsibilities of government. We cannot continue any longer our wasteful ways at the expense of the workers of this land or of our children.

Since 1960 our government has spent $5.1 trillion; our debt has grown by $648 billion. Prices have exploded by 178 percent. How much better off are we for all that? We all know, we are very much worse off.

Need to Act

When we measure how harshly these years of inflation, lower productivity, and uncontrolled government growth have affected our lives, we know we must act and act now.

We must not be timid.

We will restore the freedom of all men and women to excel and to create. We will unleash the energy and genius of the American people—traits which have never failed us.

To the Congress of the United States, I extend my hand in cooperation and I believe we can go forward in a bipartisan manner.

I found a real willingness to cooperate on the part of Democrats and members of my own Party.

To my colleagues in the Executive Branch of government and to all Federal employees I ask that we work in the spirit of service.

I urge those great institutions in America—business and labor—to be guided by the national interest and I'm confident they will. The only special interest that we will serve is the interest of all the people.

We can create the incentives which take advantage of the genius of our economic system—a system, as Walter Lippmann observed more than 40 years ago, which for the first time in history gave men "a way of producing wealth in which the good fortune of others multiplied their own."

Our aim is to increase our national wealth so all will have more not just redistribute what we already have which is just a sharing of scarcity. We can begin to reward hard work and risk-taking, by forcing this government to live within its means.

Over the years we've let negative economic forces run out of control. We've stalled the judgment day. We no longer have that luxury. We're out of time.

And to you my fellow citizens, let us join in a new determination to rebuild the foundation of our society; to work together to act responsibly. Let us do so with the most profound respect for that which must be preserved as well as with sensitive understanding and compassion for those who must be protected.

We can leave our children with an unrepayable massive debt and a shattered economy or we can leave them liberty in a land where every individual has the opportunity to be whatever God intended us to be. All it takes is a little common sense and recognition of our own ability. Together we can forge a new beginning for America.

Thank you and good night.

PRESIDENT REAGAN'S
ECONOMIC PROPOSALS TEXT

Following is the text of the address as delivered by President Reagan to a joint session of Congress on February 18, 1981.

Mr. Speaker, Mr. President, distinguished Members of Congress, honored guests, and fellow citizens:

Only a month ago, I was your guest in this historic building and I pledged to you my cooperation in doing what is right for this Nation that we all love so much.

I am here tonight to reaffirm that pledge and to ask that we share in restoring the promise that is offered to every citizen by this, the last, best hope of man on earth.

All of us are aware of the punishing inflation which has, for the first time in some 60 years, held to double digit figures for 2 years in a row. Interest rates have reached absurd levels of more than 20 percent and over 15 percent for those who would borrow to buy a home. All across this land one can see newly built homes standing vacant, unsold because of mortgage interest rates.

Almost eight million Americans are out of work. These are people who want to be productive. But as the months go by, despair dominates their lives. The threats of layoffs and unemployment hang over other millions, and all who work are frustrated by their inability to keep up with inflation.

One worker in a Midwest city put it to me this way: He said, "I'm bringing home more dollars than I thought I ever believed I could possibly earn, but I seem to be getting worse off." And he is. Not only have hourly earnings of the American worker, after adjusting for inflation, declined 5 percent over the past 5 years, but in these 5 years, Federal personal taxes for the average family increased 67 percent.

We can no longer procrastinate and hope that things will get better. They will not. Unless we act forcefully, and now, the economy will get worse.

National Debt

Can we who man the ship of state deny it is somewhat out of control? Our national debt is approaching $1 trillion. A few weeks ago I called such a figure—a trillion dollars—incomprehensible. I've been trying ever since to think of a way to illustrate how big a trillion is. The best I could come up with is that if you had a stack of $1,000 bills in your hand only four inches high you would be a millionaire. A trillion dollars would be a stack of $1,000 bills 67 miles high.

The interest on the public debt this year we know will be over $90 billion. And unless we change the proposed spending for the fiscal year beginning October 1, we'll add another almost $80 billion to the debt.

Adding to our troubles is a mass of regulations imposed on the shopkeeper, the farmer, the craftsman, professionals and major industry that is estimated to add $100 billion to the price of things we buy and it reduces our ability to produce. The rate of increase in American productivity, once one of the highest in the world, is among the lowest of all major industrial nations. Indeed, it has actually declined in the last 3 years.

I have painted a pretty grim picture but I think that I have painted it accurately. It is within our power to change this picture and we can act with hope. There is nothing wrong with our internal strengths. There has been no breakdown in the human, technological, and natural resources upon which the economy is built.

Four-point Proposal

Based on this confidence in a system which has never failed us—but which we have failed through a lack of confidence, and sometimes through a belief that we could fine tune the economy and get a tune to our liking—I am proposing a comprehensive four-point program. Let me outline in detail some of the principal parts of this program. You will each be provided with a completely detailed copy of the entire program.

This plan is aimed at reducing the growth in Government spending and taxing, reforming and eliminating regulations which are unnecessary and unproductive or counterproductive, and encouraging a consistent monetary policy aimed at maintaining the value of the currency.

If enacted in full, this program can help America create 13 million new jobs, nearly 3 million more than we would have without these measures. It will also help us gain control of inflation.

Tax Increase Rate Reduction

It is important to note that we are only reducing the rate of increase in taxing and spending. We are not attempting to cut either spending or taxing levels below that which we presently have. This plan will get our economy moving again, increase productivity growth, and thus create the jobs our people must have.

And I am asking that you join me in reducing direct Federal spending by $41.4 billion in fiscal year 1982, along with another $7.7 billion user fees and off-budget savings for a total savings of $49.1 billion.

This will still allow an increase of $40.8 billion over 1981 spending.

Full Funding for Truly Needy

I know that exaggerated and inaccurate stories about these cuts have disturbed many people, particularly those dependent on grant and benefit programs for their basic needs. Some of you have heard from constituents, I know, afraid that social security checks, for example, were going to be taken away from them. I regret the fear that these unfounded stories have caused and I welcome this opportunity to set things straight.

We will continue to fulfill the obligations that spring from our national conscience. Those who through no fault of their own must depend on the rest of us, the poverty stricken, the disabled, the elderly, all those with true need, can rest assured that the social safety net of programs they depend on are exempt from any cuts.

The full retirement benefits of the more than 31 million social security recipients will be continued along with an annual cost of living increase. Medicare will not be cut, nor will supplemental income for the blind, aged, and disabled, and funding will continue for veterans' pensions.

School breakfasts and lunches for the children of low income families will continue, as will nutrition and other special services for the aging. There will be no cut in Project Head Start or summer youth jobs.

All in all, nearly $216 billion worth of programs providing help for tens of millions of Americans—will be fully funded. But government will not continue to subsidize individuals or particular business interests where real need cannot be demonstrated.

And while we will reduce some subsidies to regional and local governments, we will at the same time convert a number of categorical grant programs into block grants to reduce wasteful administrative overhead and to give local government entities and States more flexibility and control. We call for an end to duplication in Federal programs and reform of those which are not cost effective.

Restore Programs to
States and Private Sector

Already, some have protested that there must be no reduction in aid to schools. Let me point out that Federal aid to education amounts to only eight percent of the total educational funding. For this eight percent the Federal Government has insisted on a tremendously disproportionate share of control over our schools. Whatever reductions we've proposed in that eight percent will amount to very little in the total cost of education. They will, however, restore more authority to States and local school districts.

Historically the American people have supported by voluntary contributions more artistic and cultural activities than all the other countries in the world put together. I wholeheartedly support this approach and believe that Americans will continue their generosity. Therefore, I am proposing a savings of $85 million in the Federal subsidies now going to the arts and humanities.

There are a number of subsidies to business and industry that I believe are unnecessary. Not because the activities being subsidized aren't of value but because the marketplace contains incentives enough to warrant continuing these activities without a government subsidy. One such subsidy is the Department of Energy's synthetic fuels program. We will continue support of research leading to development of new technologies and more independence from foreign oil, but we can save at least $3.2 billion by leaving to private industry the building of plants to make liquid or gas fuels from coal.

We are asking that another major industry, business subsidy I should say, the Export-Import Bank loan authority, be reduced by one-third in 1982. We are doing this because the primary beneficiaries of tax payer funds in this case are the exporting companies themselves—most of them profitable corporations.

High Cost of Government Borrowing

This brings me to a number of other lending programs in which Government makes low-interest loans. Some of them at an interest rate as low as 2 percent. What has not been very well understood is that the Treasury Department has no money of its own. It has to go into the private capital market and borrow the money. So in this time of excessive interest rates the government finds itself borrowing at an interest rate several times as high as the interest rate it gets back from those it lends the money to. This difference, of course, is paid by your constituents, the taxpayers. They get hit again if they try to borrow because Government borrowing contributes to raising all interest rates.

By terminating the Economic Development Administration we can save hundreds of millions of dollars in 1982 and billions more over the next few years. There is a lack of consistent and convincing evidence that EDA and its Regional Commissions have been effective in creating new jobs. They have been effective in creating an array of planners, grantsmen and professional middlemen. We believe we can do better just by the expansion of the economy and the job creation which will come from our economic program.

Welfare and Unemployment Programs

The Food Stamp program will be restored to its original purpose, to assist those without resources to purchase sufficient nutritional food. We will, however, save $1.8 billion in fiscal year 1982 by removing from eligibility those who are not in real need or who are abusing the program.

Even with this reduction, the program will be budgeted for more than $10 billion.

We will tighten welfare and give more attention to outside sources of income when determining the amount of welfare an individual is allowed. This plus strong and effective work requirements will save $520 million in the next year.

I stated a moment ago our intention to keep the school breakfast and lunch programs for those in true need. But by cutting back on meals for children of families who can afford to pay, the savings will be $1.6 billion in fiscal year 1982.

Let me just touch on a few other areas which are typical of the kinds of reductions we have included in this economic package. The Trade Adjustment Assistance program provides benefits for workers who are unemployed when foreign imports reduce the market for various American products causing shutdown of plants and layoff of workers. The purpose is to help these workers find jobs in growing sectors of our economy. There is nothing wrong with that. But because these benefits are paid out on top of normal unemployment benefits, we wind up paying greater benefits to those who lose their jobs because of foreign competition than we do to their friends and neighbors who are laid off due to domestic competition. Anyone must agree that this is unfair. Putting these two programs on the same footing will save $1.15 billion in just 1 year.

Federal Regulation Burden

Earlier I made mention of changing categorical grants to States and local governments into block grants. We know, of course, that the categorical grant programs burden local and State governments with a mass of Federal regulations and Federal paperwork.

Ineffective targeting, wasteful administrative overhead—all can be eliminated by shifting the resources and decision-making authority to local and State government. This will also consolidate programs which are scattered throughout the Federal bureaucracy, bringing government closer to the people and saving $23.9 billion over the next 5 years.

Our program for economic renewal deals with a number of programs which at present are not cost-effective. An example is Medicaid. Right now Washington provides the States with unlimited matching payments for their expenditures. At the same time we here in Washington pretty much dictate how the States are going to manage these programs. We want to put a cap on how much the Federal Government will contribute but at the same time allow the States much more flexibility in managing and structuring the programs. I know from our experience in California that such flexibility could have led to far more cost-effective reforms. This will bring a savings of $1 billion next year.

Space and Postal Agencies

The space program has been and is important to America and we plan to continue it. We believe, however, that a reordering of priorities to focus on the most important and cost-effective NASA programs can result in a savings of a quarter of a billion dollars.

Coming down from space to the mailbox—the Postal Service has been consistently unable to live within its operating budget. It is still dependent on large Federal subsidies. We propose reducing those subsidies by $632 million in 1982 to press the Postal Service into becoming more effective. In subsequent years, the savings will continue to add up.

The Economic Regulatory Administration in the Department of Energy has programs to force companies to convert to specific fuels. It has the authority to administer a gas rationing plan, and prior to decontrol it ran the oil price control program. With these and other regulations gone we can save several hundreds of millions of dollars over the next few years.

Defense Spending

I'm sure there is one department you've been waiting for me to mention, the Department of Defense. It is the only department in our entire program that will actually be increased over the present budgeted figure.

But even here there was no exemption. The Department of Defense came up with a number of cuts which reduced the budget increase needed to restore our military balance. These measures will save $2.9 billion in 1982 outlays and by 1986 a total of $28.2 billion will have been saved. Perhaps I should say will have been made available for the necessary things that we must do. The aim will be to provide the most effective defense for the lowest possible cost.

I believe that my duty as President requires that I recommend increases in defense spending over the coming years.

I know that you are aware but I think it bears saying again that since 1970, the Soviet Union has invested $300 billion more in its military forces than we have. As a result of its massive military buildup, the Soviets have made a significant numerical advantage in strategic nuclear delivery systems, tactical aircraft, submarines, artillery and antiaircraft defense. To allow this imbalance to continue is a threat to our national security.

Notwithstanding our economic straits, making the financial changes beginning now is far less costly than waiting and having to attempt a crash program several years from now.

We remain committed to the goal of arms limitation through negotiation. I hope we can persuade our adversaries to come to realistic balanced and verifiable agreements.

But, as we negotiate, our security must be fully protected by a balanced and realistic defense program.

Let me say a word here about the general problem of waste and fraud in the Federal Government. One government estimate indicated that fraud alone may account for anywhere from 1 to 10 percent—as much as $25 billion—of Federal expenditures for social programs. If the tax dollars that are wasted or mismanaged are added to this fraud total, the staggering dimensions of this problem begin to emerge.

New Inspectors General

The Office of Management and Budget is now putting together an interagency task force to attack waste and fraud. We are also planning to appoint as Inspectors General highly trained professionals who will spare no effort to do this job.

No administration can promise to immediately stop a trend that has grown in recent years as quickly as Government expenditures themselves. But let me say this: waste and fraud in the Federal budget is exactly what I have called it before—an unrelenting national scandal—a scandal we are bound and determined to do something about.

Tax Proposals

Marching in lockstep with the whole program of reductions in spending is the equally important program of reduced tax rates. Both are essential if we are to have economic recovery. It is time to create new jobs. To build and rebuild industry, and to give the American people room to do what they do best. And that can only be done with a tax program which provides incentive to increase productivity for both workers and industry.

Our proposal is for a 10 percent across-the-board cut every year for three years in the tax rates for all individual income taxpayers, making a total cut in tax rates of 30 percent. This 3-year reduction will also apply to the tax on unearned income, leading toward an eventual elimination of the present differential between the tax on earned and unearned income.

I would have hoped that we could be retroactive with this, but as it stands the effective starting date for these 10 percent personal income tax rate reductions will be called for as of July 1st of this year.

Again, let me remind you that while this 30 percent reduction will leave the taxpayers with $500 billion more in their pockets over the next five years, it's actually only a reduction in the tax increase already built into the system.

Unlike some past "tax reforms," this is not merely a shift of wealth between different sets of taxpayers. This proposal for an equal reduction in everyone's tax rates will expand our national prosperity, enlarge national incomes, and increase opportunities for all Americans.

Some will argue, I know, that reducing tax rates now will be inflationary. A solid body of economic experts does not agree. And tax cuts adopted over the past three-fourths of a century indicate these economic experts are right. They will not be inflationary. I have had advice that in 1985 our real production of goods and services will grow by 20 percent and will be $300 billion higher than it is today. The average worker's wage will rise (in real purchasing power) 8 percent, and this is in after-tax dollars and this, of course, is predicated on a complete program of tax cuts and spending reductions being implemented.

The other part of the tax package is aimed directly at providing business and industry with the capital needed to modernize and engage in more research and development. This will involve an increase in depreciation allowances, and this part of our tax proposal will be retroactive to January 1st.

The present depreciation system is obsolete, needlessly complex, and is economically counterproductive. Very simply, it bases the depreciation of plant, machinery, vehicles, and tools on their original cost with no recognition of how inflation has increased their replacement cost. We are proposing a much shorter write-off time than is presently allowed: a 5-year write-off for machinery; 3 years for vehicles and trucks; and a 10-year write-off for plants.

In fiscal year 1982 under this plan business would acquire nearly $10 billion for investment. By 1985 the figure would be nearly $45 billion. These changes are essential to provide the new investment which is needed to create millions of new jobs between now and 1985 and to make America competitive once again in the world market.

These won't be make-work jobs, they are productive jobs, jobs with a future.

I'm well aware that there are many other desirable and needed tax changes such as indexing the income tax brackets to protect taxpayers against inflation; the unjust discrimination against married couples if both are working and earning; tuition tax credits; the unfairness of the inheritance tax, especially to the family-owned farm and the family-owned business, and a number of others. But our program for economic recovery is so urgently needed to begin to bring down inflation that I am asking you to act on this plan first and with great urgency. Then I pledge I will join with you in seeking these additional tax changes at the earliest date possible.

Overregulation

American society experienced a virtual explosion in Government regulation during the past decade. Between 1970 and 1979, expenditures for the major regulatory agencies quadrupled, the number of pages published annually in the *Federal Register* nearly tripled, and the number of pages in the *Code of Federal Regulations* increased by nearly two-thirds.

The result has been higher prices, higher unemployment, and lower productivity growth. Overregulation causes small and independent businessmen and women, as well as large businesses, to defer or terminate plans for expansion, and since they are responsible for most of our new jobs, those new jobs just aren't created.

We have no intention of dismantling the regulatory agencies—especially those necessary to protect [the] environment and to ensure the public health and safety. However, we must come to grips with inefficient and burdensome regulations—eliminate those we can and reform the others.

I have asked Vice President Bush to head a Cabinet-level Task Force on Regulatory Relief. Second, I asked each member of my Cabinet to postpone the effective dates of the hundreds of regulations which have not yet been implemented. Third, in coordination with the task force, many of the agency heads have already taken prompt action to review and rescind existing burdensome regulations. Finally, just yesterday, I signed an executive order that for the first time provides for effective and coordinated management of the regulatory process.

Much has been accomplished, but it is only a beginning. We will eliminate those regulations that are unproductive and unnecessary by executive order, where possible, and cooperate fully with you on those that require legislation.

The final aspect of our plan requires a national monetary policy which does not allow money growth to increase consistently faster than the growth of goods and services. In order to curb inflation, we need to slow the growth in our money supply.

We fully recognize the independence of the Federal Reserve System and will do nothing to interfere with or undermine that independence. We will consult regularly with the Federal Reserve Board on all aspects of our economic program and will vigorously pursue budget policies that will make their job easier in reducing monetary growth.

A successful program to achieve stable and moderate growth patterns in the money supply will keep both inflation and interest rates down and restore vigor to our financial institutions and markets.

'Economic Recovery' Proposed

This, then, is our proposal. "America's New Beginning: A Program for Economic Recovery." I don't want it to be simply the plan of my Administration—I am here tonight to ask you to join me in making it our plan. [Applause, members rising.]

I should have arranged to quit right there.

Well, together we can embark on this road, not to make things easy, but to make things better.

Our social, political and cultural as well as our economic institutions can no longer absorb the repeated shocks that have been dealt them over the past decades.

Can we do the job? The answer is yes, but we must begin now.

We are in control here. There is nothing wrong with America that we can't fix. I am sure there will be some who will raise the familiar old cry, "Don't touch my program—cut somewhere else."

I hope I've made it plain that our approach has been evenhanded; that only the programs for the truly deserving needy remain untouched.

The question is, are we simply going to go down the same path we've gone down before—carving out one special program here, another special program there. I don't think that is what the American people expect of us. More important, I don't think that is what they want. They are ready to return to the source of our strength.

The substance and prosperity of our Nation is built by wages brought home from the factories and the mills, the farms and the shops. They are the services provided in 10,000 corners of America; the interest on the thrift of our people and the returns for their risk-taking. The production of America is the possession of those who build, serve, create and produce.

For too long now, we've removed from our people the decisions on how to dispose of what they created. We have strayed from first principles. We must alter our course.

The taxing power of government must be used to provide revenues for legitimate government purposes. It must not be used to regulate the economy or bring about social change. We've tried that and surely must be able to see it doesn't work.

Spending by Government must be limited to those functions which are the proper province of Government. We can no longer afford things simply because we think of them.

Next year we can reduce the budget by $41.4 billion, without harm to Government's legitimate purposes or to our responsibility to all who need our benevolence. This, plus the reduction in tax rates, will help bring an end to inflation.

In the health and social services area alone the plan we are proposing will substantially reduce the need for 465 pages of law, 1,400 pages of regulations, 5,000 Federal employees who presently administer 7,600 separate grants in about 25,000 separate locations. Over 7 million man and woman hours of work by State and local officials are required to fill out government forms.

I would direct a question to those who have indicated already an unwillingness to accept such a plan. Have they an alternative which offers a greater chance of balancing the budget, reducing and eliminating inflation, stimulating the creation of jobs, and reducing the tax burden? And if they haven't, are they suggesting we can continue on the present course without coming to a day of reckoning?

If we don't do this, inflation and the growing tax burden will put an end to everything we believe in and our dreams for the future. We don't have an option of living with inflation and its attendant tragedy, millions of productive people willing and able to work but unable to find a buyer for their work in the job market.

We have an alternative, and that is the program for economic recovery.

True, it will take time for the favorable effects of our proposal to be felt. So we must begin now.

The people are watching and waiting. They don't demand miracles. They do expect us to act. Let us act together.

Thank you and good night.

Data on the 1980 Election

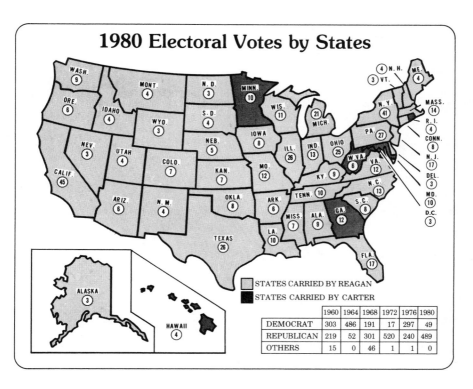

1980 Electoral Votes by States

WASH. 9
ORE. 6
MONT. 4
N.D. 3
MINN. 10
WIS. 11
MICH. 21
N.Y. 41
N.H. 4
VT. 3
ME. 4
MASS. 14
IDAHO 4
WYO. 3
S.D. 4
IOWA 8
ILL. 26
IND. 13
OHIO 25
PA. 27
R.I. 4
CONN. 8
NEV. 3
UTAH 4
NEB. 5
W.VA. 6
VA. 12
N.J. 17
DEL. 3
CALIF. 45
COLO. 7
KAN. 7
MO. 12
KY. 9
N.C. 13
MD. 10
D.C. 3
ARIZ. 6
N.M. 4
OKLA. 8
ARK. 6
TENN. 10
S.C. 8
MISS. 7
ALA. 9
GA. 12
TEXAS 26
LA. 10
FLA. 17

ALASKA 3
HAWAII 4

☐ STATES CARRIED BY REAGAN
■ STATES CARRIED BY CARTER

	1960	1964	1968	1972	1976	1980
DEMOCRAT	303	486	191	17	297	49
REPUBLICAN	219	52	301	520	240	489
OTHERS	15	0	46	1	1	0

1980 PRESIDENTIAL ELECTION RESULTS*

(270 Electoral Votes Needed to Win)

State	POPULAR VOTE			PERCENTAGE		
	Carter	Reagan	Anderson	Carter	Reagan	Anderson
Ala.	626,934	640,621	15,844	48	50	1
Alaska	31,408	66,874	8,091	26	55	7
Ariz.	243,498	523,124	75,805	28	61	9
Ark.	397,919	402,946	21,057	48	48	3
Calif.	3,040,600	4,447,266	727,871	36	53	8
Colo.	368,906	650,749	130,580	31	55	11
Conn.	537,407	672,648	168,260	39	48	12
Del.	106,650	111,631	16,344	45	47	7
D.C.	124,376	21,765	14,971	76	13	9
Fla.	1,366,365	1,937,269	178,011	39	55	5
Ga.	870,483	631,470	33,842	12	41	2
Hawaii	135,879	130,112	32,021	45	43	11
Idaho	109,410	290,087	27,096	25	67	6
Ill.	1,949,985	2,342,450	344,807	42	50	7
Ind.	835,541	1,231,295	107,090	38	56	5
Iowa	508,735	676,556	114,589	39	51	9
Kan.	324,974	562,848	67,535	34	58	7
Ky.	609,687	625,820	29,843	48	49	2
La.	707,981	796,240	26,198	46	52	2
Maine	220,387	238,156	53,450	42	46	10
Md.	706,327	656,255	113,452	47	44	8
Mass.	1,048,391	1,054,390	382,044	42	42	15
Mich.	1,519,474	1,808,832	258,924	42	50	7
Minn.	897,882	824,007	166,066	47	43	9
Miss.	428,948	439,843	11,828	48	50	1
Mo.	917,663	1,055,355	76,488	44	51	4
Mont.	109,940	191,208	27,492	33	56	8
Neb.	164,270	413,338	44,024	26	66	7
Nev.	66,468	154,570	17,580	27	64	7
N.H.	109,080	221,771	49,295	28	58	13
N.J.	1,119,576	1,506,437	224,173	39	52	8
N.M.	164,794	245,191	28,400	37	55	6
N.Y.	2,627,959	2,790,498	441,863	44	47	7
N.C.	875,947	913,949	52,375	47	49	3
N.D.	71,544	173,825	21,749	27	64	8
Ohio	1,744,226	2,202,212	255,555	41	52	6
Okla.	399,292	683,807	38,051	35	60	3
Ore.	445,352	555,859	109,363	39	48	10
Pa.	1,932,392	2,251,058	285,094	43	50	6
R.I.	185,319	145,576	56,213	48	37	14
S.C.	422,029	445,414	14,877	48	50	2
S.D.	103,909	198,102	21,342	32	61	6
Tenn.	781,464	787,156	35,927	49	49	2
Texas	1,779,025	2,433,290	103,431	41	56	2
Utah	123,447	435,839	30,191	21	73	5

State	POPULAR VOTE			PERCENTAGE		
	Carter	Reagan	Anderson	Carter	Reagan	Anderson
Vt.	81,409	93,443	31,670	39	44	15
Va.	745,600	979,871	92,769	40	53	5
Wash.	583,299	763,631	165,368	38	49	11
W.Va.	353,508	326,645	30,499	49	46	4
Wis.	988,255	1,089,750	159,793	44	48	7
Wyo.	49,123	110,096	12,350	28	62	7
Total	34,663,037	42,951,145	5,551,551	41	51	7

*Based on nearly complete, unofficial return compiled by the News Election Service. Returns for third party candidates and write-ins were scattered. Total reported for Ed Clark (Libertarian) was 876,557 (1%); for Barry Commoner (Citizens), 220,769.

PRESIDENTIAL VOTING BY REGIONS, 1976-1980

	1976			1980			
	Turnout (in millions)	Carter	Ford	Turnout (in millions)	Carter	Reagan	Anderson
East	22.1	51%	47%	21.4	43%	47%	9%
South	20.6	54	45	22.6	44	52	3
Midwest	24.2	48	50	24.5	41	51	7
West	14.7	46	51	15.8	35	54	9
Total	81.6	50%	48%	84.3	41%	51%	7%

NOTE: The 1976 results are official; the 1980 results are based on nearly complete but unofficial returns compiled by the News Election Service.

The Contributors

CECIL V. CRABB, JR. is professor of political science at Louisiana State University (Baton Rouge); he served as chairman of the department from 1968-1980. He is the author of numerous books and articles on international relations and American foreign policy, including: *Bipartisan Foreign Policy: Myth or Reality?; Nations in a Multipolar World; American Foreign Policy in the Nuclear Age; Invitation to Struggle: Congress, the President and Foreign Policy;* and *The Doctrines of American Foreign Policy* (forthcoming).

ERWIN C. HARGROVE is professor of political science at Vanderbilt University and director of the Vanderbilt Institute for Policy Studies. Formerly on the faculty of Brown University, he is author of *Presidential Leadership, Personality and Politicial Style; Professional Roles in Modern Society: The English Case; The Power of the Modern Presidency;* and *The Missing Link: The Study of the Implementation of Social Policy.* He is currently writing a book on the American presidency with Michael Nelson.

CHARLES O. JONES is a Maurice Falk Professor of Politics at the University of Pittsburgh. He will join the faculty of the University of Virginia as a Robert Kent Gooch Professor of Government and Foreign Affairs, effective September 1981. He has written several books and articles on Congress, political parties, and public policy. He served as managing editor of the *American Political Science Review*, 1977-1981.

NEIL MacNEIL, chief congressional correspondent for *Time* magazine since 1958, has written three books: *Forge of Democracy, the House of Representatives; Dirksen, Portrait of a Public Man,* and *The President's Medal, 1789-1977.* A graduate of Harvard College, he has covered national politics since the 1940s. In 1976, he was chairman of the United States Assay Commission.

CLIFTON McCLESKEY is professor of government and foreign affairs and director of the Institute of Government at the University of Virginia. He has published articles in the fields of political parties, voting, elections, state and local government, and public law; he has authored one book, *The Government and Politics of Texas,* and co-authored two others: *Party and Factional Division in Texas* and *The Politics of Mental Health.*

STEPHEN L. McDONALD is professor of economics at the University of Texas at Austin, where he has taught for 25 years and served as chairman for five years. He is a former professor and chairman at Louisiana State University, economist for Humble Oil and Refining Co. (now Exxon, USA), and staff associate of The Brookings Institution. He is the author of *Federal Tax Treatment of Income from Oil and Gas* (Brookings, 1963), *Petroleum Conservation in the United States* (Johns Hopkins, 1971), and *The Leasing of Federal Lands for Fossil Fuels Production* (Johns Hopkins, 1979), and numerous articles in professional journals.

MICHAEL NELSON is assistant professor of political science at Vanderbilt University. A former editor of *The Washington Monthly,* he also has written for the *Journal of Politics, Virginia Quarterly Review, The Public Interest, Saturday Review,* and *Newsweek* and has won awards for articles on classical music and baseball. He is co-editor of *The Culture of Bureaucracy* and currently is writing *How the Government Works: The Case of CETA* for Congressional Quarterly Press.

ELLIS SANDOZ is professor of political science and chairman of the department at Louisiana State University (Baton Rouge). He has published numerous articles in the fields of political philosophy and American thought and two books: *Political Apocalypse: A Study of Dostoevsky's Grand Inquisitor* (1971) and *Conceived in Liberty: American Individual Rights Today* (1978). Two others are forthcoming: *The Voegelinian Revolution: A Biographical Introduction* (LSU Press) and *Eric Voegelin's Thought: A Symposium* (Duke University Press).

RICHARD M. SCAMMON is director of the Elections Research Center in Washington, D.C., a visiting fellow at the American Enterprise Institute, a trustee of the National Council on Public Polls, and an elections consultant for NBC News. He is a former director of the U.S. Bureau of the Census, was a member of the U.S. delegation to the 1973 General Assembly of the United Nations, and has served on numerous commissions and delegations, including the president's Commission on Registration and Voting Participation. He is editor of *America at the Polls,* co-author of *This U.S.A.* and *The Real Majority,* and is editor of the *America Votes* series.

JAMES L. SUNDQUIST has been a senior fellow at The Brookings Institution, Washington, D.C., since 1965. He is the author of *Dynamics of the Party System: Alignment and Realignment of Political Parties in the United States* (1973); *Politics and Policy: the Eisenhower, Kennedy, and Johnson Years* (1968), and other books and articles on government and politics. In practical politics, he has served as assistant to the Democratic National Chairman, as secretary to the platform committee at two Democratic national conventions (1960 and 1968), and as a staff assistant in several presidential and senatorial campaigns.

Suggested Readings

Alexander, Herbert E. *Financing Politics.* 2d ed. Washington, D.C.: Congressional Quarterly Press, 1980.

Asher, Herbert. *Presidential Elections and American Politics.* Homewood, Ill.: Dorsey Press, 1980.

Barber, James David, ed. *Choosing the President.* Englewood Cliffs, N.J.: Prentice-Hall, 1974.

_____. *Race for the Presidency: The Media and the Nominating Process.* Englewood Cliffs, N.J.: Prentice-Hall, 1978.

Bartlett, Bruce R. *Reaganomics: Supply Side Economics in Action.* Westport, Conn.: Arlington House, 1981.

Bass, Jack and DeVries, Walter. *The Transformation of Southern Politics.* New York: Basic Books, 1976.

Bishop, George; Meadow, Robert G.; and Jackson-Beeck, Marilyn, eds. *The Presidential Debates: Media, Electoral, and Policy Perspectives.* New York: Praeger Publishers, 1978.

Broder, David. *The Party's Over: The Failure of Politics in America.* New York: Harper & Row, Publishers, 1971.

Broder, David; Cannon, Lou; Johnson, Haynes; Schram, Martin; and Harwood, Richard, et al. *The Pursuit of the Presidency 1980.* New York: Berkley Books, 1980.

Burnham, Walter Dean. *Critical Elections and the Mainsprings of American Politics.* New York: W. W. Norton & Co., 1970.

Campbell, Bruce A. *The American Electorate: Attitudes and Action.* New York: Holt, Rinehart & Winston, 1979.

Converse, Philip E. *The Dynamics of Party Support: Cohort-Analyzing Party Identification.* Beverly Hills, Calif.: Sage Publications, 1976.

Crabb, Cecil V., Jr. and Holt, Pat M. *Invitation to Struggle: Congress, the President and Foreign Policy.* Washington, D.C.: Congressional Quarterly Press, 1980.

Cronin, Thomas E. *The State of the Presidency.* 2d ed. Boston: Little, Brown & Co., 1980.

Crotty, William J. *Political Reform and the American Experiment.* New York: Thomas Y. Crowell Co., 1977.

_____. *Decision for the Democrats: Reforming the Party Structure.* Baltimore: Johns Hopkins University Press, 1978.

Davis, James W. *Presidential Primaries: Road to the White House.* 2d ed. Westport, Conn.: Greenwood Press, 1980.

Diamond, Martin. *The Electoral College and the American Idea of Democracy.* Washington, D.C.: American Enterprise Institute for Public Policy Research, 1977.

Epstein, Edward Jay. *News from Nowhere: Television, Politics and the News.* New York: Random House, 1973.

Fishel, Jeff, ed. *Parties and Elections in an Anti-Party Age.* Bloomington: Indiana University Press, 1978.

Flanigan, William H. and Zingale, Nancy H. *Political Behavior of the American Electorate.* 4th ed. Boston: Allyn & Bacon, 1979.

Graber, Doris. *Mass Media and American Politics.* Washington, D.C.: Congressional Quarterly Press, 1980.

Hargrove, Erwin C. *The Power of the Modern Presidency.* New York: Alfred A. Knopf, 1974.

Hofstetter, C. Richard. *Bias in the News: Network Television Coverage of the 1972 Election Campaign.* Columbus: Ohio State University Press, 1976.

Kirkpatrick, Jeane. *The New Presidential Elite.* New York: Russell Sage Foundation, 1976.

Kraus, Sidney and Davis, Dennis. *The Effects of Mass Communication on Political Behavior.* University Park: Pennsylvania State University Press, 1976.

Kraus, Sidney, ed. *The Great Debates, 1976: Ford vs. Carter.* Bloomington: Indiana University Press, 1979.

Ladd, Everett C. *Where Have All the Voters Gone?* New York: W. W. Norton & Co., 1978.

Ladd, Everett C. and Hadley, Charles D. *Transformations of the American Party System.* 2d ed. New York: W. W. Norton & Co., 1978.

Lipset, Seymour Martin, ed. *Emerging Coalitions in American Politics.* San Francisco: Institute for Contemporary Studies, 1978.

Miller, Warren E. and Levitin, Teresa E. *Leadership and Change: Presidential Elections from 1952 to 1976.* Cambridge, Mass.: Winthrop Publishers, 1976.

Mulcahy, Kevin V. and Katz, Richard S. *American Votes: What You Should Kow about Elections Today.* Englewood Cliffs, N.J.: Prentice-Hall, 1976.

Nie, Norman H.; Verba, Sidney; and Petrocik, John R. *The Changing American Voter.* Cambridge, Mass.: Harvard University Press, 1976.

Neustadt, Richard E. *Presidential Power: The Politics of Leadership.* 2d ed. New York: John Wiley & Sons, 1980.

Patterson, Thomas E. and McClure, Robert D. *The Unseeing Eye: The Myth of Television Power in National Politics.* New York: G. P. Putnam's Sons, 1976.

Polsby, Nelson W. and Wildavsky, Aaron B. *Presidential Elections.* New York: Charles Scribner's Sons, 1980.

Pomper, Gerald, ed. *The Election of 1976.* New York: David McKay Co., 1977.

President Reagan. Washington, D.C.: Congressional Quarterly, 1981 (forthcoming).

Ranney, Austin. *Curing the Mischiefs of Faction: Party Reform in America.* Berkeley and London: University of California Press, 1975.

Scammon, Richard and Wattenberg, Ben J. *The Real Majority.* New York: Coward, McCann & Geoghegan, 1970.

Schram, Martin. *Running for President.* New York: Stein & Day Publishers, 1977.

Seagull, Louis M. *Youth and Change in American Politics.* New York: New Viewpoints, 1977.

Smith, Hedrick; Clymer, Adam; Silk, Leonard; Lindsey, Robert; and Burt, Richard. *Reagan the Man, the President.* New York: Macmillan Publishing Co., 1980.

Sundquist, James L. *Dynamics of the Party System.* Washington, D.C.: Brookings Institution, 1973.

_____. *Politics and Policy: The Eisenhower, Kennedy, and Johnson Years.* Washington, D.C.: Brookings Institution, 1968.

Wayne, Stephen J. *Road to the White House: Politics of Presidential Elections.* New York: St. Martins Press, 1980.

Witcover, Jules. *Marathon: The Pursuit of the Presidency, 1972-1976.* New York: New American Library, 1977.

Wooten, James. *Dasher.* New York: Warner Books, 1979.

Index

Abramowitz, Alan I. - 111
"Abscam" investigation - 75
Adams, John - 47
Adams, Sherman - 60
Afghanistan - 157, 172, 174
Africa - 173-176
AFL-CIO. *See also* Labor Unions - 15
Alliance for Progress - 180
Americans for Constitutional Action (ACA) - 133
Americans for Democratic Action (ADA) - 133
Anderson, John - 9, 12, 15, 21, 129-130
Angola - 174
Apartheid - 174-176
Argentina - 180-181
Ashley, Thomas - 79
Asia - 177-180

Baker, Howard (R Tenn.) - 77, 109, 130
Baker, James - 60
Bass, Jack - 44
Bauman, Robert (R Md.) - 78-80
Bayh, Birch (D Ind.) - 23, 83, 103, 110, 130, 200
Bell, Coral - 188
Berelson, Bernard R. - 63, 136
Bibby, John F. - 110
Biemiller, Andrew - 67
Bipartisanship - 5, 35, 162-163
Blank, Robert H. - 17
Block, John R. - 161
Bolling, Richard (D Mo.) - 77
Bone, Hugh A. - 17
Bowman, William W. - 137
Brademas, John (D Ind.) - 23, 73-74, 77, 79-80, 108
Brazil - 180-181
Brock, William - 69

Broder, David S. - 19, 63
Brown, Harold - 169
Buchanan, Christopher - 110
Buchanan, John - 83-84
Buckley, William F., Jr. - 188
Budget
  estimation - 151
  problems - 56-59
  reductions - 150-151
Bullock, C. J. - 18
Bumpers, Dale - 96
Bureaucracy - 207
Burger, Warren - 11
Burke, Edmund - 7
Burnham, Walter Dean - 43, 136
Burns, James MacGregor - 17
Bush, George - 12, 32, 129, 209
Byrd, Harry, Jr. (Ind Va.) - 23, 200
Byrd, Robert (D W.Va.) - 76-77, 82, 86, 95

Cabinet - 37, 60-61
Caddell, Pat - 18, 79
Camp David accords - 171
Campaign financing - 13-14, 74-76
Campaign spending - 71, 100-102, 201-202
Carter, Jimmy - 32, 46, 52-53, 61, 76, 131
  Africa - 174
  campaign strategy - 12-13, 21
  China - 177
  concedes 1980 election - 1-2, 79-80
  congressional relations - 162, 209
  debate with Reagan - 21
  economic issues - 139-143
  failure of - 209
  interest groups - 50
  mass media - 205
  Middle East - 171
  national defense - 164-165
  Nicaragua - 183

nomination - 12-13
popular vote - 130
presidency - 196
supporters of - 21-22
unpopularity - 14-15, 20-21, 25-26, 68-69
"Carter Doctrine" - 170
Central America - 180-184
Chace, James - 186
"Challenge primary" - 135
Chambers, William - 136
Chile - 182
China, Nationalist - 177-178
China, People's Republic of China (PRC) - 173, 177-178
Christian lobby. *See also* Moral Majority - 123
Christian Voice - 83
Christopher, Warren - 190
Church, Frank (D Idaho) - 23, 83, 96, 102-103, 130, 200
Clark, Dick (D Iowa) - 123
Clymer, Adam - 185
Cobb, Major Tyrus W. - 187
Cohen, Richard E. - 111
Committee for the Survival of a Free Congress - 14, 83
Communism. *See also* Soviet Union - 164, 169, 182-185
Comprehensive Employment and Training Act (CETA) - 58
Congress. *See also* House of Representatives; Senate
"Abscam" investigation - 75
bipartisanship - 162-163
disunity in - 49, 163
foreign policy - 204
lobbying - 200
1980 election - 23
public opinion - 203
Reagan programs, 59-60, 85-86
Congressional Club - 14
Conservative Caucus - 83
Conservatism - 123, 181, 194-195
"New Right" - 28-31, 83-84, 123-124
1980 election - 130
and the presidency - 53-56
in the Senate - 86, 96, 104-107
Constitution of the U.S. - 7-11
Cook, Rhodes - 137
Coolidge, Calvin - 52
Corman, James - 73-74, 80, 108
Council of Economic Advisers - 58
Cranston, Alan (D Calif.) - 103
Crawford, Alan - 43
Cronin, Thomas - 17, 48-49, 63
Crowe, Beryl L. - 17
Cuba - 174, 182
Culver, John (D Iowa) - 23, 103, 130, 200
Cutler, Lloyd - 50, 63

Cycles in American politics - 52-56

Dale, Richard - 188
Dart, Justin - 83
Debate, presidential - 21, 78-80
Defense, national - 160-167
Democracy
and interest groups - 124
and mass media - 119-123
Democratic convention - 12
Democratic National Committee - 75, 82, 116
Democratic party
black voters - 39
campaign financing - 74-76, 82
campaign spending - 101-102
campaign tactics - 21
constituency - 21
corruption in - 75
disunity - 4
economic issues - 51
future of - 37-38, 208-209
House leadership - 72-74
labor unions - 22
New Deal coalition - 24-28
opposition party role - 27-28, 58-59, 131
policy alternatives - 59
presidential primaries - 115-116
reform - 62
in the South - 38-40, 90-92, 96
Desegregation - 56
Détente - 167-168
de Tocqueville, Alexis - 17
Deviore, Samuel - 80
DeVries, Walter - 44
Dewar, Helen - 17
Dole, Robert (R Kan.) - 3, 76
Dornan, Robert (R Calif.) - 83
Draft, military - 166

Eaton, William J. - 18
Eagleton, Thomas (D Mo.) - 96, 103
Economic issues in 1980 elections - 51, 55, 76-78, 139-156
Education - 58
Egypt - 173
Eisenhower, Dwight - 34-38, 46, 52-53, 108, 159, 182
Eisenstat, Stuart - 63
Eldersveld, Samuel - 117, 136
Elections, U.S.:
election of 1800 - 47
election of 1828 - 5, 47
election of 1860 - 5, 47, 193
election of 1896 - 5
election of 1932 - 5, 24-28, 47, 130, 192
election of 1952 - 34-38
election of 1964 - 103, 130
election of 1974 - 103

election of 1976 - 116
Election of 1980. *See also* Carter, Jimmy;
  Congress; Democratic party; Reagan,
  Ronald; Republican party
  "Abscam" investigation - 75
  campaign spending - 69-71, 74-75
  campaign strategies - 12-14
  Carter concedes - 1-2, 79-80
  congressional races - 23
  conservative revival - 28-34
  Democratic strategy - 68-70
  economic issues - 76-78, 139-156
  electoral vote - 2
  financing - 13-14
  fiscal policy - 75-76
  foreign policy - 16
  gubernatorial races - 3
  House of Representatives - 2-3, 65-86
  incumbents in - 80-81, 202-204
  Independents in - 40-42
  key states in - 11
  mandate - 129-130, 158, 201
  mass media - 13, 118-123, 204-207
  moral issues - 76-78
  "new era" - 193-196
  "New Right" - 83-84
  party membership - 133
  political action committees - 14, 102-103
  political realignment - 15-16, 40-42
  popular vote - 130
  presidential race - 21-23, 45-62
  primaries - 11-13, 116
  procedures - 9-11
  projections - 94-96, 109
  public opinion - 8, 14
  Republican strategy - 70-72, 103
  results - 2-3
  Senate results - 2, 89-110
  in the South - 38-40
  voting in - 8, 126
  women in - 84-85
  youth in - 8
Election of 1982 - 3
Electoral college - 10
El Salvador - 182-183
Emerson, Rupert - 188
Energy crisis - 54, 148-149, 151-153, 208
Environmental problems - 55, 149
Epstein, Edward J. - 120
Equal Rights Amendment - 23, 29
Ethiopia - 174
Ethnic minorities - 22
Europe, Western - 168-170

Falwell, Jerry - 14
Farley, Jim - 135
Federal Bureau of Investigation - 75
Federal Election Commission - 82-83
Federal Reserve System - 145, 149, 155-156

Federalist party - 5
Fenno, Richard F. - 100
Ford, Gerald - 32, 46, 52, 54, 71, 116, 188
Ford, Wendell (D Ky.) - 102
Foley, Michael - 89-90, 110
Foley, Thomas (D Wash.) - 73-74, 79
Fontaine, Roger W. - 189
Foreign aid - 159, 174, 185
Foreign policy
  Africa - 173-176
  Asia - 177-180
  China - 177-178
  conservative views - 28-30
  continuity of U.S. - 159
  détente - 167-168
  disunity in - 160-163
  domestic problems - 159, 161, 184
  foreign aid - 159
  interventionism - 166
  Japan - 178-180
  Latin America - 180-184
  Middle East - 171-173
  military strength - 160
  NATO - 168-170
  1980 election - 157-159
  Persian Gulf - 170
  public opinion - 30
  Reagan administration - 157-185
  South Korea - 179-180
  Third World - 185
Foust, Mary L. - 102
Frost Belt - 11, 51

Gabriel, Ralph H. - 17
Gallup Poll - 21-22, 42
Game theory - 55-56
Garner, John N. (D Texas) - 72
Giaimo, Robert (D Conn.) - 76-77
Goldwater, Barry (R Ariz.) - 32, 103
Gordon, Robert J. - 156
Grande, William Leo - 190
Great Britain - 169
Great Depression - 25-26
Great Society - 53, 56, 62
Gross national product (GNP) - 140-143
Grotpeter, John - 188
Guatemala - 182

Haig, Alexander - 60, 161, 168, 175, 178
Haldeman, H. R. - 60
Hamilton, Alexander - 5, 118
Hamilton, Walton - 113
Hanna, Mark - 135
Harding, Warren - 52
Hart, Gary (D Colo.) - 96
Hart, Peter D. - 18
Havard, William C., Jr. - 44
Hawkins, Paula (R Fla.) - 85
Hayakawa, S. I. (R Calif.) - 200

Heinz, John (R Pa.)- 90
Helms, Jesse (R N.C.) - 6, 14
Hill, David B. - 137
Hodgson, Godfrey - 48
Holt, Pat M. - 186
Hoover, Herbert - 52
House of Representatives - 2-3, 65-87
  "Abscam" investigation - 75
  Democrats in - 28-29
  elections in - 9, 65-86, 98-99
  incumbents in - 108
  women in - 84-85
Howe, Russell W. - 188
Hughes, Thomas L. - 160
Human rights - 175
Humphrey, Hubert (D Minn.) - 116, 202

Income in the U.S. - 141-143
Industry deregulation - 148-149
Independents, political - 9, 40-41
Inflation - 51, 139-146, 149, 151-154, 198
Inouye, Daniel - 96
Interest groups. *See also* Lobbying; Political action committees - 50, 82-83, 124-125, 131, 199-201, 207-208
Iran - 21, 28, 68, 157, 161, 171, 173
Iraqi-Iranian war - 172
Israel - 172

Jackson, Andrew - 5, 47
Jamaica - 183
Japan - 152, 157, 178-180
Javits, Jacob (R N.Y.) - 102
Jefferson, Thomas - 5, 45, 47, 118
Jenrette, John (D S.C.) - 80
Jewish voters - 22
Johnson, Harold (D Calif.) - 73, 80
Johnson, Lyndon - 37, 48, 52-53, 62, 86, 130, 197
Johnstone, John W. C. - 137
Judiciary - 203, 207

Kamiya, Fuji - 189
Katz, Elihu - 136
Kelly, Richard (R Fla.) - 75
Kemp, Jack (R N.Y.) - 26
Kemp-Roth bill - 26, 55
Kennan, George F. - 177
Kennedy, Edward (D Mass.) - 12-13, 36, 68, 116, 208
Kennedy, John F. - 34, 37, 52-53, 180
Kessel, John - 136
Kessler, Richard L. - 189
Keynes, John Maynard - 55
Kirkpatrick, Jeane - 85
Knauerhase, Ramon - 188
Korea, South - 179-180
Korean War - 21, 35

Labor unions - 14, 22
Ladd, Everett C. - 136
Lanouette, William J. - 111
Latin America - 180-184
Laxalt, Paul (R Nev.) - 95, 109
Lazarsfeld, Paul F. - 63, 136
Levine, Robert M. - 189
Lewis, Anthony - 96
Liberalism - 30-32, 59, 89-90, 136
Lincoln, Abraham - 7, 16, 47, 193
"Linkage" - 167-168
Lisagor, Peter - 48
Lobbying. *See also* Interest groups; Political action committees - 199-201, 207-208
Long, Russell (D La.) - 3
Longworth, Nicholas (R Ohio) - 72
Lucey, Patrick - 9
Lugar, Richard (R Ind.) - 200
Luttbeg, Norman R. - 137

Madison, James - 5, 7, 10
Magnuson, Warren (D Wash.) - 103
Mahon, George (D Texas) - 71
Main, Jackson Turner - 17
Makielski, S. J., Jr. - 137
Martin, Joseph W. - 72-73
Mass media - 13, 49, 69-70, 99-100, 118-123, 128-129, 132, 204-207
Maynes, Charles William - 186
Mayo, Charles G. - 17
McClure, Robert D. - 137
McGovern, George (D S.D.) - 23, 31-32, 83, 103, 116, 119, 130, 200
McKinney, Joan - 17
McPhee, William N. - 63, 136
Meese, Edwin - 60
Merriam, Charles E. - 115
Mexico - 180-181
Michel, Robert (R Ill.) - 66, 81, 85
Middle East. *See also* Persian Gulf area - 171-173
Monetary policy - 145-146, 153-156
Moore, Frank - 79
Moral issues - 76
Moral Majority - 6, 14, 29, 83, 134, 200
Moynihan, Daniel P. (D N.Y.) - 14, 31
Multipolarity - 159
Murphy, John (D N.Y.) - 75
Muskie, Edmund - 90
Myers, Michael (D Pa.) - 75, 80, 203

Nader, Ralph - 19
National Committee for an Effective Congress - 200
National Conservative Political Action Committee (NCPAC) - 83, 103, 134, 200

North Atlantic Treaty Organization (NATO) - 165, 168-170
National Republican Congressional Committee - 70, 84
National Republican Senatorial Committee - 102
Neutron bomb - 164
"New conservatism." *See also* Conservatism - 28-29, 194-195
New Deal. *See also* Roosevelt, Franklin D. - 19, 22-28, 41, 47, 50-53, 132-133, 192
New Frontier - 53
Newman, John M. - 189
"New Right." *See also* Conservatism - 6, 83-84, 123-124
Nicaragua - 183
Nickles, Don (R Okla.) - 104
Nixon, Richard - 6, 13, 21, 46-48, 52-54, 59, 62, 119, 159, 197, 203
Nominating process. *See also* Primary elections - 115-116
Nuclear weapons - 48

O'Neill, Thomas P., Jr. (D Mass.) - 15, 66-68, 72-73, 76-82, 85-86, 201
Organization of Petroleum Exporting Countries (OPEC) - 54, 140, 145-146, 157

Packwood, Robert (R Ore.) - 96
Pakistan - 173
Palestine Liberation Organization (PLO) - 172
Panama - 182-183
Patronage - 116
Patterson, Thomas E. - 137
Peltason, J. W. - 17
Persian Gulf. *See also* Middle East - 170-173
Philippines, Republic of - 180
Phillips, Howard - 18
Phillips, Kevin - 17, 19, 43
Political action committees (PACs). *See also* Interest groups; Lobbying - 14, 74, 82-83, 100, 199-202
Political aggregation - 5, 125-126
Political alienation - 126-129
Political machines - 127-129
Political mobilization - 127-129, 131
Political parties. *See also* Democratic party; Political system; Republican party - 114-118, 127-129, 133-136
Political system, American - 3-7
  aggregation in - 125-126
  amateurism - 31-32
  apathy in - 126-129
  campaign spending - 201-202
  coalitions in - 5-7

conflicts in - 122-123
consensus - 6-7
conservatism - 30-34
Constitution - 7-9
cycles in - 35-36, 40-41, 52-56, 195-196
dealignment - 40-42
decentralization - 116-117
de-institutionalization of - 113-136
divisions in - 50
ethical questions - 55
functions of - 115
incumbents - 202-203
independents in - 40-41
institutions in - 113-114
liberalism - 30-34
media in - 118-123
mobilization - 127-129
nominating process - 115-116
parties in - 31-32, 114-118
patronage - 116
protest vote - 35
and public opinion - 118-123
realignment - 14-16, 24-28, 46-48, 191-209
reform of - 62
regional changes - 38-40
religious groups - 83-84
revolution in - 45-48
rewards in - 134
rotation in - 45-50
single-issue politics - 29
third parties - 9-11
ticket-splitting - 41-42
"trivialization" of - 121-122
Portillo, José López - 180
Power, of U.S. - 158-159, 164-167
Pragmatism - 192
Presidency - 196-199
  congressional relations - 108
  cycles - 35-38, 52-56, 195-196
  electoral procedures - 10
  images of - 48-50
  reform of - 50, 62
  Reagan administration- 56-62
  rotation in office - 46-50
  Senate relations - 107-109
  style of - 59-62
  theories of - 52-56
  weakening of - 162
Presidential primaries - 115-116
Preyer, Richardson (D N.C.) - 79
Primary elections - 11-13, 115-116, 135
Productivity
  American - 140, 152-153
  European - 152
  Japanese - 152
"Proposition 13" - 68
Protectionism - 179
Public opinion - 14-15, 120-121

alienation - 127-129
ambiguity - 160
consensus in - 55, 160, 162, 184
economic issues - 26
foreign policy - 29, 157-159
mass media - 118-123
presidency - 48-50
presidential campaign - 78-79
Reagan administration - 132
Public opinion polls - 13, 15-16

Quayle, Dan (R Ind.) - 83, 104, 110
Quester, George - 186

Range, Peter Ross - 18
Rapid Deployment Force (RDF) - 172-173
Rayburn, Sam (D Texas) - 72-73, 86
Reagan, Ronald. *See also* Republican party - 116
Africa - 173-176
Asia - 177-180
background - 12
budget cuts - 147-148, 150-151
cabinet - 60-61
campaign strategy - 109
congressional relations - 59-60, 85-86, 162-163, 209
conservatism - 31, 194-195
defense budget - 165
debate with Carter - 21
economic issues - 55-59, 139-156, 197-199
environmental policies - 149
Europe - 168-171
executive branch - 61, 161-162
federal budget - 26
fiscal policies - 147-149
foreign policy - 157-185
historical significance - 32
House Democrats - 81
human rights - 175
ideology - 37
inauguration - 11
inflation - 149
interest groups - 131
Iran - 172-173
Israel - 172
Japan - 178-179
Latin America - 180-184
mandate of - 129
mass media - 205
Middle East - 171-173
montary policies - 147-148
1980 election - 1-2
nomination - 12, 21
Panama Canal - 183
policies of - 134
political leadership - 135
political strategy - 32-33
presidential office - 196-199

public opinion - 132-134
relations with Democrats - 131
Senate relations - 108-109
Soviet Union - 167-168
supporters of - 22
style of - 59
tax policies - 76, 146-149
trade policies - 178-179
Recession of 1980 - 139-143
Religious groups. *See also* Christian lobby;
Moral Majority - 10, 17, 83-84
Religious Roundtable - 83
Republican convention - 12
Republican National Committee - 69
Republican party - 194
campaign spending - 71, 100-102
campaign strategy - 69-72
China - 177-178
congressional election - 23
economic program, 26-27, 51
Eisenhower period - 34-38
future of - 198-199, 207-209
leadership by - 135
mandate of - 129-130
mass media - 205
New Deal - 24-28
1980 election - 2-3
Senate - 90-91, 107-109
in the South - 38-40
unity - 4
Rhodes, John (R Ariz.) - 70, 73, 77-78, 80
Riding, Alan - 189
Riordan, William - 137
Robbins, Carla Anne - 190
Roberts, Steven V. - 186
Robinson, Michael - 137
Roman Catholic voters - 22
Roosevelt, Franklin D. *See also* New Deal -
5, 19, 24-28, 47, 50, 52, 54, 61, 130-133,
192, 194
Roosevelt, Theodore - 52, 158
Rosenbloom, David L. - 136
Roth, William (R Del.) - 26, 200
Rumsfeld, Donald - 60

Sadat, Anwar - 173
Safire, William - 95-96
Sandinista Movement - 183-184
Saudi Arabia - 73
Schattschneider, E. E. - 7, 17
Schlesinger, Arthur, Jr. - 134
Schmitt, Harrison (R N.M.) - 200
Sears, John - 18, 32
Senate - 2
campaign spending - 100-102
changes in - 104-109
committee chairmen - 106-107
conservatism in - 96, 104-107

elections in - 9-10, 23, 89-110
  ideological divisions - 86
  incumbents - 90-100
  media coverage - 99-100
  Reagan presidency - 86, 108-109
  Republican gains - 90-91
  staff changes - 107
  tax cut - 76
  trends in - 89-91
  women in - 84-85
Shapiro, Isaac - 189
"Single-issue" politics - 29
Sinnott, Nancy - 84-85
Skelton, George - 18
Slawski, Edward - 137
Smith, Adam - 16
Smith, Hedrick - 187, 188
Smith, Peter H. - 189
Somalia - 174
Sorauf, Frank - 136
South - 38-40, 51, 91-92, 127-128
South Africa - 174-176
Soviet Union - 184-185
  Afghanistan - 172
  Africa - 174
  China - 177-178
  détente - 167-168
  internal developments - 164
  Japan - 178
  military power - 163-165
  United States - 28, 158-159, 163-168, 170, 172, 174, 178, 183
State Department - 160-163
States Rights Party - 39
Stevenson, Adlai (D Ill.) - 35
Stockman, David - 57
Stone, Marvin - 186
Strategic Arms Limitation Talks (SALT II) - 68, 164
Sun Belt - 11, 51
"Supply-side economics" - 147
Supreme Court - 29, 116, 207
Sussman, Barry - 18
Suzuki, Zenko - 178
Sweeney, William - 84
Synar, Mike (D Okla.) - 84
Symms, Steven (R Idaho) - 102

Taft, William H. - 52
Talmadge, Herman (D Ga.) - 91, 102
Tammany Hall - 127-128
Tax policy - 76, 146-149
Teeter, Robert M. - 18
Television. *See also* Mass media - 69-70, 121-122
Thompson, Frank (D N.J.) - 75, 80
Thompson, James - 14
Thurmond, Strom (R S.C.) - 39

Thurow, Lester - 138
"Tide of discontent" - 2, 209
Third parties - 9-11
Third World - 185
Torrijos, Omar Herrera - 182
Tower, John (R Texas) - 39, 74
Trade - 177-180
Truman, Harry S - 13, 21, 52-54, 159
Tugwell, Rexford - 63
Two-party system. *See also* Political system - 9-11

Udall, Morris (D Ariz.) - 73, 79
Ullman, Al (D Ore.) - 23, 73, 79, 108
Ullman, Richard H. - 186
Unemployment - 140
Union of Soviet Socialist Republics. *See* Soviet Union

Van Buren, Martin - 135
Vance, Cyrus - 161
Vander Jagt, Guy (R Mich.) - 2, 70-74, 78, 80-81
Vietnam War - 29, 160, 162, 166, 197
Volcker, Paul - 148
Voting behavior - 126
  blacks - 126
  congressional elections - 23, 78-80, 99-100
  conservative-liberal - 30
  during New Deal - 24-28
  ethnic minorities - 22
  labor unions - 22
  mobility - 127-128
  1980 election - 8, 20-29
  party identification - 133
  regions - 22
  religious groups - 22
  sex - 22-23
  in the South - 126-127
  women - 84-85
  youth - 126-127

Walker, Thomas W. - 190
Warsaw Pact - 165, 169
Watergate - 6, 39, 48, 59, 67, 197, 203
Watson, Richard A. - 18
Wattenberg, Ben J. - 63
Weidenbaum, Murray - 58
Welfare programs - 57-59
West Germany - 152, 169
Weyrich, Paul - 14, 84
White, John - 75
White, Theodore H. - 11, 19
White House staff. *See also* Presidency - 60, 161
Whitney, Craig R. - 187
Williams, Harrison (D N.J.) - 75
Wills, Garry - 62

Wilson, James Q. - 136
Wilson, Woodrow - 52
Wirthlin, Richard - 15
Witt, Evans - 18
Women, voting by - 22, 84-85

World War II - 25
Wright, James (D Texas) - 73-74, 79

Zagoria, Donald - 187
Zimbabwe - 176

DATE DUE	